My Isl@m

My Isl@m

How Fundamentalism
Stole My Mind—and
Doubt Freed My Soul

Amir Ahmad Nasr

St. Martin's Press
New York

www.stmartins.com

Library of Congress Cataloging-in-Publication Data

Nasr, Amir Ahmad.
    My Isl@m : how fundamentalism stole my mind—and doubt freed
my soul / Amir Ahmad Nasr. — 1st ed.
        p. cm.
    ISBN 978-1-250-01679-9 (hardcover)
    ISBN 978-1-250-01648-5 (e-book)
    1. Islamic fundamentalism.   2. Nasr, Amir Ahmad.   3. Muslims—
Malaysia—Biography.   I. Title.   II. Title: My Islam.
    BP166.14.F85N374 2013
    297.09'051—dc23

                                                        2013004044

St. Martin's Press books may be purchased for educational, business, or
promotional use. For information on bulk purchases, please contact
Macmillan Corporate and Premium Sales Department at 1-800-221-7945
extension 5442 or write specialmarkets@macmillan.com.

First Edition: June 2013

10   9   8   7   6   5   4   3   2   1

In memory of

all the digital activists

and

freedom fighters

of the Arab Uprisings

who died for liberty

Contents

viii CONTENTS

A Note to the Reader

While the message of this book is a deeply philosophical one, I wanted to spare both myself and you the reader the more arduous task of wading through a philosophical treatise. Therefore, I've chosen to write *My Isl@m* in a way that's personal, conversational, and from the heart. I've written it for the layperson as well as the scholarly minded. Everything you're about to read is based on true stories—reconstructed and retold using blog and e-mail archives, relevant documents, and the best of my memory. However, please note that some of the names and nationalities of some characters have been changed out of respect for privacy. The quoted dialogues have also either been copied word-for-word from online archives and edited for slight grammatical corrections, or paraphrased loosely and appropriately. Finally, I've kept the English spellings of Arabic words simple and used only Yusuf Ali translations for all Qur'anic material.

Prologue

He smacked her across the face—a violent thundering slap. The television seemed to reverberate with the impact. It was the climax of the show, and I had entered the living room uninvited.

"Why did he hit her?" I asked my mom. "Shush, not now," she replied, her eyes still fixed on the screen.

I hated being ignored. "What happened? What did she do?" I continued, insisting that I get an answer. "I said, not now!" Mama snapped back, now obviously annoyed.

The woman collapsed on the floor and broke down in tears. The man who had hit her, clearly still enraged, stood tall above her, and then shouted in her face, "You're divorced. Divorced. Divorced!"

The words marched out of his mouth, decisively and with absolute vengeance. I didn't want to risk getting a similar response from my mom, but I couldn't resist. "Why did he say that three times? What happened, Mama?" "How many times do I have to tell you, not now," Mama shot back, still not fully acknowledging my presence. "Will you tell me later then?" I asked, desperate to know if I would ever get to find out what the mystery was all about. "*Khalas*, fine, yes," she assured me.

My mom was busy watching an Egyptian series, and I was bored out of my six-year-old mind. I did my best to amuse myself, but neither my brother's Michael Jackson tape, nor my Ninja Turtle action figures, nor my well-worn superhero fantasies did the trick. After what seemed like forever, I sensed movement outside my room. My mom was done with her television show, so I rushed out to demand my answer. "Will you tell me what happened now, Mama? Why did he hit her? And what was that thing he said three times?" "He got angry at his wife and divorced her," she responded at last.

Still, I wasn't satisfied. "Why did he get angry? What did she do?" I continued. "Later, Amir, later," Mama replied.

Later—many years later—I'd finally come to better understand part of what happened in that memorable scene.

Generally speaking, in the Islamic tradition, a man can divorce his wife up to three times, after which it becomes extremely difficult—even virtually impossible—to remarry her. If a marriage is in trouble, but there is a chance of reconciliation, a husband will make the divorce proclamation, "You're divorced," just once to his wife. This leaves the door open for a change of heart. Even if, enraged or disillusioned, he makes the proclamation twice, hope is not lost.

Only deeply troubled, irreconcilable marriages end in a "three-proclamations divorce" and a mushroom cloud of heartbreak and anger like the one portrayed in that Egyptian television series.

Over the years, I often found myself recalling that scene, and wondering about the remaining questions. What did the wife ever do to deserve getting divorced with three fierce proclamations? Did her husband love her, and if he did, what changed? And why the hell did he have to hit her?

One day, however, I partly understood. I experienced that kind of rage, the agonizing pain of feeling betrayed by one that I had loved unconditionally. I, too, longed to end it with that fierce finality. But my love was not a woman. It was my faith.

Growing up, I loved my sci-fi cartoons. I loved my toys. I loved my LEGOs. I loved what I loved especially when it lit up my creative imagination freely and in all its magical glory. But above all, I loved Islam.

Therein lay all the heartbreak.

For a while, there was a beautiful, spiritually liberating, mystical Islam that I loved as a child; later, entwined with it, came another Islam, that dictated that I should hold on to certain beliefs or risk burning in hell for all eternity. It erected tall suffocating barriers between me and the magical curiosity and imaginative free thought I loved as a child.

I didn't like that Islam. It was mean. It made me uneasy, but it was so thoroughly fused to the other one I revered and loved that I could no longer tell the difference.

And so I believed without questioning. Like a young man wedded to a stranger in a forced arranged marriage that he accepted for fear of betraying his family, I devoted myself to my faith. I practiced, worshipped, and swept doubt under the rug whenever it surfaced.

I memorized long passages of the Qur'an, joined national recitation competitions, won, and got featured in the newspaper. I listened to my bearded teachers, trusted them, and followed their instructions. I became wary of non-Muslims.

I hated Jews, hated secularism, and doubted democracy. I had a love-hate relationship with the West and its leader, the "Big Satan," the United States of America.

Finally, at the height of my deeply held jihadist euphoria, I wished I could die and martyr myself for Islam and occupied Palestine.

I was eleven years old.

What followed will not only surprise you, but it is my hope that it will inspire you to see various forms of religion in a fresh and more nuanced light. It includes tales about haunting melodic calls to prayer, a French girl named Doubt, anti-Muslim bigots, five pillars and a teddy bear, a sexy belly-button ring, a soulful three-eyed beauty nicknamed Trinity, American bombs raining on a pharmaceuticals factory, and an accidental blog that turned my life upside down.

This book is my story. Part memoir, part manifesto for liberty, it's about my relationship with Islam and its guardians. It's about my journey from arranged marriage to infidelity to the brink of irreconcilability . . . and back.

It's a meditation on blogging and the Internet, and how they've forever altered yesterday's dictatorial politics of ignorance and ushered in a new politics of knowledge that helped trigger and facilitate the so-called Arab Spring. It's about courageously following your heart's cause, finding your tribe, and doing what you can to help change the world. It's about the search for identity, meaning and, ultimately, Truth.

If you're someone who's had a difficult relationship with religion, or you have a deep interest in it; someone who's got a burning desire to help advance freedom, human dignity, and justice on our increasingly shrinking planet; someone who's passionate about personal and cultural transformation and self-empowerment, what I write is for you.

If having your beliefs challenged boils your blood, this book is probably not for you.

Lastly, if you value evidence, and if you passionately believe that God (or "God" if you wish) shouldn't be reduced to ink on paper, but should instead be experienced, expressed, and honored freely in love and ecstasy, and without coercion, then this book is certainly for you.

PART I

The Arranged
Marriage

I

The Chessboard

"Publish."

I had clicked that button more than a thousand times, but this time I was hesitating. This was not just another blog post. I paused for a few seconds, but I knew I had to do it.

"Is there anything else I can get you?" asked the beautiful young Norwegian waitress, in perfectly accented American English. "Thanks, I'm good," I replied, without taking my eyes off the screen of my MacBook Pro, where the familiar administrator panel of my WordPress blog now contained a threshold, exhilarating but a little frightening, over which I was about to step.

I was visiting Norway to share the stage with Nobel Peace Laureates and former presidents at the 2011 Oslo Freedom Forum to speak on a panel entitled "Dawn of a New Arab World." It had already been nearly four months since the "#Jan25" Egyptian uprising, and a week since the killing of Osama Bin Laden. The world I lived in felt like it had changed immensely, and here I was, about to change my world forever, too.

"Publish."

Taking a deep breath, I clicked the button, and with that, updated my blog and stepped out from behind the curtain of anonymity that I felt had protected me for so long. There I was, in black and white, for all the world to see: "My name is Ahmad. Amir Ahmad, known to you for the last five years as Drima. I am the blogger behind 'The Sudanese Thinker'. . . ."

Instantly, I felt relief. The anonymity that had once given me so much freedom—the freedom to question the religious dogma of my upbringing, to become infatuated with atheism, to converse with Jews in Israel and an American soldier in Baghdad, and even to infiltrate online jihadist forums—had in recent years become suffocating. I felt newly liberated, despite the occasional nagging concerns at the back of my mind that I tried to ignore. "What kind of e-mails will I receive now from the haters among my blog readers? Will I get another death threat? Will the Sudanese government start troubling me?" I wondered with a smile as I walked through Oslo's breezy streets back to the 130-year-old Grand Hotel. But these concerns had little hold over me. The fear I had grown up with, like millions of other Arab youths, had lost its potency, and now, with the uprisings that were sweeping the Arab world, I knew something fundamental had shifted. We had finally found our voice, and the means through which we were going to express it passionately, ferociously, and with utter conviction.

This wave of change was what brought me to Norway. The panel on which I was speaking was going to be opened by Wael Ghonim, the Egyptian Google executive who helped energize the youth-led revolution in his nation after an emotional televised interview. I was also going to be joined on stage by three other activists and bloggers: Ghazi Gheblawi, a Libyan, Lina Ben Mhenni, a Tunisian, and Maryam al-Khawaja, a Bahraini girl whom I ran into that night in the hotel lobby.

"*Salam*. Maryam, right?" I greeted her, recognizing her face from a CNN interview. I was not sure if she was going to shake my extended hand, but she did. Knowing her harrowing story, I tried to offer my consolation. "I'm really sorry about what your family is going through in Bahrain. I hope your father gets released from prison soon." She did not seem in need of sympathy, however. Maryam was strong in her resolve and had a great sense of humor. "He got beaten up severely and badly tortured, but his spirits are high," she told me. "My mom finally got to see him. Anyways, we're kind of used to it by now. It's not the first time they've arrested him. He's always been a brave and stubborn human rights activist," she said with a chuckle.

As I listened to Maryam detailing her father's ordeal, my thoughts drifted back to my latest blog post, and my nagging concerns re-emerged. What if someone were to come after me or to intimidate my family? Would I be able to handle the beatings and torture? Would I break under pressure? I didn't know. But all I knew was that there was no going back now, and I was glad. It seemed like my whole life had been leading to this moment, when I could finally be myself.

I took my first breath in August of 1986 in the dusty city of Khartoum, the capital of Sudan, my homeland, a North African Arab nation still suffering to this day from its Afro-Arab identity crisis. Khartoum is located at the convergence of the White and Blue Niles, which join together, cut through

Northern Sudan, then Egypt, and finally pour into the Mediterranean Sea.

Soon after I was born, I left my homeland and moved with my family to the small nearby oil-rich Arab Gulf nation of Qatar on the Arabian Peninsula. By 1992, I had started school there. Things were already a lot calmer in the Arab world compared to a year earlier, when Saddam Hussein had invaded nearby Kuwait, and annexed it into Iraq. Qatar was under threat, but luckily the Americans and allied forces arrived just in time and bombed Hussein's army into retreat before it could reach us. If his army had reached us, we would very likely have been forced to flee back to Sudan, and my academic career would have started there instead. But Qatar was destined to be the backdrop for my early formative years.

Our early years were normal by Qatar's comfortable standards. I remember my father returning home from work each day, dressed in one of his many suits and ties, with the day's Qatari newspapers pinned under his arm and his black metal briefcase clenched in his fist. He had a secure job as a research consultant that paid well, and provided us with the large villa we would live in for a decade.

"So, tell me, tell me. How was school today? What did they teach you?" my father would inquire after hugging and kissing me.

"We learned a lot of things! Adding numbers, drawing and coloring, how to pray—many things, Baba!" I replied enthusiastically.

At the office, people called Baba "Doctor Ahmad." This wasn't because he treated patients. It was because he held a Ph.D. in oral-traditions folklore, which he had received over a decade before from the University of Wisconsin-Madison in 1977, where he had also taught Arabic.

"I studied hard when I was young, son, and because of that, I graduated from the University of Khartoum as a top student. That's how I got my scholarship to complete my postgraduate studies in America," he told me, more times than I could count. "And that's why you need to study hard and do well in school, too. If you want to succeed in life, you have to read many books and become well educated. Islam commands us to seek knowledge, think, and grow."

"Listen to what your father says," my mom would chime in, sensing my mild annoyance at feeling like I was being preached at. Both would then proceed to tell stories of how wonderful Wisconsin was and how they were still in touch with a few of their American friends whom they got to know there. It was an all-too-familiar scene.

Moments later, all five of us gathered around the kitchen table for our usual late lunch, while my baby sister, born a year earlier, slept in a nearby room. I was hungry and immediately began digging into my meal. "Did you say *bismillah* before starting, Amir?" asked Baba. I was silent. "Remember to say it next time, so that your food will be blessed. You need to be thankful and grateful to God for what you have. Learn to appreciate it," he advised gently. Then one of my older brothers chimed in, commenting on my eating habits. "Didn't they teach you Islamic hygiene at school? Always try to eat with your right hand only. The left hand is for dirty tasks, and when you eat with it, Satan will eat along with you, too. He joins you during your meal," he warned.

I tried picturing the possibility. What did the Devil look like? Was he a big red creature with horns like I had seen in

cartoons? Given what I had heard, Satan sure did seem powerful. So then, why would he need to eat? I mean, hello, he's
not human. He's made of fire. Heck, would he even enjoy
Mama's cooking? Could he even taste it?

After lunch, I followed Daddy upstairs to the master bed-
room and flipped though the day's newspaper next to him in
bed. I performed this ritual on an almost daily basis for the
next few years. It helped kill my boredom.

Printed in the newspaper were pictures of bad things happening to people all over the world. I read, struggling to understand as much as I could, and whenever something didn't
make sense, I asked Baba about it. Sometimes I tended to get
on his nerves with my many questions, especially if he was
really sleepy and wanted to take his habitual post-lunch nap
sooner than usual.

One day, as he yawned, I asked him, "Who makes this
newspaper, Baba?"

"This? You mean who publishes it? Ah, it's all controlled,
son. It's all just nonsense, empty talk!"

" 'Nonsense'? What do you mean, Baba? You read it every
day!" I remarked, confused and utterly baffled.

"Well, what else is there to read? I still need to at least
have an idea of what's going on in the world," he replied, his
voice heavy with frustration.

"But what do you mean by 'nonsense'?" I asked again.

"*Khalas*, enough, Amir. Later. I want to sleep now. I'm
tired. Go do your homework."

My homework usually consisted of rote learning tasks that
only increased my boredom. Either I had to memorize things,
or copy entire portions from my Arabic textbook into my

exercise book. Often the Arabic textbooks I studied contained stories that glorified the Islamic Golden Age, which supposedly began in the eighth century, and bitterly lamented its collapse five centuries later. They blamed the collapse on Muslim moral decadence and the enemies of Islam and the Arabs. I hated the homework, but as students, we weren't encouraged to question our teachers' wisdom or instructions. It was considered very rude and disrespectful.

In the evening, before sunset, my dad would wake up from his nap and head to the nearby neighborhood mosque to perform the sunset prayer. After the prayers, Baba sipped the chai tea that Mama prepared for him, and watched the evening news that aired on Qatar's national Arabic channel. He preferred it over the other Qatari channel, which aired programs in English. We didn't have any more channels available in our household, and when the opportunity to get more through cable arose a few years later, Baba never seized it. I overheard him once discussing the matter with Mama. My ears only caught snippets. "Naked women . . . Kissing scenes . . . He lets his kids see *Baywatch.* . . . Dirty songs . . . Them watching things like this . . . Shameful."

By evening, I would already be bored of my action figures and had no more *Majid* magazines left to read and reread, and so I often watched the news with my parents, struggling to understand what I saw. Many daily stories disappeared as quickly as they appeared. Others, however, were the center of attention for weeks, if not months.

I'll never forget the images of death and destruction that were always aired during the first Palestinian Intifada.

"The Zionist enemy has killed seventeen innocent civilians, and wounded twenty-three."

"These filthy cursed people! Look! Look at how they're killing innocents. Look at how they're destroying homes!"

Nothing in the news seemed to make my parents angrier than what Israel did to the Palestinians. It was horrible. Little children my age died under Israeli bombs and bullets. Worse, the stories hardly changed over time. It seemed as if Israel was simply hell-bent on killing as many Palestinians as possible.

"Baba, what happened? Why is she crying?" I asked, trying to understand the scene on our television screen. "Wait! I'm watching, Amir!" my father replied. Disappointed, I turned to my mom and pulled on her arm, hoping she'd pay attention. "They killed her son. Okay? Now let us watch, Amir, please, just wait one minute."

There were days when I really hated the news because it made Mama and Baba moody and unhappy. "Times have changed my son, there's no more mercy in this world," my mom usually declared after a heavy dose of terrible headlines. Then she'd go to chat on the phone with a friend or prepare dinner. My dad would leave to perform the last of the five daily prayers.

One late evening, my father sat me and my big brother down for what was obviously going to be a serious talk. I was about eight years old.

"Listen, boys, you're all grown up now, and soon you're going to be men with mustaches and beards. You're not children anymore. Do you agree?" he asked us. We nodded, somewhat hesitantly. We sensed there was a catch.

"Fine then, I shall talk to you as adults. Listen to what I'm about to tell you carefully, my sons. When God created us . . ."

"Wonderful," I thought to myself, "a lecture."

". . . He asked us to do certain things. One of them is that we must perform the daily five prayers. In fact, this is why He created us. He created us so we can worship Him. Now, while this isn't obligatory for children, it is for grown-ups."

"But why do we have to worship, Baba? What if we don't?" I asked. While I had learned about the steps involved in performing prayer at school, I still wondered about the reasons behind it.

"You worship and praise God because that's how you show that you're grateful for what He's given you. If you don't pray, God will ask you on Judgment Day why you didn't. What are you going to say? That you were too lazy? That's not a good excuse. Are you going to say you forgot? That's not a good excuse, either.

"God doesn't like liars, and He will also question you about your actions and deeds. All of your good actions are recorded by an angel on your right, and all of your bad ones are recorded by another on your left. They're always there, keeping track of everything you do. Everything. And when your turn comes during the Day of Judgment, the angels will measure your deeds on a weighing scale."

Daddy paused for a breath, and looked from one silent face to the other.

"The good deeds will be weighed on the right side, and the bad deeds, on the left one. If the right side is heavier, you will end up in Heaven and be rewarded for all the good you've done in your life. If the left side of the scale outweighs the right one, you're in trouble. God will put the sinful ones in Hell as punishment for the bad they've done. My sons, as of today, you must begin paying attention to all that you do.

Do not lie. Do not steal. Do not treat others with ill manners. Do not be lazy. Avoid jealousy. Listen to what your parents tell you. Do not skip your five prayers." Baba looked stern. "Now that you're not children anymore, you're going to be held accountable for all your actions. Understood?"

My brother was the first to speak. "What happens if someone steps up to be judged, and both sides of the scale weigh exactly the same?"

"Allah forgives him, and he goes to Heaven," my father reassured him.

While my brother seemed to be looking for loopholes, I was starting to get worried. "How can I be sure that on Judgment Day my right side will weigh heavier, Baba?"

"Just follow what God tells you and be a good person."

"But what if my left side is still heavier? What if my good actions still aren't enough? How can I ever be sure? What will happen to me then? Will I go to Hell together with all the bad people?"

Sensing my anxiety, Baba explained that I shouldn't really think about Hell. But how could I not? Wouldn't that be risky?

My father put his hand on my shoulder. "I'm trying to simplify the things I'm explaining to you as much as possible," he said, "but when it comes to prayer, there is something else I didn't mention. It's called *al-nafs al-mutma'innah*, the tranquil self. Your goal in life should be to purify your heart and achieve this state of being through the practice of dedicated prayer. You do it by not giving in to the voice of *al-nafs al-ammaarah bissu'*, the carnal self. That's the voice that tempts you to do bad things; it's the whispers of Satan. You must resist it. If you give in to it, the voice that then scolds you is *al-nafs al-lawwama*, the admonishing self. These two selves are always in conflict with each other within all of us. This is the *jihad* of the self, the greatest form of jihad. Prayer helps you in this jihad. It brings you peace of mind, and if you maintain it sincerely throughout your life, you will eventually reach the level of the tranquil self. If you achieve this and die, your spirit will be reunited peacefully with God in Heaven for all eternity."

I felt a lot better, and in a matter of minutes, I scurried away to pray.

Thinking about the fires of Hell made me a little scared. I envied my older brother's ability to remain laid-back in the face of Baba's cautioning. Truth is, my own fear of punishment was one of the reasons I prayed as often as possible. However, ultimately, the main reason I developed and maintained the habit of praying was simply because I liked it. I found prayer to be a calming and soothing form of meditation. I discovered it was not just a set of "up and down" movements, and no, it didn't require a ton of effort.

In fact, when I practiced prayer sincerely, with love and devotion, it was absolute bliss.

After some time, I also chose to accept my dad's invitations and accompany him once in a while to the nearby neighborhood mosque.

The mosque was blessed with a reverberating interior and a young charismatic Indian Imam possessing a mesmerizing voice. His call to prayer, echoing five times a day through the minaret's speakers, was haunting, melodic, and had the ability to generously raise my spirits like how Aladdin's magic carpet raised Jasmine all the way up to the heavens. The

Imam could recite and "sing" the Qur'an so beautifully, my mind got swept away to a peaceful realm where my worries were released. I wanted to move people just like he did.

As the months passed, every now and then, my dad would check with me: "Hey, did you pray today?"

"Yes."

"All four of them so far?"

"No."

His response was always encouraging. "Okay. Well, don't worry about the ones you missed. You'll get used to it, step by step. Soon, *insha'allah*, you'll perform all five. Anyway, I'm heading out to the mosque now. Would you like to come with me?"

"No, not today, Baba, I want to play with my LEGOs now," I replied, still focused on my toys.

"Okay, no problem. As you wish."

As I look back, I am and always will be grateful to have been raised by parents who did not forcefully shove religion down my throat. They nudged. They recommended. They sometimes used guilt to prompt me to action, but they never forced. Other folks were not so gentle, however, and apparently even had the sacred textual support to back up their beliefs and their methods.

At school, for example, one teacher once told us about a saying of the Prophet Muhammad that supposedly encouraged the beating of boys if they still refused to pray after reaching the age of eight. Not only that, but she as well as other teachers routinely caned and beat us into submission, sometimes severely, if we were rowdy or inattentive.

My parents, on the other hand, implied a different opinion that suggested I won't get spanked for not praying. More importantly, they lived by their principles. This was the start of my subtle confusion.

Who was right? Who was wrong? My teachers, or my parents? I didn't know, and so the annoying confusion persisted, along with the inevitable boredom of childhood. Eventually, at least the boredom was cured thanks to a new and exciting source of entertainment.

Given that Baba refused to install cable or satellite television at home, one of my brothers came up with an innovative solution so we could watch our favorite singers' MTV music videos. He got his fortunate cable-owning MTV-obsessed friends to record the videos on blank VCR tapes, and then we secretly played them at home. No wonder Mama and Baba didn't like the idea of cable television. Scantily dressed girls dancing. Hips shaking to Sir Mix-A-Lot's "I like big butts, and I cannot lie." Bodies swaying. It was awesome, but still, for me, there was nothing that beat video games.

By then, the Atari was history. So was the Nintendo Family. SEGA was the new big hit. Every kid in town wanted it, and I owned one. Before the day Baba took us out to buy it, I stayed up the entire night dreaming of hugging it in my arms. After we bought it, hours of gaming soon ensued, until Baba decided we were only allowed to play SEGA on Fridays. Sometimes, though, he made exceptions.

In Qatar, Friday was the off-work, off-school day. It was also the day of Friday prayers, and the preceding long sermons, which tended to end with the usual, sometimes indignant, proclamations and appeals to God. "*Allahumma*, forgive the faithful, those who are alive and those who are dead . . . *Allahumma*, forgive the faithful, and destroy your enemies, the enemies of the faith . . . *Allahumma*, destroy the Jews, and orphan their children . . . *Allahumma*, destroy them! Destroy them! Destroy them, and bring victory to the Muslims in Palestine!"

"Amen!" we hummed collectively, and then we'd rise up to pray.

Thursdays were different from Fridays. When we lived in Qatar, virtually every Thursday, the last day of the workweek, we either visited other Sudanese in Doha, or they came to visit us. Regardless of where we congregated, it usually meant tea-fueled political discussions in the men's seating area, and tea-fueled gossip in the women's seating area.

If there were kids my age, I played with them. If there weren't, I hung around the grown-ups and listened in on their conversations.

I can still hear the echoes of their voices and remember their faded faces.

"Ah, these Americans, always saying they want peace. What a bunch of cursed people. If they really did want peace, they'd stop those filthy Jews from killing the Palestinians, instead of supporting them," someone sitting in the men's area would comment.

"The problem isn't the Americans. They're not bad people. It's their stinking corrupt government!" another would angrily respond.

"By the way, Omar, speaking of America, how's your oldest son doing? Are you still sending him to study for his university there? *Insha'allah*, God willing, it will go well for you. We wish you success," a third voice would add, changing the topic of a heated conversation into something more relaxed.

Meanwhile, over where the women gathered, the talk was

about other women. Sometimes they discussed the wedding celebrations they planned on attending once they returned to Sudan for the holidays.

"Awadiyya's daugther is getting married soon, *insha'allah*. The boy she's getting married to is Fatma's nephew's brother-in-law. I believe he's related to you through Abdallah, right? Anyway, we'll be attending their wedding ceremony next month during our holiday in Sudan. We're very, very excited! Come, attend it with us!"

Mosquitoes. Flies. Scorching heat. Frequent electric power outages. Innumerable aunts and uncles having grown-up conversations in the afternoons. Visiting Sudan for annual holidays was one of my least favorite childhood pastimes. But for reasons I couldn't grasp at the time, my parents performed the ritual every year as if it was the sixth pillar of Islam.

"Listen, boy, Sudan is your country, and one day we may very well probably return forever!" my mother lectured me after I once again begged her to cut our visit short. "Never," I shot back. "I'm never going back for good!"

The jet plane takeoffs were the highlight of those trips. As we pierced through the clouds, and I watched the buildings below shrink into blue nothingness, I felt the presence and greatness of God. Indeed, He lifted up the skies without pillars so we may see them.

I was always in awe of being so high up in the sky, but I wanted more. "Mama, if the plane went up a bit higher, will we be able to exit into space?" I asked. "No, Amir, the plane can't fly any higher than this," she replied. Dismayed, I glued my face even harder onto my small window, and looked up in hopes of seeing other galaxies like those I saw in my favorite Arabic-dubbed Japanese sci-fi cartoons. But there was nothing.

At the airport in Khartoum, we were usually greeted by uncles and cousins from my mother's side of the family. In my younger days, Grandpa accompanied them, but as he got older, he waited for us at our home in al-Amaraat with my aunts and Grandma.

"Amir! Look at you! You've changed! You've grown taller and gotten bigger, *masha'allah*, as God has willed," exclaimed my aunts as soon as they saw me, to which I usually replied, "Every year you repeat the same thing. Seriously, how lame are you, don't you have anything else to say?"

The rude retorts were my attempt at keeping at bay the suffocating hugs and slimy kisses. But to no avail. "Ha! Well, it looks like your tongue is still long and sharp, that's for sure," an aunt would reply. Then they would all attack and squeeze every last breath out of me with their big bosoms and strong chubby arms.

At night, since it didn't rain much and there were frequent power outages, most of us usually slept outdoors on beds lined up along our large balcony. Whenever I laid in mine, I stared up at Allah's star-studded canopy and tried counting the bright stars. Was God out there somewhere behind the stars? Did he know how deeply I desired to be a good Muslim? Was he pleased with me and my behavior? I didn't want to upset my Lord.

At dawn, I sometimes woke up momentarily, thanks to the loud call to prayer blasting through the minaret speakers of the nearby mosque at Souq 41. It was annoying as hell. The Imam could have really used some vocal training from his colleague at our neighborhood mosque in Qatar.

An uncle or two would rise up, and off they'd go to the mosque, returning about forty minutes later. A few aunts would head downstairs to pray. On the other hand, most of us, including me, never heeded to the Imam's message that "prayer is better than sleep." We simply snored away like Caterpillar trucks, but when the sun rose, and the buzzing flies emerged, we had no choice but to get out of bed.

I tried to be either one of the first or the very last to go downstairs. Brushing teeth and showering required that people wait in line or reserve a sink. Getting up early meant beating the traffic, and getting up late meant the traffic was over. Such was the condition of our home in al-Amaraat when it was full of vacationing cousins, aunts, and uncles returning for the big annual reunion. My mother had nine siblings.

Luckily, I had a hobby to pass the time during those long holiday visits: chess. I spent a great many afternoons learning and playing chess with my maternal grandfather, Jiddo, who was an avid player and former champion in his younger days. My paternal grandfather had already passed away by then, so I didn't know him, but Jiddo, who was still alive and well, introduced me to the game after I came to him with a chess set that I discovered in his room when I was bored one day.

"My son, life is like a chess game," he explained as we played one afternoon. He seemed stressed. "In life, just like in chess, you always need to understand what goes on around you. Before you make your moves, you must assess your opponent and the positions of all his pieces. Don't be distracted by a single move or two. Observe his moves, but always see the pattern. Never miss the pattern or how it forms."

"I don't understand, Jiddo. What do you mean by 'pattern'?"

"Later, when you become a grown-up, you'll need to know where you're going in life. To know, you need to see where you're standing, because if you don't know where you're standing, the circumstances you're in, and how you got there, if you don't understand all the factors involved, well, you won't know how to progress. The pattern is in the relationships. It's in how the dots connect. Do you understand me?"

I didn't fully get what Jiddo meant, but as I played more with each passing holiday, I got better at chess—a lot better. Little did I know, as Grandpa and I planned our moves and played them out against each other, that bigger moves were being played out over our heads by the government throughout Sudan.

2

Bullied into Belief

The harsh oppression of the Sudanese people by the National Islamic Front, totalitarian Islamists who had seized power in 1989 after a coup that deposed a democratically elected government, was cruelly raping and tearing the country apart. At the time of my childhood holidays in Khartoum during the nineties, the NIF (nicknamed "the Salvation") was led by military commander Omar Hassan al-Bashir and "spiritual" leader Dr. Hassan al-Turabi, the charismatic man responsible for hosting Osama Bin Laden in Sudan before he was expelled due to international pressure.

Al-Turabi was a smart strategist who gave the people the kind of promises they wanted to hear. He cleverly mixed Islam with his self-serving rhetoric, rendering it more believable and convincing. Sometimes my mother debated Sudanese friends of hers who saw al-Turabi as a true Islamic revolutionary and supported him. My mother didn't. She loathed him.

"Al-Turabi? Fighting for Islam? What Islam? All of them are just a bunch of corrupt filthy men merely using the name of Islam. Look at how they're stealing peoples' money in broad daylight, taking all of it and lining their own pockets. Islam, indeed. Such nonsense!"

This Sudanese crisis wasn't straightforward to understand. Hence, as the conversations of the adults continued to revolve around politics, so did my thoughts. I didn't choose to be stuck there—either physically or mentally. I just was.

While al-Bashir was the muscle of the regime, al-Turabi was propagandist in chief, effectively casting a magic spell on too many Sudanese Muslims who passionately—and blindly—rallied behind Sudan's new abusive police state. It wasn't pretty, and my cousin Suad knows this all too well. During the war, her son was shipped off to fight in the South, brutally killed, and called a martyr. She wept and screamed, her cries muffled by the dusty winds of Khartoum's new overwhelming misery. There had been better times and happier days, not just for her but for many mothers like her, some of whom were forbidden by state security from mourning their losses publicly.

In those days, people's frustration—the wrong kind—was more abundant than the air of Khartoum's sandy skies. It was passive, reactionary, and tragically aimless.

Economically, the nation was struggling, thanks to the ongoing fighting. Jiddo's wealth, which he had amassed mostly during his years as a businessman in Saudi Arabia after working in Sudan with Shell, was steadily shrinking. New taxes imposed by the regime didn't help, either. Politically, the country was repressed. A new legal code was introduced. Socially, newly married couples celebrating their weddings were sometimes harassed for having parties with music and traditional Sudanese dances, and girls in universities were forced to cover their hair.

Our African Christian and animist fellow countrymen in the South, we were told in the early nineties, were collaborating with the infidel "crUSAders" and devilish Zionists in order to destroy our faith and Islamic way of life. Our economic grievances were apparently caused by dark external forces, the same ones financing and arming the Southern Sudanese. The NIF's vision of Islamic law needed to be implemented all over the country. Jihad needed to be unleashed, apparently, and so war was declared.

The change was drastic.

Newspapers critical of the government were shut down. Even the slightest criticism was not tolerated. Dissenting editors and journalists were often thrown into dungeons and some were mercilessly tortured in *beiyut al-ashbaah*, ghost houses. Television and radio fell under the government's firm grip. Both regularly beat the drums of war and broadcasted news of glorious victories in Southern Sudan. I still remember the images on Sudanese television, the decomposing corpses of Southern rebels followed by scenes of marching Northern government troops. Nationalistic songs accompanied the grim footage.

Meanwhile, in Khartoum, high school students were forced to shed their old uniform and replace it with a new one—camouflage fatigues, as if to always remind them that they were in a holy struggle against an evil enemy. Enrollment in the Popular Defense Forces (PDF), an organization ideologically and militarily allied to the NIF, became a compulsory prerequisite for boys graduating high school and entering university. Young kids were taken to the numerous PDF training camps, which, besides being designed to prepare them for armed battle against the Southern Sudanese, also served as religious indoctrination camps in which the NIF's propaganda machine was happily at work planting fervor and hatred with frightening success into the hearts and minds of youngsters.

Once, a few dissident kids tried to escape their PDF training camp. They were gunned down from behind as they ran away.

Not surprisingly, politicians in the NIF and other privileged Sudanese easily managed to excuse their sons from enduring the harsh conditions of training in PDF camps by conveniently obtaining medical reports explaining their numerous "health problems."

Of course, not everybody who went for the training did so reluctantly. Some went very willingly, either because they believed al-Turabi or pictured the war to be an exciting Rambo-like adventure. They included some of my distant relatives. Others were kidnapped off of the streets of Khartoum's poor neighborhoods and coerced into fighting. A few were reportedly even forcefully dragged out of their homes in front of their crying mothers. Too many eventually perished in the South, never to return to their families in the North.

Higher education wasn't spared from the NIF's games. In Khartoum, faculty members who opposed the education reforms in their universities were sacked and replaced by members of the ruling party or figures friendly toward it. English, declared by the NIF as the language of the infidels, was substituted by Arabic as the new language of instruction in universities.

Media, check. Education, check. Silencing dissent, check. The Internet didn't exist in Sudan then, so no check. The politics of ignorance were chillingly effective. The NIF cooked up the recipe for its contagious self-beneficial virus and spread it systematically through the various available channels. It spread it and spread it until a big enough portion of the population began doing precisely the same—spreading the infectious virus. Ideological supporters, check.

We, the people, had become the chess pieces.

One hot afternoon, I went to visit my friend Sameer, who lived a few houses down the dusty street from ours in al-Amaraat. His home had a large garden where we played football. That day, we were joined by Sameer's youthful uncle and the Southern Sudanese kid whose parents took care of cooking and keeping the house clean. When I returned home tired and a little sweaty, one of my aunts asked me if I wanted my lunch right away.

"No thanks, I already ate at Sameer's house," I replied.

"You what? Don't eat at their home again!" shouted my aunt. I was taken aback by her reaction.

"Do you know who cooks their food? The Southerner lady! Who knows if she even washes her hands. Sameer's grandma is lazy and crazy for letting her prepare their meals. Who knows, Amir, their food is probably dirty. Don't eat there again!"

That same holiday, my older brother came back home after spending time nearby at Souq 41 with a cousin. He looked nervous, and my mom pulled him aside to quietly ask him if something was wrong.

"Nothing, Mama. Nothing."

"*Ma takzib ya walad*, don't lie, boy. What's going on?"

"It's Hisham, Mama. He did it. I didn't do anything!"

"Did what? *Itkallam*, speak. Speak the truth!"

The ceiling fan spun above us, hardly moving enough air to keep our skins comfortable.

"We . . . we went inside the church near Souq 41. We wanted to see how it looks, and how they pray. As we walked around, Hisham was awfully quiet. Then, suddenly, when nobody was looking, he spat on one of the Christian statues."

"He what? *Intu majaneen*, are you crazy?"

"I didn't do anything! He's the one who did it. I should have known. He was accumulating all the saliva he could in his mouth."

Mama was furious. "Why? Why all this hatred? Is it really necessary? Would you like it if a Christian did this in a mosque?"

"How am I supposed to know? It wasn't me who did it, Mama! I didn't do anything. Hisham did it. Talk to him. He says they deserve it because they're fighting Islam."

My mom shook her head disapprovingly and muttered repeatedly, "Nonsense, I swear to God. Utter nonsense." She was visibly disappointed and upset, as if she was mourning something bigger than the incident itself. When my brother turned around to walk away, she asked with a worried look on her face: "Are you sure nobody saw you?"

"Nobody saw us, Mama."

"Good. Now listen to me. Don't you ever hang out with Hisham again. Never! And don't you ever go with him near that church!"

"Yes, Mama," my brother replied, his gaze lowered, and then he vanished into the shadows.

The war's engine roared on relentlessly and as the NIF's golden profits flowed, so did the blood of countless innocent women and children. What the Southern Sudanese had to endure was worse than the hell Darfur would go through about a decade later. Such horrors, and previous tragedies sent enormous numbers of Sudanese, including yours truly, into numerous corners of this planet, effectively giving birth to today's large Sudanese Diaspora.

Again, my mom was right, because in various ways, Islam was exploited and dragged through the mud, after being reduced to nothing but an effective political tool to use and be shielded behind. But she was also wrong. Later when I grew up, I was traumatized to discover that a number of key troublesome things the NIF preached and carried out—like aspects of the violent jihad they waged—were in actuality supported by the religious texts. What kind of support those texts provided to the NIF's agenda, and how, isn't as simple as one, two, three. It's a matter of complex and controversial debate, one that too many Muslims today are afraid to critically examine, or lack the knowledge to engage in, thanks mostly to blind reverence and beliefs like my teachers in Qatar instilled in me and my fellow students—beliefs that have been instilled by other teachers in generation upon generation of Muslims, past and present.

When I was about ten years old, the bearded Egyptian ustaz Ashraf was the head Imam at our neighborhood mosque in Qatar. I attended his Qur'an recitation and memorization class with other kids who lived nearby, after I returned home from my all-female-teachers private school in the afternoon. I found the recitations moving and comforting. They soothed my heart, especially when I had a bad day at school.

At the time, school wasn't going too well, because I was getting regularly bullied. For months, I let the notorious

Nizar and his friends beat me without much fighting back on my part. When I tried, the beatings got worse, and bigger, meaner bullies from the grade above joined in. If they were caught, or if my complaints and my parents' didn't fall on deaf ears, the bullies got caned, but that only kept them away from me temporarily.

Even when I tried to make peace with Nizar and his friends, they still continued. Even on board the school bus, and on the way back home, they continued, but what hurt the most was not the fists. It wasn't the kicking. It wasn't the hair pulling or the strangling. It was what they said, how they said it, and when they said it, particularly in light of abla Ameena's diatribes.

Abla Ameena was our Islamic teacher at school. In her early thirties, she was from *Bilad al-Sham*—the region that includes Jordan, Palestine, Syria, and Lebanon—and had come to Qatar to work as a teacher. Whenever she lectured, her voice was squeaky but loud. Her eyes had an intimidating, penetrating look. Even if you sat in the last row in the classroom, there was no way you could escape her falcon gaze. Her eyes would still hunt you down, and while her body was thin and short, her immense presence made up for it, especially when she lectured passionately, and she sure did.

"Okay, boys, today we're going to have an open lecture, so go ahead, close all your books, and put them back in your bags. Oh, and don't worry, I'm not going to give you any homework at all. All you have to do is listen to today's story," instructed abla Ameena.

We rejoiced.

"Boys, listen. Every one of you is going to grow up and

become someone. You all have dreams and ambitions, right? Answer me, you all have hopes and dreams, right?"

"Yes, teacher!" we shouted in unison.

"Mahmood, what do you want to be when you grow up?" asked abla Ameena.

"Engineer!" he yelled enthusiastically.

Pointing at another student, she inquired, "What about you, Ali?"

"Doctor!" he cried back. Each kid was more excited than the one before.

"Good, then pay attention, boys, because there are people out there in this world who want to destroy your dreams. They've been conspiring against us since the coming of Islam. These people are the Jews!

"The Jews are our enemies. They stand against us in everything. In Palestine, they're killing innocent people every day. They're destroying their homes. Children as little as you are dying terrible deaths. The Jews drink their blood.

"People have no food, no water, and no safety. Many children lose their parents, because the Jews kill them. Do you hear me, boys? They kill them! Imagine if someone approached your mama and your baba with a gun and threatened to kill them, would you love this person?"

Invigorated and upset, we yelled, "No!"

"Tell me, how many of you here love our Prophet. Do you love the Prophet?"

Determined to make our voices louder, we all shouted, "Yes!"

Abla Ameena could have easily been a rapper telling his responsive, stoned audience, "Say oh! Say yeah! Now scream!"

Except we weren't high on weed. We were ten-year-olds high on fervor.

"Well, guess what the Jews tried to do to our Prophet when he was alive? They tried to kill him. Yes, the Jews tried to kill our beloved Muhammad. Listen to me, boys. You are the Muslim Ummah's and the Arab world's hope for a better future and a free Palestine. We, the Arabs, must stand up to the Jews and fight them. Jihad is our duty! This jihad can be fought with knowledge that helps Muslims build powerful weapons. It can be with money donated to help fund our struggle. It can be with Muslim-manufactured medicines to help us end our dependence on medicines made by the West. It can be with anything.

"Jihad does not only need to be fought through actual physical fighting. Therefore, use whatever means you'll have at your disposal later when you grow up, and use them with dedication in the cause of God. God loves those who fight in His name, and eventually, the victory will be ours anyway, because before The Hour, Islamic prophecies predict that Muslims will defeat the Jews."

Was this politics, religion, or both? I didn't know. The question never occurred to me. I just did what any good student was expected to do. I listened. I responded, loudly, when prompted. And as I did, I felt a surge of excitement rush up through my body.

During break time, my Jordanian friend Mahmood professed to me, "I really like abla Ameena. She's right. We're the future generation, and we need to stand up for all Arabs! When we become grown-ups, we need to fight the Jews!"

If fighting the big bad guy in the last level of video games like Street Fighter and Mortal Kombat lit up the flames of excitement inside my chest, abla Ameena's oratory bomb-shells ignited the volcanoes of my very purpose, as a righteous person, as a Muslim, as an Arab.

"Yes, we the Arabs must the fight the Jews!" I declared, and for some reason, I felt exhilarated. At the height of my ji-hadist fervor, I longed to martyr myself for Palestine. At least the bullying would stop, and soon my family would be re-united with me in Paradise, God's reward for those who per-sist in the face of evil, and do good. A worthy reward of the highest order, where I would have everything I'd ever wanted. A place where all dreams and desires are fulfilled with the Lord's blessings. What more could you want?

Unfortunately, even in the midst of uniting against a common enemy, "we the Arabs" couldn't get along on the playground. In the eyes of my bullying adversaries who still continued to occasionally persecute me, there was no "we." They were fair skinned and from *Bilad al-Sham*, the Levan-tine countries. I wasn't. Most of them were big and tall. I wasn't. They saw themselves as "pure" Arabs. I wasn't.

"Shut up, you charcoal . . . Get lost, chocolate . . . Guys, bring the white chalk and draw on this blackboard . . . *Inta abd Sudani*, you're a Sudanese slave! You're not an Arab!" Sometimes spit burst through the air along with their fists. And it got worse any time abla Ameena praised me in class, or after Nizar and his gang got caned, and found an opportu-nity to secretly bash me again.

But who cares, right? It's not like they were right, right? It's not like what they said was true, right? I was the top student. They weren't. I was smart and clever in class. They weren't. I was liked by my teachers. They weren't. I found comfort in knowing that, and most of the time, it helped.

Most of the time.

When it didn't help, I reminded myself of what ustaz Ashraf taught us, his diverse group of students, at my neighborhood mosque after the Qur'an recitations: "In God's eyes, we're all equal. Do you hear me boys? We're all equal. It doesn't matter what race, nationality, or tribe you're from. The only thing that differentiates a good Muslim from a bad one is the strength of his faith. Always remember that, and always keep your faith strong."

The more I attended ustaz Ashraf's classes, the more I grew fond of him. He spent most of his time teaching us the rules of Qur'an recitation through his own beautiful melodic demonstration, and then asked us to repeat from our Qur'ans what he had just recited. Next, we were instructed to sit alone and memorize certain Surahs. Following that, we took turns to recite to ustaz Ashraf from memory.

Often, I arrived at the mosque earlier than others to recite the Qur'an loudly and enjoy having the reverberating interior all to myself. I also memorized the expected Surahs the ustaz taught, starting with the short ones, faster and better than all my fellow students. This earned me the sought-after praise of the ustaz himself, and he began paying special attention to me, until at last, I gained that magical ability I had always admired in gifted Imams who lead their congregations in prayer.

"*Masha'allah*, Amir. Your recitation is beautiful. I actually felt it," exclaimed ustaz Ashraf one day. I wanted to jump with joy. Soon after, he registered me and a few other qualifying students for Qatar's biggest Qur'an recitation contest. When the day came, I competed in my group, and won. Baba and Mama were proud. Days later, Baba cut out the page that featured my name and picture in the newspaper, folded it, and kept it.

Sometimes, ustaz Ashraf and his new teaching partner spent significant time lecturing us after the recitations were over. They told us stories about our beloved Prophet Muhammad and the various messengers of God before him, such as Noah and Jesus. They also explained to us with fervor the importance of Sharia, Islamic law, and why all Muslim societies had to live by it and why it had to be spread all over the world to everyone.

"In the West, women walk around naked, inviting all kinds of obscene stares. They're hardly covered, and they call this freedom! Freedom! God's Sharia prevents this. It restores dignity and respect to a woman. It gives her freedom but it also preserves her honor."

Then I remembered MTV.

"The infidels must be guided to the truth, and Sharia has to spread. This is why jihad is important."

Week after week, almost daily, the lectures went on. "Hell is a terrible place. . . . The infidels are waging war on Islam. . . . Don't listen to the Devil's whispers. . . . God is almighty, all-knowing, and all-powerful. . . . When the Day of Judgment comes, every man, no matter how powerful he was during his life, will have to answer to God!"

As I walked back home after class, at times, I wondered about the things ustaz Ashraf said. Some of it just didn't make sense. If God is almighty and all-powerful, why couldn't

He just stop the Devil? Since He is all knowing, did He already know if I was going to end up in Hell or Heaven? If He did, then how can life be a test?

With every question I pondered, my heart beat faster, and my chest grew heavier. My thoughts shifted to the bullies at school, and I wondered if they, too, were a test. But after one fateful day, I wondered no more.

I saw him at the basketball court: Nizar, the chief bully. School was over and I was walking toward the bus. Then he waved and shouted from across the court, "Hey charcoal!" His friends laughed. I walked slower, and when his friends left almost immediately, I stopped just as Nizar turned around and gave me his back.

Heart racing, body shaking, I dropped my bag on the hot asphalt, charged at my nemesis, and brought him down like a professional NFL player. Crowds of students gathered.

The seconds or minutes that followed were inaudible, and blurry. I punched and punched, but felt and heard nothing, losing my awareness, only to regain it moments later when I heard my bus driver running toward us, shouting at me to stop. Nizar's face was covered in blood, his nose leaking like a broken sewage pipe. But I hadn't had enough yet, and so I kept punching his face repeatedly, albeit much slower now.

I panted. Knuckles numb, lungs shrunken, and heart releasing explosive pulses through my body, I stopped, now also aware of the red stains on my white school shirt. I had emptied months of bottled-up anger and frustration in the blink of an eye, and it sure felt pretty damn good.

The next day, to my surprise and my father's, Nizar was expelled. The school principal had been receiving a growing list of serious complaints against him from other students and

their parents. After hearing my story of persecution in gruesome detail, she had decided it was enough and forgave me.
No one ever bullied me again. Violence had paid off.

At a time when I was having too many nightmares, Baba used
to read me bedtime stories to help me sleep. He read to me
about the creation of the universe, and how Moses stood up
to Pharaoh. How God gave Moses a staff that enabled him to
perform miracles. How Yunus survived in the belly of a
whale for days. How Abraham was thrown into a fire that
failed to burn him. All these stories and more evoked in me a
sense of awe. They also triggered more questions.

"How did he survive in the whale's belly, Baba? How come
he didn't get digested?" I asked in the middle of a yawn.

"Because God willed it. If He can create this whole universe, He can will anything, right? He's God!"

"Baba is right," I thought to myself as I gently wrestled
with my novice religiosity.

One day at the neighborhood mosque however, unlike the
verbal tiptoeing of before, I vocally let out all my questions
to ustaz Ashraf in front of the entire class. Something in the
looks other boys gave me told me they too sensed what I
sensed. "If He already knows everything, including my fate
on Judgment Day, how can I be sure I will get to Paradise?
What if I do good but my fate is already written anyway?
How can life be a test then?"

"My son, God is merciful."

"But it doesn't make sense!"

When class was over, and everyone rose to leave, ustaz
Ashraf gave me a strange look and said, "Amir, please don't
go back yet. I need to speak to you in private."

We sat down under the remaining lights in pin-drop silence. "*Ya ibni*, my son, Amir," began ustaz Ashraf. "You're
starting to worry me, my boy. Your questions are not comforting, to be frank."

"I just want to understand, ustaz," I replied, slouching a
little defensively.

"Listen to me. These thoughts, these questions . . . when
they come to you, do you get an unpleasant feeling in your
chest? Do you feel it getting heavier?"

I was surprised. How did he know? "Yes! Yes, ustaz Ashraf,
I feel it all the time!"

He kept silent for a moment, drew closer to me, looked
me straight in the eye, and began speaking in a whisper.

"My son, that feeling—the one you get in your chest—
that's the Devil. That's Satan whispering to you and trying
to lead you astray. He's working through you, Amir. He wants
you to doubt. And when you voice your doubts, you make
others around you doubt as well. So not only do you sin for
your own doubts, you also acquire the sins of those who
doubt because of you, because of your misdeeds and how
you confuse them. Amir, nothing makes Satan happier than
when the faithful doubt their faith."

My ears began to heat up.

"Amir, believe me, I care about you, my boy, and I don't
want you to lose. I don't want to see your faith weaken. The
Devil—Satan—He . . . He does not want anything good for
you. He is determined to lead you, lead us, all of us, into the
fire pits of Hell."

I felt my heart beating in my throat, and when I gulped, it
still remained there. Ustaz Ashraf's face was now much
closer to mine, speaking in whispers through lips surrounded

by a thin trimmed mustache and a large beard hanging down like a big black bush.

"Do you know what happens to people in Hell, Amir? They undergo the worst possible torture imaginable."

My heart was now playing dubstep music beats and was about to pop out of my mouth.

"Amir, on the Day of Judgment, God orders the angels to throw the evil-doers into the fires of Hell, where they're tormented forever. Your body will burn gradually, slowly. The fire will eat up your skin. Then it will sear into your flesh, and char your face. Your eyeballs will melt, and finally your private parts will shrivel into dust. But that's only the beginning, because once it's all over, God re-creates you back, and the torture begins again."

I almost stopped breathing.

"It never stops, Amir. Never! It just goes on. For all eternity. Hell's tiniest spark is as powerful and dreadful as red-hot flowing lava from earth's biggest volcanoes."

My mouth had dried up. My stomach felt empty. I sat, silently, slouching ever more. I struggled to breathe.

"Is it the same feeling in your chest again? Ask for forgiveness, my son. Seek refuge in your Lord. Every time you hear those doubts in your head, those questions, pray and seek forgiveness. Protect your faith. The Devil's whispers will go away, and God will watch over you."

As soon as I emerged out of the mosque, I burst into tears and ran home, terrified at how I had sinned, murmuring a prayer every step of the way in the middle of panting breaths, seeking forgiveness and refuge in my Lord.

No more doubting. No more questioning.

3

Warning Signals

"Why is she kneeling down and putting his dick in her mouth? What are those pictures?" I grumbled aloud with unease at Ahmed. He held up the image under a tree outside school for some classmates to see.

"It's called a fucking blow job, you idiot!" he shouted back. "And these pictures are called porn," he added with a slight smugness. Everyone burst out laughing.

The lovely scene took place sometime around 1999. After a decade of living in Qatar, my family decided to move to Kuala Lumpur, the capital of Malaysia—a multicultural and multireligious beautiful mosaic nation of Malays, Chinese, Indians, and indigenous people—where we arrived in January 1997. My parents made the decision because my dad felt uncertain and anxious about our future in Qatar due to the increasing financial instability of his employer at the time. So when he received an offer to be a professor at a well-known Malaysian university and the contract stipulated that his kids' private school education would be fully paid for, he accepted. He also liked the fact that Malaysia is a relatively progressive

Muslim-majority country, which to him meant a modern-ized environment with Islamic values for us to grow up in.

A few weeks after arriving in KL, a much more Western-ized and liberal city compared to Qatar's Doha in the early 1990s, I enrolled into a British-system international school with a radically different environment from the one in which I had spent my previous formative years. We existed in a bubble beyond the confines of conservative Malay society. It was a disorienting transition, and from the start, the cultural and linguistic barriers were a challenge. Switching from an Arabic-language educational system into an English one wasn't something I was prepared for. Hence, I joined special English class for a little over half a year, starting with Mr. Anbu.

The students were divided into three groups. Group A, B, and C, based on competency levels and age. I was placed in Group B, the intermediate level even though based on my younger age I was supposed to be in Group C. The lessons were extensive. All we did all day was learn and practice En-glish. And to my surprise, Mr. Anbu encouraged us to ques-tion him and challenge his ideas and stories.

The classroom was quite diverse, too, and mix-gendered. It consisted of Koreans, Arabs, Taiwanese, Iranians, a few Europeans, and other nationalities. Lucky for me I hadn't hit puberty yet, so being around girls in short skirts wasn't awk-ward. I had after all grown up with many Sudanese friends of the opposite gender as a kid in Doha. What *was* awkward at first was being around so many non-Muslims. Or as ustaz Ashraf would've said: *kuffar*, infidels.

The kids in class were very friendly, and I was starting to become quite close with some of them, but deep inside, a voice kept telling me, "Something is not right, Amir."

My new friends at school were nice kids. Just good, regular, nice kids.

They weren't supposed to be.

One day I came back home and asked my mom, "Ummi,
can I be friends with all the kids in school? Some of the boys
I play with during break-time aren't Muslim."

"What kind of a question is that?" She turned away from
the pot she was stirring and asked with firmness. "What's
wrong with playing with other boys if they're not Muslim?
What's the matter with it?" she inquired.

"I remember that ustaz Ashraf told us in some lessons
that we shouldn't be friends with the *kuffar*, and that we
should be weary of them. He said they cannot be trusted," I
casually replied.

"What sort of nonsense were they teaching you? Is this
what he told you?" she said, now clearly frustrated and quite
baffled. "Listen," she continued with a stern look, "when we
used to live in Sudan a long time ago, our neighbors were Cop-
tic Christians, and we were very good friends with them, and
them with us, your aunts and uncles. So there's no issue or
problem being friends with Christians and non-Muslims. The
important thing is that your friends are decent and respectful
people. *Bas*, that is all. Don't let such empty talk affect you."

"How do *you* know whether or not it's an issue? You didn't
even study religion like ustaz Ashraf!" I lectured my mom
and gestured at her with my hand. I was annoyed by her dis-
missive attitude. But the truth was deeper than that because
my annoyance was a cloak triggered by my mother's response
in order for me to hide my inner insecurity and sense of in-
validation.

"There's no such thing in religion. The Qur'an doesn't

teach that," my mom asserted back. "*Khalas, fihimta?* Understood? So it's not a problem, you can be friends with those boys," she concluded.

It was a convenient choice for sure, and so I settled for friendship regardless of religion's supposed dictates, not because I felt convinced of the truth of the matter, but because it was an easier path to take, and I knew it. I didn't want to fool myself. I had no way of assessing things then and knowing if my mom was right or wrong, so I let it be and soon I forgot about it.

The school workload was unbearable at times, but I studied hard and finished at the top of my group in special English class. I was elated, and I couldn't wait to begin real school with the other kids in primary six. I pictured myself excelling in my studies, making new friends, and having a lot of fun.

Boy, was I wrong.

The first semester of primary six was pure hell. Too many of the kids in it were of a different breed. They were little monsters—boys *and* girls—who loved to pick on other kids and play pranks on them. I was the new student in class, and thanks to my funny accent and relatively weak English, I stood out and became an easy target for mean jokes. The bullying that I thought I had defeated and left behind in Qatar returned, but this time, I fought back quickly and stopped it.

Quizzes and tests soon started, and I usually either failed in a few or got marks in the sixties or seventies out of a hundred. I was crushed. I was not used to this lower level of academic performance. My self-esteem took a painful kick in the face followed by a nosedive into oblivion. Worse, I lost my love for books and learning.

Nineteen ninety-seven was a difficult year for me and for my family. We all struggled to adjust to our new life in Malaysia. I became particularly depressed, and even contemplated suicide at one point. I felt ashamed and as if I was being punished for something, so I prayed to God to forgive me if I had sinned, and I remember finding some comfort in those prayers.

Then the Asian economic crisis hit us by the end of the year. The Malaysian currency and Kuala Lumpur Stock Exchange both lost about 50 percent of their value, causing my dad, who had financial commitments, to adjust our spending significantly and tighten things in our household in a dramatic way I had never experienced before.

School continued to get more challenging for me as well, and my parents were sometimes extremely frustrated with my bitching and apocalyptic whining.

"This is it. I'm finished. I'm a failure. It's over for me. I'm finished!" I once tearfully proclaimed.

In August of 1998, I was in Sudan yet again with my family, performing our usual annual holiday ritual in Khartoum.

"Ummi, it looks like it's going to rain. There's no need to take the mattresses outside. Let's take them back in," I cautioned my mother one evening before sunset.

I was out in the garden and had just seen and heard what I thought were the strangest lightning and thunder occurrences. My mom came outside and noticed no pregnant clouds. She insisted I furnish my grandparents' beds with their mattresses and went back in.

But I soon saw more ominous-looking flashes above and heard what was now becoming more clearly audible: rumbles and sounds of explosions in the distance.

Then the sounds got buried in my uncle's panicked shouting. "Guys, everyone, come. Come and watch. Bill Clinton is live on CNN. They're dropping bombs on us!"

More than a dozen of us gathered around the television room.

"Our target was terror," read Clinton. "Our mission was clear. To strike at the network of radical groups affiliated with and funded by Osama Bin Laden, perhaps the preeminent organizer and financier of international terrorism in the world today," he declared.

Cruise missiles were launched from U.S. naval ships in the Red Sea to target and destroy an alleged chemical weapons factory in the Sudanese capital. The attack was in retaliation for the bombing of the U.S. embassies in Kenya and Tanzania days earlier.

United States intelligence linked the alleged chemical weapons factory to Bin Laden and his associates. Later, independent investigations revealed that the facility was merely what many knew it to be: a *pharmaceuticals* factory. Stories also emerged about individuals like then-CIA analyst Mary O. McCarthy, who had reportedly protested against the bombing plans because they relied on inconclusive evidence.

Years later, a similar fiasco involving alleged weapons of mass destruction would repeat itself in Iraq, albeit on a much bigger scale.

Predictably, there was immense anger in Khartoum which Omar al-Bashir's military-Islamist regime fully exploited for political gain. The nation was whipped up into an anti-American frenzy and distracted from domestic troubles, including corruption, repression, and war with South Sudan.

Rumors emerged that more air strikes targeting bridges

were expected, which made me scared we'd get bombed and I'd die every time I was in a car crossing a bridge over the Nile.

"Cruise Missiles. I spit on them. Cowards! Dropping their bombs from up above. Let them come and face us like real men on the ground. We'll slaughter them like they slaughtered them in Vietnam."

"Man, by Allah's grace, they won't even be able to handle our mosquitoes. They'd get bitten and will all die from malaria."

Such were the sentiments on the streets.

For as long as I can remember, one of the most striking characteristics of Khartoum that has always stood out and troubled me was its sharp wealth contrasts.

A donkey cart overtaken by a brand-new BMW on the same road might seem like an impossible scene, but it is a real one residents and visitors witnessed throughout the later Bashir-dominated years. The huge economic gap between the rich, disappearing middle class and the poor was obvious for anyone to see. In fact, my entire family in Sudan, including my extended maternal and paternal relatives, were to some extent a microcosm of this reality. Some were rich and very comfortable, and others, far from it. But what troubled me most was the apathy shown by many privileged Sudanese in Khartoum toward the less fortunate who mainly tended to be displaced Southern Sudanese. Perhaps being surrounded by a great deal of suffering can overwhelm and corrode our sense of empathy.

One day I was out in the city with my uncle. I waited inside his parked car while he entered an upscale shop to buy some groceries. Before he got down, he took out some money from a bundle of cash, which he hid in the glove compartment and warned me not to touch it.

Then an old, light-brown-skinned Northern Sudanese woman knocked on my window and gestured at me with her open palm begging for money. She was covered in dust and looked extremely poor and worn out. Separated by thin glass, we were worlds apart. The sight was devastatingly heartbreaking.

I was used to seeing poor old black Southern Sudanese women begging on the streets. It was "normal," and I rarely gave them money because there were so many of them. However, I had never seen such an old Northerner in such dire circumstances before. Her situation elicited much stronger feelings in me.

At the risk of my uncle finding out and getting scolded by him, I stole a few notes of money from his bundle of cash and slipped them to the old lady through the window. She took the money and left visibly happier.

For a lonely moment, I sat still slouching in my car seat, feeling a mixture of sadness, heartache, and self-loathing.

Where were her sons and daughters? Did she even have any? How did she end up on the street? Didn't she have a home she could go to or any relatives who could take her in? Why was I born into a comfortable family and class, while others had to endure such miserable injustice? What did I do to deserve the opportunities I enjoyed and that others are denied? Why can't God help her and ease her pain? I wondered and wondered.

"That old woman could have been my grandmother or a friend's for God's sake," I thought in despair.

Then my thoughts got interrupted by a poor black-as-night Southern Sudanese woman who knocked on the window to beg for money, too.

In a depressing epiphany that would stay with me forever, my young conscience was confronted with the ugly truth and how I had been caught up in it. Even though by that time the government's politicized religious propaganda against the Southern Sudanese had no effect over me anymore, in an instant, I became aware of how the invisible structural prism of race and class I was blind to and embedded in affected me repulsively and distorted my moral compass. Constructs of "us" and "them." Greed. Affinity. Identity. Tribalism and self-interest. All were revealed before my heart and mind in one big fell swoop.

I felt a deep sense of shame suddenly running through me, and before I could hand the woman some cash notes, my uncle returned with plastic bags full of food and fresh vegetables. *"Allah kareem*, God is generous," he gently told her before getting into the car and driving off.

Back in school in Malaysia, further contrasts were reinforced in other ways. It was early 1999. My English improved, thanks partially to singing Will Smith hit songs. I also became more comfortable in my new environment. I had already finished primary six and form one, and I was now in form two, feeling the contrasts worsening.

In Qatar, one of my life's features was my inability to reconcile the tension I felt between the open religious environment of my home and the much more rigid and politicized environment at my school and the Qur'an classes at the neighborhood mosque.

In Malaysia however, the situation was flipped. I struggled to reconcile the sometimes severe tension I felt between my school's more open and Westernized liberal environment, and my home's conservative traditional context. A culture war was slowly brewing within me.

I didn't have a term for what I was experiencing at the time, but I was becoming what the sociologists Ruth E. Van Reken and David C. Pollock termed a third-culture kid (TCK). There I was, a youngster struggling to assimilate elements of my parents' culture and other cultures in which I was immersed into a third colorful culture of my own. I was straddling East and West.

Wearing a necklace at school was totally fine. At home, I got a lecture for it, because "only women wear necklaces." Hanging out and mixing freely with boys and girls in school was a casual norm. Telling my parents I was going out on the weekend with a group of boys and girls from class required nuanced explanations and assurances. Seeing students sell pornography became something I dismissed disapprovingly. Had my parents known about it, it would have triggered immense disgust and fury.

There were too many days on which I felt like a guilty sinner. I'd come back home from school confused, then I'd pray and ask God for forgiveness and guidance to ease my predicaments. I'd carefully check with myself if I had committed anything potentially wrong and promise God that I'd do my best to not repeat it again. At times, the emotional burden was heavy to carry.

I was filled with questions, and so I prayed and cultivated a reservoir of patience, but still, I had no inner answers or sense of peace.

My relationship with Islam was becoming dysfunctional. I felt stuck.

In late 1999, my younger sister and I enrolled in an unusual new school. My relationship with Islam and its guardians was about to take an abusive turn.

My father had to transition to a new office, which was far away from his old office building, and where we lived and went to school during our first few years in KL. Hence, we moved into a large apartment near his upgraded work building. The apartment building was located in a very religious Muslim neighborhood close to my new international school.

The idea for the private school was said to have been dreamed up by an American Arab Muslim who advocated the Islamization of knowledge. Soon, the school was set up and cleverly marketed as an institution that offered the best of American education served in an environment bound by orthodox Islamic rules, and which nurtured in its students stronger faith and Islamic values.

The proposition looked good on paper and all Muslim parents who heard about it including my father liked the idea.

I hated the school from day one. With *zealous* passion. But I understood and accepted that it was the nearest international school from where we lived at the time. Necessity dictated that I had to study there. At least for a while.

For the first time, my sister had to cover her hair with the hijab. All girls did—some willingly and by their own choice, and others like my sister, because of the rules. It was school regulations. Boys and girls were segregated and stood in their different designated sections during the morning assembly, which needless to say, was conducted more like a religious ritual.

The girls had to dress in long garments and "behave modestly." The boys had to lower their gaze and "purify" their "evil thoughts." Conversations between the genders, with the exception of short and necessary ones, were discouraged and looked down upon. (Yet the measures failed to prevent sexual indiscretions.)

It all felt so conspicuously phony. The energy was dull and stifling, and the air, heavy to breathe and reeking of a fake enforced "piety." And it was precisely that that bothered me so much. Not the religiosity itself, but its forced imposition on us by authoritarian figures who were so adamantly self-righteous and determined to mold us as they saw fit.

It seemed like a far cry from the beautiful inner aliveness I felt during my childhood prayers under the echoing dome of my neighborhood mosque in Qatar. And it certainly was a whole other world compared to my previous school and its teachers' philosophy of learning. The mode of teaching in our classes did not rely on dialogue and two-way exchange. It was a monologue.

I wasn't alone in my feelings and perceptions. Other students felt the same way, too. Many were dragged kicking and screaming by their parents from the "morally corrupt," "overly Western" international schools they studied in before. I can empathize with why their parents made such a decision, and how they must have been worried about their children possibly deviating from their tradition's path. I knew my parents worried about the same things, too. It was an understandable sentiment from their perspective. It doesn't mean I liked it though.

Most students in the school were Arabs, South-East Asians, Indo-Pakistanis, and Malaysians. So were the teachers, along with a few white British and American converts to Islam. Why they converted and how were questions that intrigued me since my first day.

Besides the Islamic rules and regulations, the school put into place "the Islamization of knowledge." The goal of the initiative was to infuse Islamic values and principles into secular knowledge, and therefore to "Islamize" it. In science class for instance, we learned about natural selection and the physical evolution of the earth, but we were taught to reject human evolution as it contradicted the teachings of the Qur'an. Not nearly as much effort was put into the teaching of science as was put into the teachings of Arabic and Islamic classes.

Musical instruments, except percussions, were also forbidden. They were not part of any art class as they were deemed to be sinful according to the orthodox teachings of the Islamic tradition. Moreover, no girls above the maturity age were allowed on stage during school events since their voices were considered "impure" and too inappropriate to be heard by us, the male students, supposedly for fear of us getting aroused to the point of ejaculation, I guess.

To put it mildly, I was neither impressed by the sexual norms displayed in the Western pornography secretly distributed by some students in my old school, nor the paranoia around girls' hijabs, hair, and hymens in my new Islamic school. Both objectify women and enforce a male-driven power paradigm in which man dominates woman.

To make matters worse, often—way too often—many teachers deviated from the main subject matter in classes and ranted long incomprehensible political lectures about how we must confront the *kuffar*, and how we must expose and fight the conspiracies all around us that seek to destroy our way of life. Among students as well as teachers, there was also a nonstop obsession with Israel and conspiracy theories that blamed the Jews for virtually all of the Muslim world's key major problems.

Apparently PEPSI stood for "pay every penny save Israel."

It felt like I was in abla Ameena's class and ustaz Ashraf's sessions all over again. This time however, the rants and tirades didn't affect me nearly as much as before. I believed the overall gist of what I was told, but I felt that the conspiracies weren't necessarily as grand or ludicrous as how everyone made them seem. They felt exaggerated and utterly fictional sometimes.

My parents were stunned and became concerned when I complained to them about what I had to put up with in classes. But my sister and I were already enrolled for the semester, so quitting or changing schools was out of the question.

The experience was emotionally exhausting, and it made me question why religion had to be such a burden and why it had to be followed so rigidly. As far as I could tell, the students in the school weren't all that happy. Neither was I.

All of that pondering unfortunately brought back something I hadn't felt so intensely in a long time: the heaviness in my chest. Satan's whispers of doubt. They were beginning to take hold over me and it royally freaked me out.

Because of this new development that meant the difference between heaven and hell, and despite everything I despised about my school, I decided to do my best to focus on my education's good aspects and my new friendships. I

decided to further cultivate my faith. Even privately if necessary and away from the suffocating conformities. It required
an enormous amount of self-motivation and commitment.
Thankfully, I succeeded at drawing both forward.

But the troubles were about to intensify.

Ustaz Raheem, our Jordanian Arabic teacher, was a well-
intentioned, pious, and God-fearing Muslim. Like numerous
other teachers, he sadly also had a tendency to go off-topic
and ramble about Israel, America, the deviance of Shia Muslims, and the importance of faith and jihad.

One afternoon, he wanted to put off the scheduled lesson
on Arabic grammar and focus instead on an issue that he felt
was more pressing: the importance of reading the Qur'an
daily.

"How many of you read the Qur'an every day? Answer
honestly," he asked us.

Only a few students raised up their hands. They did so
with great pride.

"My sons, every day in our lives we inevitably commit
sins. Some of us lie. Some of us cheat and steal. And some of
us do much worse things. As we do all these things, we acquire many bad deeds that we'll be judged for. One of the
ways we can protect ourselves is by reading the Qur'an every
day and memorizing as much of it as we can," he explained.

"It's so sad how so many young Muslims today have no
problem memorizing the lyrics of lewd Western songs but
they can't even recite by heart a long *surah* from the Qur'an.
Not only that, but by listening to music, they actually acquire more sins! Don't they know that listening to music is
haram—religiously forbidden?" he continued.

At that moment, Abdul Qader, a short Algerian student eyed me from in front of the class and quipped loudly to ustaz Raheem about how I liked to play guitar and sing. He complained to the teacher about my defense of playing musical instruments, and warned him that I was not convinced playing guitar was *haram*.

Ustaz Raheem asked me if this was true, and I acknowledged it. He dutifully responded with a forceful lecture in front of everyone about how I needed to repent and beware of the consequences.

"Amir, on Judgment Day, God rounds up those who spent their lives playing instruments and listening to music, and fills up their ears with hot molten silver," he warned.

His warning didn't have a strong effect. It's not like I was singing lewd lyrics or dancing in a rap music video. I simply enjoyed playing soothing and uplifting melodies on my guitar, so I couldn't understand why that was so wrong.

Nevertheless, what he warned us about next definitely made me fearful of God's wrath.

"Many of us who commit sins will actually have to endure a smaller torture before the tortures of Hell. This smaller torture is called the 'torture of the grave.' The souls of those who die righteous will dwell comfortably in a large space, unaware of the passage of time, and will be awoken on Judgment Day to earn their reward of Heaven. They'll avoid the torture of the grave. However, those who die in sin will suffer throughout the entire period between their deaths and the Final Hour. For example, if a man engaged in fornication or adultery during his lifetime, then his penis will be bitten repeatedly by a large snake as punishment. Each bite will be more painful than the one before," cautioned ustaz Raheem.

"There's a way you can be sure you'll avoid the torture of the grave for your sins. All you have to do is read Surat al-Mulk every night before you sleep. That way, even if you die in your sleep, you'll be fine and protected," he revealed.

I was gripped by fear.

In keeping with the commitment I made to myself to be more devoted to my faith, on that night I read Surat al-Mulk and re-memorized it. I read it from the Qur'an right after praying the last of the five prayers and before going to sleep.

One night though, I jumped out of bed terrified and ran to the bathroom outside my room to perform the water ablution ritual.

My mother, who was still awake, noticed my anxious state. "*Fe shino ya waladi?* What's wrong my son? Why do you look scared and why are you wet? Did you perform the *wudu* to pray *ishaa*?" she asked.

"I already prayed it, but I forgot to read Surat al-Mulk before sleeping," I replied, and explained to her what ustaz Raheem told us.

She was furious.

"*Mutkhallif!* What an idiotic backward ignoramus! Don't believe what he says. God is kind and merciful. Read the Qur'an when you want to. Don't read it out of fear," she insisted.

Again, out of a desire for convenience and emotional comfort, I relied on my mother's authority. The fear of the torture of the grave gradually faded, and I went back to reading the Qur'an occasionally whenever I felt like it, and especially whenever Ramadhan arrived.

One evening before sunset, I was returning with a friend back to my neighborhood, and we heard the call to sunset prayer blaring from the mosque's speaker. My friend headed to the mosque and I continued toward my apartment to shower and pray at home instead since I was sweaty.

My neighbor, an old Afghan man, approached fast from behind. He was nicknamed Santa Claus by the kids who hung around at the playground because of his long and thick white beard.

Suddenly, I felt a violent pull by the back of my T-shirt's collar.

I almost fell.

"Boy! Where are you going? Can't you hear the *azaan?* Go to the mosque and pray *maghrib* with the others now!" he commanded.

I wanted to punch him in the face but I kept my cool, yanked my collar away from his grip, and said, "I'm going to pray at home. I want to shower first. Now mind your own business please."

"It *is* my business," he responded angrily. "When God decides to punish you, my family and I might be affected. Don't you know what happened to Noah's people? God sent the Flood and drowned them all! Who knows, God can do the same to us here!"

He wasn't kidding.

"Then maybe you should go knock on every single apartment door in the neighborhood and make sure everybody prays tonight," I challenged him sarcastically.

"You don't disrespect me! I'm going to tell your father," he threatened.

"Tell him," I said with a smile before walking away.

My father essentially told him exactly what I did.

"Mind your own business."

• • •

Every Friday, large buses took us, the male students, from school to a gigantic mosque about a twenty-minute drive away for Friday prayers. The sermons were rarely interesting or relevant on a practical level. So we often didn't pay much attention. Each of us spent time distracting one's self or whispering to a nearby friend. Sometimes we drew patterns with our fingers on the thick maroon floor carpeting.

One Friday ustaz Yaas told us about a Hadith—a reported authentic saying of the Prophet supposedly—and warned us, "Boys, don't make me catch you playing with the carpet. When you don't pay attention to the sermon and spend it fidgeting around, all your *hasanaat*, your good deeds, for that prayer get nullified."

"Here we go again with the annoying bullshit," I secretly thought.

The famous Muslim Sufi mystic and Persian poet Jalal ad-Din Muhammad Rumi once said, "Your task is not to seek for love, but merely to seek and find all the barriers within yourself that you have built against it."

But what if those barriers were built against it by our very own guardians—the communities that raised us and whom we seek to honor and cherish? To them, what do we say?

The fathers who marry their daughters off against their own will. The lovers whose hearts get crushed when they're forced to spend the rest of their lives, not with each other, but with spouses they didn't choose. The mothers who stand by idly watching in silence, or worse, participate in these injustices.

What do we say to them? What do we say to such heart-wrenching cultural practices often justified by religion, and packaged in it?

And what do we say when religion itself seeks to shove its weight down our throats; when too many of Islam's current crop of scholars and guardians seek to impose their vision of faith on us forcefully and through indoctrination; when the justification for such imposition is derived from the religious texts themselves; when orthodox and militant interpretations high on the fervor of their gatekeepers react viciously against others that are more tolerant and rationally grounded; when reverence for the wrong things keeps us blind and afraid to speak up?

What do we say to such travesties?

For nearly six long excruciating months, in spite of the resentments I felt, I renewed my commitment to Islam over and over again. Still held on tightly, but with every renewal, a seemingly celestial hammer was swung downward. Hard. Imposingly. *Painfully*. To ensure my submission and complete subordination.

In a short period, my relationship with Islam—at times loving, at times dysfunctional, at times abusive—had become a loveless, dysfunctional, and abusive affair all at once.

With my parents' full support, my sister and I left that miserable school.

In early 2000, I joined my third international school in Malaysia and enrolled in the first semester of form three. Later, my family also moved out of our apartment into a larger three-story home near my new school, in a friendlier neighborhood where people did actually mind their own business. The new school would end up being the one my sister and I graduated from with British GCE O-Levels certificates.

Awash in a vast open sea of relief and waves of diversity, I reveled in my regained sense of freedom. At last, gone was the tyranny of conformity and banished were the anxieties. Religious concerns took a backseat and were mostly replaced by apathy and hurried robotic performances of the basic rituals. By then, my relationship with my faith began resembling that of a troubled married couple who opted to continue their uninterested and uninteresting near-loveless partnership for practical reasons. What took center stage instead in the period that followed were struggles with my Afro-Arab identity, and what every teenage boy in hormone-raging circumstances eventually had to deal with: girls.

"Mention your name and where you're from. And tell the class something about yourself."

One by one, students introduced themselves on our first day in class.

"My name is Lee. I'm from South Korea."

"My name is Alexandria McCarthy, and I'm from the United States."

"My name is Ahmad. I'm from Egypt."

"My name is Amir," I told my classmates. "And I am from . . . Sudan," I said after a second of hesitation.

Sudan. My country of origin. Its name rolled of my tongue lazily. While everyone mentioned their country of origin with pride, I mentioned mine disconnectedly, like it held no meaning. Like I had unknowingly disowned it, and was all of a sudden reminded of it when I didn't want to be.

Sudan in my mind had become too associated with war, repression, and lowly realities. A place full of indignities and indignation. What was there for one to be proud of? Perhaps it was because I had never really lived in Sudan and never felt fully a part of it, or it of me.

Such emotions leave one feeling ungrounded, and at times rather bitter.

The need to belong is a universal one all humans share, and in my inability to feel a deep connection and longing for my country of birth and community, I found resonance with those who didn't fully feel they belonged to theirs, either.

A son of a Malaysian diplomat, Affie, who was my junior, once told me, "Man, I can't stand Malaysia and this damn school. Dude, I don't belong here. I hate it here. I just want to go back to New York."

An irony given his father's arguably nationalistic role and responsibilities. But it was the quintessential remark of a privileged third-culture kid. I recognized it and where it was coming from because I had made many similar remarks in the past.

There was also my close Pakistani friend, Ali, who lived away from Pakistan for a long period and couldn't relate to "typical" Pakistanis anymore. The same sentiment was shared and felt by two Iranian school friends we had in common. And then there was my cherished "Chirish" Aimee, who was half Chinese-Malaysian and half Irish, and her stories about how some "silly" Chinese she knew treated her differently because of her half-whiteness, in a way that indicated an inferiority complex.

I was able to relate to every story they shared. Their experiences sounded all too familiar, and the new school I was now in ensured more such experiences for myself, specifically two recurring themes I would eventually go through due to my mixed Afro-Arab heritage.

Whenever I first visited the homes of Muslim Malay friends who had conservative parents, my "Arabness" appealed to them more than my "Africanness," because it meant I could read and understand the Qur'an in Arabic, in its original sacred form. The Arabness was looked up to with some sense of reverence and respect. My Africanness was either ignored or dismissed. Alternatively, once the MTV hip-hop craze arrived at the shores of Malaysia, having a token black friend (and sometimes potential boyfriend) became a hot commodity among international high school teens who got swept up in the "black is cool" trend.

"Yo, Amir, wanna come out with us to O-range this weekend? Yo, it's gonna be hot, and there's gonna be some loud banging music," Shazia told me one day after school was over with a suggestive look in her eyes.

The blackness that attracted racist abuse from some kids in my school in Qatar was now a factor that attracted attractive girls. *Lustful* attractive girls.

The reversal in fortune wasn't lost on me.

Satan would soon return, but not before a calamity that shook the world.

"Make a wish," I said to my older brother before he blew out the candles.

We weren't really ones to celebrate birthdays, but that late evening my family made an exception since my uncle was vacationing with us from Sudan, and my oldest brother and aunt were visiting from the United States. It was an excuse for us to enjoy some tea and cake.

Sipping from my cup, I turned on the television and shouted

to my brothers, "Hey, guys, come and check out this awe-some action movie. I think it's new."

My oldest brother came to check, and noticed something. "Wait, hold on a minute, this isn't HBO. Shit, shit, it's CNN."

"People, there's a disaster unfolding. It's happening live," he alerted the rest.

Just like we had done in Khartoum years earlier, the family gathered in front of the screen and watched in confusion. Minutes later, my mom's screeching voice broke out.

"Oh, no, another one, another one!"

Horrified screaming.

The metallic beast pierced into the building and exploded into a scorching fireball, slaughtering many helpless lives in an instant.

This wasn't an accident. It was *intentional*.

Then in what resembled a doomsday scenario, the tower-ing twin structures came crashing down in the midst of more horrified screeches, and as they shattered downward, so did my perception of America as an invincible giant.

The sheer scale of the devastation and the horrifying vi-sual spectacle shocked everyone.

CNN's banner now read: "America Under Attack."

Not long after the attacks, a name I heard many times before in Sudan—Osama Bin Laden—became the talk of everyone in the news and in town.

The next day, during the morning school assembly, our Malay principal expressed his sadness at what happened in America and told us we should be grateful for the safety we enjoy in our lives.

Standing behind me in line, my Russian friend murmured, "Fuck them. They deserve it."

Beyond my school walls, debates ensued in Muslim circles.

"I don't support what happened, but now at least they have a taste of what the Palestinians go through everyday under Israeli occupation and killing."

"They're trying to frame Islam and Muslims. Bin Laden is a CIA agent. It's the Jews who are behind this crime!"

"This was legitimate jihad. They got what they deserved. Enough with the bullshit sensitivities please. This is war, and they started it."

"No, the attacks were un-Islamic because they targeted innocent civilians. I support the one against the Pentagon, because it's a military target, but not the attack in New York."

"But the attack on the Pentagon was still carried out using a plane with innocent civilians on board. Islam's rules are clear. You can't deliberately kill innocent noncombatants, especially women and children."

"Listen, if they wanted to really kill innocent civilians, they could have targeted a baseball stadium full of spectators and crashed a plane into it. They didn't. Instead, they targeted America's financial center and its military headquarters."

"What's that thing the Americans always say as their excuse? Collateral damage, right? Well, this is collateral damage, and in war, innocents die. So too bad."

Looking to my parents for some guidance to make sense of things, I found a mom loathing how Islam's name got dirtied, and a dad who insisted that "what happened is not jihad." He argued, "What kind of jihad kills innocent people on purpose? That's craziness," and would add that, "If the Americans really want to fix things, they can't just combat extremists, they need to solve the Palestinian issue and stop the Israeli injustices. Otherwise, the hatred will continue."

And so my parents' stances became my stances. They made sense, but to an extent so did Bin Laden's message and advocacy. His words were eerily familiar. I heard them before. The United States, or at least its government, was indeed Islam's enemy and so were the Jews. But did that justify the attacks and how they were carried out? And could the Jews really have been the ones actually responsible for what happened as some suggested?

I chose to be distant and detached from those heavy matters, and so I continued playing computer strategy games like Star Craft, and stuck with my conclusion that the attacks were utterly wrong and perpetrated by al-Qaeda.

She slid my hand under her shirt and watched me draw in a deep breath.

"What are you doing, Shazia?" I asked nervously.

"Do you like it?" she asked me with a look in her hazel eyes oozing with sex. "Touch it. Can you feel it? It's nice, right?"

"It is," I replied, feeling extremely aroused and a little shaky. "Did it hurt when they pierced it?" I asked curiously in an attempt to continue a more normal conversation.

"No, not really. It was quick and quite painless actually. Only the moment you're pierced hurts and stings a little." She responded with a flirtatious smile and caressed my fingers while they rested on her bellybutton ring.

I was now on the verge of exploding in my pants.

"Listen, you know where I live, right? It's close to where

you stay. Walking distance actually. Why don't you come over later, after school? My mom is away, and it will be fun for us to hang around," she said in a soothing voice, and then immediately left.

When I arrived home, I ran up to my room, and walked around in circles like a madman. I didn't have a condom. Heck, I had never even bought or put one on before. And what was I about to commit anyway? One of the biggest sins in the eyes of God, certainly. But I was aroused, and going unbearably crazy.

She knew how to torture me.

I was sixteen and I wanted to have sex. Badly. I wanted to enjoy its legendary pleasures. I wanted to have bragging rights among my mostly still-virgin guy friends.

But sex was a pleasure of the flesh—the forbidden kind—unless you were married, which meant I would have had to wait at least another twelve years or so, an awfully long period, and it felt unfair. Absolutely, ridiculously unfair. I didn't want to have sex tomorrow or in ten years. No, I wanted to have sex *now*. Today. On *that* very day.

But the last time I tasted smaller physical intimacies with a girl, I returned home filled with conflicting feelings of shame, pride, and guilt and asked God for forgiveness. Lots of it.

So I looked up above and begged my Lord for his guidance and mercy, all while still walking around in circles. But nothing happened. Nothing, and it made me want to kill myself out of my own misery. So I sat at the corner of my bed and tried to pray again. Quietly. With more focus. More devotion. Really, really hard with my eyes closed.

Then all of a sudden, my room was filled with the extremely bright flash of a catastrophically loud thunder bolt that startled the sexual urges out of me.

The sky opened its floodgates.

It had not rained that heavily in many months.

God had saved me.

By 2003, my guitar had become my best friend. Whenever I wanted to confide my deepest feelings in someone, it was there for me. Whenever I was bored, it was there for me. Whenever I wanted to lose myself in a tranquil place beyond time, it was there for me. It neither judged me nor complained about my misdemeanors. It was just there. Present. In all its carved-out wooden beauty, just as my music-making software programs were.

And so I wrote lyrics, made beats, and produced my own original creations: house, jazz, lounge, hip-hop, rock, you name it. Then I sat for hours listening to what I created, wondering how it came out of me. Such was my relationship with music. It was more heartfelt and alive to me by that point than my relationship with my faith.

I loved music so much that when I graduated from high school, I wanted to study sound engineering and music production at the Malaysian branch of SAE, the international School of Audio Engineering, but I was discouraged by my parents, who demanded I get a "real" education.

"We didn't raise you and educate you so you could go and learn music. No, go and find a real interest. Engineering. Accounting. IT. Something useful," they instructed.

I stubbornly refused. Then I considered going to America to study engineering and stay with my oldest brother in

Chicago, but he convinced me to stay in KL and study business and information technology.

"First of all, you'll have a degree that will help you get a job in business or IT-related fields. Your job opportunities will be wider and more varied. Secondly, once you've made enough money, you can start your own music studio or even a record label if you want. Both your business and IT knowledge will be helpful," he explained persuasively. I followed his advice.

Little did I know I would end up spending a great deal of time learning neither about business nor IT.

The mighty tantalizing blogosphere awaited me.

4

Blogs, Bastards, and Heretics

On a dull rainy afternoon in January 2006, I sat at my keyboard trying to find a lost part of me through Google. It was on that fateful day that I made an accidental discovery that in just three short years would dramatically change my life forever. With one click, I set into motion a series of events that not only went on to transform my inner and outer worlds, but also influenced my career path, and introduced me to a network of some of the most inspiring, courageous, and intelligent acquaintances and friends I'd ever met. Young, progressive, defiant, and tech-savvy men and women—bloggers, rebels and digital activists—who together, five years later would help instigate and facilitate the biggest political earthquake the Arab world had known in forty years, shaking it to its core.

Sitting hunched close to my computer screen that rainy day, I Googled away, looking for information about the ancient Nubian civilization and Taharqa, the Nubian Pharaoh from modern-day northern Sudan, who had conquered and ruled Egypt and the Kingdom of Kush from 690 BC to 664 BC.

My years of living overseas as a member of the Sudanese

Diaspora left me yearning for a more deeply rooted identity in something I could be proud of, something valid that held meaning. So I searched for articles about the history of my people, the Nubian-Arabs of north Sudan.

About a dozen or so queries later, I found something oddly intriguing.

"The Big Pharaoh."

I clicked the Google search result and stumbled upon a strange-looking "blogspot" site containing content that had nothing to do with Taharqa, Nubian pyramids, or ancient Egypt. But I was intrigued by it, because of the topics the site talked about and how it talked about them: women's rights, sex, Islam, democracy, terrorism. An enticing list of topics. The thoughts—written in English—were irreverent, and the opinions were unique, fresh, and unthinkably heretical to me.

"What the hell is this? And who's writing these things?" I wondered with a mixture of shock, fascination, and extreme curiosity. I had never read anything like that before.

The Big Pharaoh was the name of an anonymous, optimistic, and outspoken liberal Egyptian blogger to whom nothing seemed taboo or beyond criticism. It was through him that I fell down the rabbit hole and landed in virtual wonderland.

I soon discovered there were many bloggers like Big Pharaoh out there—most of them anonymous—and the more I found and read, starting with Big Pharaoh's recommended list, the more obsessed I became. In fact, I became so obsessed, I went from a diligent university student who had scored a GPA of 3.79 out of 4.00 the previous year, to a lower-performing one who found way more stimulation right in the heart of the Arab blogosphere.

The Arab blogosphere's discourse was anything but bor-

ing. It was influenced by the backdrop of a post-9/11 world
that was dark, complex, and very polarized. The Danish cartoons controversy the previous year had just triggered a great
deal of understandable anger in the Muslim world along with
some pretty inexcusable "medieval stupidity," as some called
it, and the memory was still fresh. The Israel-Palestine conflict continued to rage with terrible consequences. Corrupt
Arab tyrants went about their daily business, doing what
they do best—oppressing the brains and souls out of those
they ruled with an iron fist. The failing war in Iraq was being
waged horrifically and incompetently by the Bush adminis-
tration in the name of democracy, while America's close
"friends" and allies, the Saudis, some of the world's biggest
human rights violators, particularly against women, continued exporting their intolerant religious Wahhabi ideology
to millions of Muslims across the globe. Discontented indoctrinated Muslim men—and sometimes even women—
continued to blow themselves up and slaughter innocents in
twisted hopes of delusional rewards and pleasures. The horrendous memory of U.S. abuse at Abu Ghraib still lingered.
And to top it off, anti-Muslim, anti-Western, and anti-
Semitic rhetoric was loud, proud, and regularly exchanged
between Muslim, Western, and Jewish commentators in the
comments sections of many blogs.

All of this contributed to a mood that was, more often than
not, sadly unsuitable for sober dialogue and understanding.
But it also created the open space for staunch and vehemently
unfettered discussions by Arab citizens with an Internet connection and the necessary will to probe controversial matters.

Iraqis—inside and outside Iraq—blogged heartfelt condemnations of Bush's war in their country, while a small but

vocal portion, most visibly the brothers behind Iraq the Model, supported the war and were strongly in favor of the removal of Saddam.

Saudi women bloggers expressed their frustrations articulately and bombarded the patriarchal norms of their society one blog post at a time. Ahmed al-Omran, the blogger behind Saudi Jeans, wrote openly under his real name, and delicately but bravely crossed lines in his critiques of the Kingdom. The Jordanian blogosphere tackled corruption and unleashed its outrage at the tradition of "honor killing" that still received lenient punishment in their country. Egyptian bloggers targeted the Islamists, Hosni Mubarak's dictatorial rule, and police abuse, among other grievances. And perhaps the most critical and irreverent of them all was none other than the English-speaking voice behind the (in)famous blog Rantings of a Sandmonkey.

Like Big Pharaoh, Sandmonkey was an anonymous and outspoken twentysomething liberal Egyptian blogger who drew in a large and loyal readership from all over the world. Unlike Big Pharaoh however, he was a foul-mouthed and self-described "extremely cynical, snarky, pro-U.S., secular, libertarian, disgruntled sandmonkey." He had spent numerous formative years as a university student in Boston, an opportunity that immersed him very deeply in American culture and gave him an intimate understanding of the American mindset.

Taking full advantage of his anonymity and derogatory pseudonym, he hilariously and bluntly tackled all kinds of sensitive issues dealing with Egypt, the United States, and the Arab world. And quite frequently, he did it from a self-critical and self-identified libertarian stance, which attracted many right-leaning American fans as well as secular-minded Arabs who appreciated him for his unconventional assessments of the region's political culture.

He wrote numerous posts mocking the Arab world's fixation on Israel conspiracy theories and regularly wrote scathing critiques of the Muslim Brotherhood. He lamented how Saudi Arabia's export Wahhabism had "mindfucked Egyptians," and he cheered for the downfall of Saddam. Not surprisingly, in doing so, he managed to piss off a lot of people who strongly disagreed with him, his style, and his issues of focus.

Initially, I found his views irritating. For a start, displaying a graphic banner that says "Buy Danish" in the aftermath of the cartoon crisis, isn't exactly the type of thing that's going to win you support from the Muslim political mainstream. When I saw the banner, I thought to myself, "What an asshole," and even after I understood its symbolism and why he displayed it to unequivocally support free expression, I felt that it went too far.

The Danish cartoons hurt the feelings of many Muslims by portraying the deeply revered Prophet of Islam in a negative light. Free speech or not, they were very offensive, so I thought, "Screw Denmark." Full stop. End of discussion. That's how I essentially saw the matter at the time. Plus, if European countries truly believed in free speech, even speech insulting to Muslims, then why is Holocaust denial a crime in places like Germany and Austria?

Yet I still returned for more of Sandmonkey's unique perspectives. I resonated with his sarcastic style. To an extent, it was similar to mine. I understood and empathized with many of his grievances, and I appreciated his blunt self-critical honesty. I was also attracted to the heated but sometimes insightful discussions in his blog's comments section.

In a moment I'll never forget and which I now find crazily absurd, one day I was completely stunned to read some comments on his blog posted by American Jews expressing their opposition to the war in Iraq.

"But how is that even possible?" exclaimed my surprised skeptical self. I wondered, "Aren't the Jews the sworn enemies of Islam? Aren't they the ones who pushed the Americans to go to war with Saddam Hussein to control and steal the oil? And don't they want to rule the Holy Land from the Nile all the way to the Euphrates River in Iraq to achieve their dreams of a Greater Israel? So then why would they oppose the war?"

Up until I stumbled upon the blogosphere, I had never knowingly interacted with any Jewish person in my life. I had never even heard of outspoken American Jewish critics of Israel before, such as Noam Chomsky. At best, I had disliked Jews or tried to ignore them, and at worst, I hated them. But in light of my past experiences at my first international school when I began having non-Muslim friends for the first time, a part of me wanted to give "those pesky Jews" the benefit of the doubt. I strongly suspected that they deserved it and weren't all that bad. The other part of me had no intention of wavering or budging. Budging was for the weak and the nonresolute.

Excited by the possibilities of the Internet, in March 2006, Nour Merza, a blogger based in the United Arab Emirates at the time, wrote that "A Revolution is bubbling underneath the shrouds of ignorance. It will not happen overnight, but every day is a step closer to it." She elaborated she did not "necessarily mean overthrow-the-government-in-a-bloody-coup type of revolution," but more specifically meant "an intellectual revolution, a social revolution, a religious revolution, a cultural revolution. Preferably, a *peaceful* revolution."

Indeed, many bloggers back then, as early as 2006, spoke of that potential for the Arab world, which in the idealistic bubble of the blogosphere was very seductive to think of sometimes.

Arab dissidents and political "heretics" of all stripes were discovering one another online and slowly forming a massive self-organized network—a lively energetic creature—that within cyberspace and the hearts and minds of many youngsters was gradually legitimizing the sort of views that would have gotten offline on-the-ground dissidents ostracized and grouped with the illegitimate "bastards" of their societies.

Principles such as freedom of speech, freedom of religion, and freedom *from* religion held no genuine legitimacy, practice, or acceptance in the real rotten world of Arabia's orthodox, authoritarian, and paternalistic circles. But online, in the liberal Arab blogosphere, such views and principles thrived and propagated.

Most beautifully of all, the various Arab and North African blogging communities linked to one another, exchanged ideas around central issues like online censorship, and established a real sense of regional solidarity. Individual bloggers weren't merely Egyptians, Saudis, or Jordanians. No, they were also Arab bloggers with transnational identities, united by a shared history, language, and cultural heritage, and a powerful impulse to speak up and confront the similar repressive realities they lived under.

As I treaded more deeply into the Arab blogosphere, I drowned myself increasingly in its thoughts and ethos of individualism, freedom, and intellectual independence. It was liberating. I wasn't alone. All those years, all those times I thought to myself secret heretical thoughts and harbored anti-orthodox suspicions reluctantly, I was not alone.

But where were the Sudanese bloggers?

In late March 2006, I made a slightly depressing realization: a Sudanese blogosphere, made up of Sudanese bloggers speaking about Sudanese issues, was nowhere to be found.

I was disappointed and annoyed, so I e-mailed Big Pharaoh and asked him for helpful information. Instead, I received back encouragement to start my own blog. And so rather than complain about the lack of Sudanese bloggers, I decided to be the first English-speaking one I knew of, writing to an international audience that wanted to learn more about Sudan and specifically Darfur, which by then was becoming a major news story. Many Arab bloggers occasionally wrote about Darfur and I felt that it would be better if a Sudanese addressed the issue and set the record straight since there were many inaccuracies and misconceptions floating around in the Western media and the blogosphere.

But besides the absence of a Sudanese blogosphere, I also had other developing reasons for my slight depression. I was pained by the anti-Islam insults I found online on Western blogs. Moreover, I was gradually beginning to wake up to a number of lies that I grew up with and wanted to further investigate: namely my belief in a grand Jewish conspiracy theory against Islam and my conceptions of an evil U.S. foreign policy.

Thus, on April 14, 2006, I launched my blog, The Sudanese Thinker on Blogger under the pseudonym Drima. I picked the name The Sudanese Thinker not because of a sense of intellectual self-importance as misperceived by some, but because growing up, I'd been accused many times of "thinking too much" and on numerous occasions, I'd been advised to just "chill out" and "stop analyzing." Moreover, I genuinely wanted to engage in a rethinking exercise to reexamine my own perspectives and correct them where flawed. With that, I ventured into the virtual desert to contemplate some truths and discuss the meaning of things with certain objectives in mind.

First, I wanted to talk about Sudan and Darfur to a Western audience in ways that were more nuanced and accurate than what they were being told in mainstream Western media. Second, I wanted to help start a Sudanese blogosphere to fill the void. Third, I wanted to discuss wider Arab–United States political issues and to start a friendly dialogue with Jews and Israelis online who were willing to engage in civil discussions. And finally, I wanted to defend Islam and wage an online jihad against the insults. Ultimately though, and more than anything else, I just wanted to think aloud and learn.

As soon as I started my blog, I told Big Pharaoh, who then generously linked back to it and instantly started sending me my first readers. I was ecstatic.

And so began my unintended exercise in intellectual and psychological self-empowerment. Had I known then where my adventures in virtual wonderland were going to take me, I might not have ventured so far in at all.

To be able to speak, to be able to have a public voice, especially when you've had none before, can be one of the most emancipating feelings any human being can experience. And once you've had a taste of it, it's near impossible to go back.

As I started my emancipatory regular practice of blogging, my previous healthy morning habits faded into distant memory and quickly got overtaken by newer ones driven by obsessive curiosity. Nearly every morning immediately after waking up in my university dorm room, the first thing I always did was to check my blog and then read other blogs.

The more actively I commented on large blogs like Big Pharaoh's and Sandmonkey's, and linked back to mine in shameless self-promotion, the more my readership grew. I then announced my blog on a Sudanese online community forum called Shamarat that I was beginning to frequent around the time to attract Sudanese readers and encourage them to begin blogging about Sudan.

Soon, my promotional efforts began bearing fruit. Checking my blog's stats counter daily became an addiction.

"Fifty-three visitors."

Yes!

"Cool, I even had one visitor from Sweden today."

Awesome!

Those were my humble beginnings, and they uplifted me greatly. After all, I was just some random nineteen-year-old Afro-Arab Muslim kid who was arguably naive, clumsy, and inarticulate, but for some reason, my seemingly inconsequential words turned out to be consequential for a tiny yet growing number of individuals: people who regularly set aside a few minutes to read what I had to say and sometimes responded with positive input. I was grateful for them.

Something I wrote resonated. Something I wrote pushed their buttons.

Some thanked me for opening their eyes and helping them realize that "not all Muslims are crazy lunatics" and that "Islam can be tolerant and understood more rationally."

There was Halalhippie, a friendly Dane who frequently commented and who wanted to engage Muslims in the blogosphere to understand why the cartoons of Prophet Muhammad triggered so much resentment in the Muslim world. Then you had Andrew, an unflinchingly pro-Israel German Jew living in Ireland who offered his interesting perspectives in discussions about the Israeli-Arab conflict, and Jim, who was raised by two lesbian mothers in 1960s America, and blogged about his experience reading the Qur'an, documenting what impressed him, and what didn't.

And of course, there was also Carmen, a favorite Egyptian-American blogger of mine who commented on my blog, and described herself in her blog bio as an "Egyptia-yorker who's spent over half her life stuck in two worlds not of her own making. Unable and unwilling to fully embrace one identity over the other, she created (is trying to create) her own place in the world where people love each other unconditionally, irrespective of artificial boundaries, and where dancing merengue is as necessary to life as breathing air." She was, in other words, someone who grew up a third-culture kid, just like me.

A whole new world full of interactions and online friendships with intriguing personalities began opening up and enriching my life.

On May 7, 2006, the Egyptian authorities detained a prominent Egyptian blogger and political activist named Alaa Abdel Fattah along with other bloggers and activists during a peaceful demonstration calling for an independent judiciary in Egypt.

Using his widely read, mostly Arabic blog, Alaa had been actively and openly pushing the boundaries of political dissent and what was tolerated in Egypt for a while. He inspired many Egyptians to start blogging and to assert their right to free speech, and his hard work was beginning to show results.

Like all his comrades, Alaa was not born an activist. No one is ever born an activist. Activists are not born, they're made. And Alaa's turning point in his making came the year before in May 2005 when he saw his mother, an activist and professor of mathematics, getting beaten up by police in a protest and jumped in to protect her. That was the defining moment that flung him into the risky world of activism. He had had enough by then. His father, a human rights lawyer, had been tortured and jailed for five years in 1983 for his political agitation, and now, Alaa was about to experience jail, too.

In response to Alaa's and the others' arrests, the Egyptian blogosphere erupted in protest and started a "Free Alaa" campaign demanding the release of all those unfairly detained. They made Alaa the face of the campaign to humanize it and establish a personal narrative for the cause.

In just a few days, the advocacy garnered the attention of the Arab blogosphere and global media. Bloggers broadcast the issue, and the global media helped amplify it. Hundreds of demonstrators—Egyptians and Westerners—protested the arrests and expressed their solidarity in front of various Egyptian embassies and consulates in major cities throughout Europe and in the United States and Canada. They took pictures of themselves and posted them online.

As for me, I did my little part by blogging about the "Free Alaa" campaign and signing online petitions that I forwarded to others. I helped spread the word.

Forty-five days after his arrest, Alaa was finally released from detention. The campaign had apparently helped publicize the issue widely and caused enough pressure and embarrassment for the Egyptian authorities.

The online campaign for Alaa's release was my little turning point, the first of bigger ones to come. It gave me my first subtle taste of what activism entailed and what bloggers can achieve together when they strategically coordinate their efforts. The campaign also showed me how Western and Arab citizens can unite in a spirit of sisterhood and brotherhood to rally behind a worthy cause.

However, the episode also raised some difficult questions for me. It was one thing to blog, but to protest on the street? Under a dictatorship? That was a whole other thing, and it just felt reckless. It felt stupid. Recklessly stupid. Did Alaa and his compatriots really believe they could change the system? And if yes, then to what extent? Influencing hearts and minds with words through blogging and writing seemed very reasonable. Protesting to change a dictatorship seemed foolish and dangerous. The risks were simply too high, and the chances for success were nearly zero, so why bother?

Well, somebody had to try at least, right? I mean, who wouldn't want more justice? More equality? More *dignity*?

Any sane person would. Reading about Alaa's passion and ordeal, I sure did, and that's why I contributed in the small, almost pathetic way I could: with petitions and a blog post. I desired to see the change, but the shameful truth was that I didn't have the courage to *be* the change. I didn't want to be the one taking the kinds of risks Alaa took. I was neither ready for nor all right with such an idea. Most of us aren't. Nonetheless, we are fine with others doing it for us though, and something about that made me cringe.

Maybe I was a coward. Maybe I just didn't have the balls to stand up to injustice bravely like others did. Or maybe, I just didn't have the *conviction*.

When I arrived at the blogosphere, I arrived in mushy form and eventually, I set myself on a quest to learn and to unlearn. To blog and to grow. To probe and to investigate. I didn't arrive with titanium-solid convictions. If anything, I was doing the opposite: chipping away at many of my older—and now suspect—convictions to make way for new, more valid ones independently. I didn't know it, but sooner or later, the new convictions were destined to emerge.

In the Islamic tradition, it is said that "Whoever mingles with a people for forty days becomes one of them." While the statement is not literally true, it is does point to a truth.

Our contexts and circumstances—familial, social, historical, environmental, theological, legal, political, educational, technological, geographical, financial, cultural, institutional— including the people we spend most of our time with, have tremendous influence on us and the formation of our attitudes.

Context affects *everything*.

Throughout my life, I had so far been blessed and cursed by the multiplicity of contexts. From my school, my home, my long holidays in Sudan, and my neighborhood mosque in Qatar's media-controlled environment, to my three international schools and liberal circles in Malaysia. The influence of constantly changing contexts on my beliefs and identity was inescapable. It is for everyone.

It transforms us, molds us, and too often preys on us—usually unnoticed, unperturbed, and largely invisible. As invisible as my semi-forced arranged marriage to the traditions I was born into and that I was expected forever to be wedded to.

In my case however, out of nowhere came the subversive blogs, bastards, and heretics of the Arab world and swiftly derailed all of that, exposing me to a world beyond my conflicting formative years and politicized religious upbringing. It was profound, but the "fun" was just starting.

A rude awakening lay around the corner.

PART II

The Fall from Grace

5

Conversations with Little Satan

In June 2006, I boarded a plane in Tokyo, Japan, to embark on a twelve-hour trip that would mark the start of an intimate and special relationship the moment I landed at my destination.

"Place your hand on the fingerprint scanner, please. Now stand in front of the camera."

With a quick scan and digital snap, I entered the system, but it was still way too early to feel relieved. I had another hurdle to overcome.

"Because you're a Sudanese citizen, we're going to have to take you through an extra screening process for security purposes. Are you familiar with this?" the black imposing immigration officer asked with rigid formality.

"Yes, the person at the U.S. embassy explained it to me," I acknowledged.

"All right, you're good to go then. Come, follow me," he said with a stiff tight-lipped smile after stamping and handing me back my passport.

From my earliest childhood days, America had always

been a place that held special significance and meaning for me, but that meaning was conflicted, and at times, conflicting.

There was the domineering imperial America, and there was the liberating America. The America that backed Israel—otherwise known as Little Satan—and consequently oppressed the Palestinians violently, and the America that helped liberate Kuwait and save Muslims from genocide in Bosnia. The America that killed over a hundred thousand Japanese civilians with two nuclear bombs, and the America that played a critical decisive role in helping free millions in Eastern Europe from the totalitarian clutches of Soviet communism. The America that held within her some of the best educational institutes and innovation hubs in the world, and the America that lived, breathed, and exported its enticing hedonism of "sex, drugs, rock and roll" to billions overseas through her Merchants of Cool.

She could be beautiful and seductive, or "bitchy" and corruptive. She could lift you up high, or bring you down low. She could deeply inspire you with her can-do attitude, or horrify you with her reckless military adventures and foreign policy double standards.

She's the junk food you eat, the education you seek, the brands you wear, the music you hear, and the scientific and technological miracle you wield. You can run away from her, but you cannot avoid her creative fingerprint. It's everywhere. In shopping malls, magazines, cinemas, television, music—even in your sleep. And often, she's there by popular demand.

It was within those dynamics that America and I fell in our long-distance love-hate relationship. And now, I was finally going to get to know her up close and personal. I was also unknowingly about to get to know Little Satan more closely than I could have ever imagined.

I grabbed my passport and luggage and followed the immigration officer. He escorted me to a small empty corner room a short distance away and left me with a young tall white guy, probably in his mid-thirties, who welcomed me warmly with a strong handshake. "Hey, how are you, buddy? You must be pretty tired from your long journey. Have a seat."

"Thanks."

I sat, and to keep myself awake, blasted some Linkin Park and Metallica into my ears, but turned down the volume when I noticed the officer speaking to me.

"Don't worry, we'll try to get this done as soon as possible and have you cleared. It's just a formal procedure we have to complete," he explained while typing behind the computer.

His friendly attitude immediately put me at ease.

"Would you like some coffee?"

"No, thanks, I don't really drink coffee," I replied.

"Well, make yourself comfortable. We're going to go through a series of questions that I need you to answer as accurately as possible, all right? Like I said, we'll try to make this fast," he said amicably.

"No worries, I understand. Take your time," I said.

He had my fingerprints and photo taken once again, and struggled to stroke some commands into the computer while I filled out a form. "Man, I hate computers!" he exclaimed.

In an attempt to break the ice, I jokingly asked if I could give the computer a try. The officer laughed. "I'm afraid I can't let you do that. Oh wait, there we go. It's working now. I'm sorry for the delay, it's just requirements," he said.

"Thanks to Uncle Sam, right?" I responded casually to which the officer laughed even more, bringing down the remaining wall of formality between us.

"Yup, you got it. Thanks to Uncle Sam. They make the rules, buddy. I just follow them and make sure we're good." Suddenly he turned quite serious, and started asking me all kinds of random questions, some of which I recognized from the visa interview I did at the U.S. embassy in Kuala Lumpur weeks before. After about an hour, he was finally done with entering the necessary information into the computer.

Contrary to the horror stories and warnings my friends had shared with me—including my Malaysian friend Lisa who went through a harsh interrogation after 9/11—my entire experience of going through U.S. airport security was a pleasant, friendly, and very professional one. At last, I could now breathe a sigh of relief.

Hello Chicago.

By late June 2006, it had already been two months since I started blogging, and half a year since I became addicted to reading sociopolitical blogs and opinion columns in mainstream media. It had also been a few weeks since I initiated my extensive online dialogue and conversation with numerous Israelis and self-identified Zionists. It felt adventurous on some level, as if I was crossing behind enemy lines and into forbidden territory.

As the logic in politically correct and well-meaning Muslims circles went: "Not all Jews are bad people. Only Zionist Jews are." But in the blogosphere, that didn't make sense, because I came across numerous self-identified "Zionist Jews" who expressed opinions that were critical of Israel's occupation of Palestine and antagonistic toward U.S. policies in Iraq and elsewhere.

So what did Zionism mean to each one of them, and how did they interpret it? And what was the true extent of the goals of Israelis and Zionists anyway? Did they and American Christians really want to destroy Islam's third holiest site in Jerusalem to rebuild their temple?

As I began exploring these questions, I adopted a very friendly tone with my Jewish and Israeli readers, because I really wanted to do my best to reach out and keep an open heart and mind to understand their perspectives directly.

In April, I took the first step with a request for an explanation on what the Israeli flag represented. Numerous Muslims I knew believed that it's proof of Israel's desire to rule from the Nile to the Euphrates. They argued that the two blue horizontal lines represented the two rivers, and the Star of David, in the middle between the two lines, represented the dream of a Jewish holy land ruled by Jews.

The blog post attracted twenty comments. In it, two commenters, Don Rodrigo and Finnpundit, said that the flag was designed to represent the traditional Jewish prayer shawl, the *Tallit*. I checked out the Wikipedia links Don posted and read other sources. I became convinced.

Finnpundit wrote that he's previously heard "a different version of the lie: the rivers were supposed to be the Tigris and the Euphrates," and noted that the argument has been used by Arab radicals for three decades. "It's interesting to note that once you start a slander, it takes on a life of its own," he said.

The post also instigated a passionate but enlightening debate between Melanie, a pro-Israel reader, and LouLou, whom I recall as a North African Tunisian-Moroccan woman.

Melanie wrote, "Arab nationals are hypocritical, especially since Israel won a war which it fought in defense, not aggression."

LouLou responded with a calm level-headedness that I admired and found quite rare in the blogosphere those days. "Well, Arabs don't see it that way, naturally. They think Israel tried to establish a state exclusively for Jews on land where Jews owned six-to-ten percent of the land. Palestinians saw this as a threat to their land. The vast majority of Palestinians at the time either worked on farms and olive groves or owned them. Very few of them had any education or any other skills. So losing land was a matter of life or death to them," LouLou argued back, and added that "Neighboring Arab countries were worried about an influx of refugees into their territory, which is exactly what happened actually."

She then stated some very interesting things. She believed that "arguing about who was in defense and who was in attack isn't going to solve anything now. I doubt that you can get both sides to agree on that," which seemed refreshingly reasonable. Then came the shocker: "As for Jews who were expelled from Arab countries, if they lost property then they're also entitled to compensation from those Arab countries and they should continue to demand it."

Again, I was stunned. Arab countries had Jews who were expelled? For real? It was the start of another new inquiry that led me to find out that my dad had a Sudanese Jewish acquaintance, whose last name was Cohen, during his university days in Khartoum. Yes, Sudan had Jews, too.

"With all due respect to both sides," continued LouLou, "I don't think this conflict deserves the attention it gets. There are much worse conflicts. Personally, I'm sick of hearing about it. It's been almost sixty years. But unfortunately I think that while it continues, this culture of blaming Israel and the West will never go away and we'll never make any progress."

One phrase stuck with me: "this culture of blaming Israel."

In one short statement, LouLou had summed up what I sometimes felt and suspected on a vague level but couldn't articulate. Victimhood: a disease that plagued the Arab and Muslim mind, based on my experience. It registered. And to a lesser extent, so did LouLou's observation about how there were "much worse conflicts." At least in terms of death and destruction, there sure were. As Sandmonkey had once blogged, Darfur was one of them, with a death toll that was estimated to be more than two hundred thousand lives. Yet the conflict didn't garner any real attention in the Arab or Muslim world. It just didn't hold the same paramount place within our psyche like the Israeli-Palestinian conflict did. Not even close. Not unless the crUSAders or Zionists were involved, I'd later come to conclude.

Our dictators—often Western-backed—had been successfully using the Israeli-Palestinian conflict for decades as a weapon of mass distraction to keep the people's focus away from local issues and direct blame at external entities, preferably with big noses and horns. In such an environment, the Arab world neither managed to actually help the Palestinians in any meaningful way nor managed to pull itself out from the hole it was in. It was stuck in an ugly cycle of anger, hatred, blame, stagnation, and frustration.

The debate in my blog post continued. Then right below the exchange between Melanie and LouLou, a final comment was posted by a Sudanese person whose name I recognized from the Sudanese forum Shamarat. The commenter suggested that the Israeli flag did really represent a conspiracy for domination, and wrote that "Israelis tried conquering Saudi Arabia, Egypt," and the "promised land extending to Iraq."

"They keep raping Palestinian women, abusing men, and slaughtering children. There is always a judgment day," he warned.

I paused, and for a second, I doubted if the Israeli flag really symbolized a Jewish prayer shawl.

For twenty-five years since 1973, the Sears Tower—a 108-story skyscraper in Chicago—proudly stood as the tallest building in the world in the middle of a concrete jungle of other massive buildings. That is until it was overtaken by Malaysia's Petronas Twin Towers in 1998.

Chicago's downtown eclipsed Kuala Lumpur's multiple times over, and its sheer breadth was breathtaking. There I was, in the city where the Oprah Winfrey Show was broadcast. The city of Michael Jordan and the Chicago Bulls. The city where my oldest brother lived and was on his way to earning a Masters in wireless telecom engineering and working in the industry. It was a great feeling to be reunited with him.

For the longest time, I had always dreamed of traveling to America and immersing myself in her famous cities. On that holiday, Chicago was my first stop followed later by Maine, New York, and a hypnotic thirty-six-hour road trip from Chicago to Los Angeles, through Iowa, Nebraska, Colorado, Utah, and Nevada.

Once I met my brother at O'Hare's arrival terminal after my long screening process, the exhaustion I felt from my long flight evaporated without a trace. I was curious and hungry for experiences. I wanted to savor America, and by my third day, for the first time, I laid eyes on a Jewish synagogue in my brother's diverse neighborhood. It was embellished with a gigantic Star of David and attended by an orthodox Jewish congregation. I viewed the crowd and passersby outside with great fascination. I found it odd that the men wore what looked to me like a black cowboy-style hat and black-and-white clothes that appeared very uncomfortable. The women wore long black-and-white garments, too, and covered their hair as well.

"They must be conservative Jews or something," I guessed.

On a sunny chill afternoon, I headed to Millennium Park in downtown Chicago for a Latin music festival where I was pleasantly impressed by the ethnic and cultural diversity I saw. It was beautiful to see a colorful crowd of people and mixed couples happily singing and dancing together—black, white, Indian, Southeast Asian, Hispanic, Afro-Caribbean, and others. Even the international schools I had studied at in Malaysia were not as diverse. Away from downtown, it was a different story.

As my brother drove back toward the suburbs, I noticed that neighborhood blocks became increasingly segregated. Along just one street, I observed storefront signs in a sequence of various languages besides English—Spanish, Italian, Polish, Japanese, Korean, Hebrew, and Arabic.

Millennium Park's delicious mixed fruit salad was no more. I thought about it and speculated that while many may enjoy mixing and may thrive in such an environment, at the end of the day they'd prefer to live with those they shared a closer language, identity, and culture with. The formula seemed to work in America, because the diversity was lived and expressed within a larger narrative and framework that made it possible: America as an aspirational idea and immigrant nation and her founding principles as codified in her constitution. Not the document itself, but how Americans—especially those who made up and supported the civil rights movement—rigorously struggled and evolved toward embodying the constitution's values and ideals more justly, equally, and appropriately in their daily social, cultural, and political lives. After all, a constitutional document is just a lifeless piece of paper. It is the abiding people who give life and meaning to it and implement it with their minds, bodies, and attitudes. And in return, they affect it with new laws, reinterpretations, and amendments, some of which can be seen as progressive or regressive. A case in point would be amendments on gay marriage, and how the subject splits American liberals and conservatives.

In downtown Chicago, even though I enjoyed the atmosphere of the Latin music festival, I was put off when I saw gay couples engaging in public displays of affection, as if to rub it in your face. "Where does the line get drawn?" I questioned. I admired Chicago's openness and diversity, but the sight of what I then saw as religious moral transgressions strengthened my opposition to secularism. And don't even get me started with how epically culture-shocked I was when I watched an episode of the television show, Maury.

"Secularism breeds immorality and encourages sin, and

we Muslims shouldn't allow it in our own countries. We *must* maintain some level of moderate religiosity and protect the Islamic morality of our societies" went my logic. I was adamant.

"How do you as a Muslim parent deal with MTV?" asked the Imam rhetorically during his Friday prayer sermon. "How do you raise your kids to follow Islam in an environment with all this media?" The congregation was very diverse and had a noticeable number of white Americans whom my brother told me were converts.

"In America, we're lucky to live in a free society," the Imam declared. "But this freedom means we can go to the mosque or go to a bar. Live by good values or adopt a materialistic lifestyle. It means you're free to do as you wish, and there's a downside to that, especially if you're a Muslim parent. What if our young teenagers choose the MTV path? What will you do? Lock them up at home? You can't force them to follow Islam, but you can patiently explain it to them. Explain to them the benefits of an Islamic lifestyle. Explain to them why the materialistic lifestyle is destructive and gives in to the *nafs*, the carnal self. Explain to them and educate them. Do your job as a parent. That's the best remedy."

At last, an Imam who gave a sermon that felt relevant, rational, and empathetic. I had not experienced anything like it before. Too often, one heard the same old sociopolitical religious tirades or something theological and doctrinal that can be easily summarized in the following: "Do this. Do that. Fear God, or else risk burning in Hell for all eternity." But not here. Not this time. Not in Chicago.

• • •

By the end of my second week in America, I was using words like "bagel," "meatloaf," and "basement" quite regularly. I had also had the fortune of visiting my aunt in Portland, Maine, and enjoying the warm friendliness of its people. It was a small town where residents greeted one another on the streets and conversed casually as if they knew one another from years before. A stark contrast compared with Southeast Asia's much more reserved social culture.

If we sped up the interactions, put the town's folks on a steady diet of Red Bull, and enlarged the buildings greatly, the experience would have more closely resembled the one I had the following week in Manhattan in New York City.

I reveled in the upbeat fast-paced energy of Manhattan. It was an iconic legendary city that lay at the heart of America's mythology of herself, and the world's view of her. Visiting it and soaking up its sounds and visuals was, as the cliché goes, a dream come true.

Throughout my four-day visit, I stayed with an Indonesian friend whose father was a high-level diplomat working in the United Nations at the time. It was a lucky combination of factors that led me through the doors of the UN building and right into the General Assembly Hall and Security Council room.

There, I stood at the UN's General Assembly podium, the same podium where many world leaders and dictators had stood and spoken before. I stood and faced an empty hall that I imagined was full of representatives from all over the world. I imagined myself speaking to them about justice and equality. Then of course I had my Indonesian friend take some pictures of me at the podium, and of me sitting in the

UN Secretary-General's seat in the Security Council room. I was nineteen, a young dreamer, an innocent idealist, and the experience did something to me. It made something inside me shift. It made me seriously think of the possibilities of what I could do and what I could contribute to help change things and fight for justice.

Maybe I had a role to play someday. Or maybe I'd just avoid the tricky task of trying to change things and focus on making lots of money instead. Back then, the two options mistakenly seemed mutually exclusive to me.

It looked just like it did on television. Except now, I was present at the site. I could sense the somber atmosphere. It had been nearly five years since the attacks, and the big hole was a gaping reminder for New Yorkers and visitors who walked by Ground Zero. What kind of thoughts ran through their minds? Did they hate Muslims? Many right-wing American bloggers sure did, and the road toward dialogue, understanding, and reconciliation would be long and often impossible.

Indeed, it would be much longer than the road trip and drive from Chicago to Los Angeles that I'd embark on days later with my brother and his friends. We left on a Thursday night at around 11:30 P.M. I was all hyped up. Hours later, as we sped down a highway separating Iowa's vast farmlands on both sides, I couldn't help but contemplate. I felt sandwiched between two worlds, between two planes of existence: the Afro-Arab Muslim engrained within me versus the liberal "Westernized" me. It's a struggle I woke up to every day. It was about the fight and search for answers to find a place where I belonged. Not a physical place, but a mental one

that I was determined to think my way to. A mental state
that I and only I could achieve for myself.

Bump.

Our Ford SUV shook a little bit and I snapped back to reality. The scenery was beautiful. America's skies are exceptional.
I had never seen such pretty skies anywhere else. Dozens of
hours later, we were drowned in darkness, driving through
Utah. And then the darkness was no more. It was Saturday, at
three in the morning, and there it was right in front of us. Las
Vegas. Sin City. Millions of tiny twinkling lights sat ahead in
the middle of the Nevada desert. By afternoon, I was enjoying
a swim in the Pacific Ocean at L.A.'s Hermosa Beach.

On July 12, 2006, a day after returning to Chicago from the
road trip to Los Angeles, yet another conflict exploded in
the Middle East, this time between Israel and Hezbollah in
Lebanon.

It would be the first war I'd come to follow closely from
start to finish, not through sensationalized Al Jazeera Arabic
or Fox News broadcasts, but via the direct humanizing raw-
ness of the blogosphere.

Simply put, according to the Israeli narrative, Hezbollah, a
terrorist organization, provoked the war by attacking Israeli
soldiers. According to the Arab and Lebanese narrative, Israel, an evil occupier, was and always has been the original
instigator of violence through its decades-long colonial and
ethnic cleansing policies. Regardless of the narratives, however, many in the blogosphere and mainstream media agreed
that Israel used excessive disproportionate force that inflicted a heavy death toll on innocent civilians in Lebanon.

The war dominated discussions in the Arab, American, and Israeli blogospheres with levels of engagement that ranged from the extremely toxic to the relatively civil. Ironically, it was then—at the height of the war and at a time when anger toward Jews and Israel was peaking throughout the Muslim world—that my feelings toward the Jewish people changed for the better. It was also around then when my romanticized view of Hezbollah and Hamas as holy resistance movements took a severe hit and irrevocably fell out of favor.

Unlike everyone else around me who was glued to a television screen, I found myself caught up in heated debates with Israelis, pro-Israeli Americans, and Arabs in the virtual terrain and comments sections of many blogs, where I witnessed a more complete spectrum of diverse Israeli opinions that I was not used to seeing before. I got familiar with Israeli views that ranged from reprehensible statements such as "a Lebanese baby before an Israeli soldier" in matters of death, to sentimental protests, such as "this is why they hate us, why are we bombing them like this?"

Many Israelis hated Hezbollah, but they also hated how Lebanon was being pummeled. They felt the Israeli military was being reckless and out of control. They reached out online to other Arabs who also reached out in a mutual spirit of dialogue. It was eye-opening.

As far as I was concerned, before the blogosphere, Jews were a monolith—a homogenous evil entity that was out to rule the world and subjugate Muslims. Until I realized the truth.

As much as I was outraged by the destruction Israel had inflicted on Lebanon, in one transformative epiphany, my

propaganda-inspired false perception of Jews as an evil
unified front collapsed and was forever shattered into pieces.

The American soldier: portrayed by most big-budget Holly-
wood movies as honorable and heroic, and by the anti–
United States machine as corrupt and murderous. So who
was he truly behind the portrayals? Or in this specific case,
who was she?

Her name was Jessica. When I "met" her through an Egyptian blog in mid-August, she was a U.S. Marine stationed in
Iraq. By the end of our August interactions, she transformed
into a fellow guitar player and music lover, one who joined
her country's army for what seemed like financial reasons
more than anything else. Unlike me, she was part of a crU-
SAder Zionist military invasion and didn't use Fruity Loops
in any of her recordings. Like me, she disliked the Republi-
can party and was a music minimalist at heart. She loved the
clean sound of acoustic guitar, drums, and vocals. She was a
fan of the Shure SM57 microphone, and found solace in a
world of Pro Tools and melodies, away from a volatile world
of death and destruction.

"But life out here isn't too bad," she said. "I'm having a
hard time grasping what all the anger is about. I mean, between religious entities and such. From my perspective,
they're all mostly Muslim. And I can't understand why Muslims want to kill other Muslims. Especially when they talk
about brotherhood so much."

"I can understand why they don't want the United States
here, because what country wants to be occupied? But right
now the Iraqis are killing each other more than they're killing U.S. troops.

"What is your personal relationship with religion?"

Her questions touched a raw nerve. They reminded me of the tragic headlines.

"Where am I supposed to begin?" I contemplated. "The repulsive heinousness of torture advocate, U.S. Secretary of Defense, Donald 'Rumsfailed'? The monstrosity of militant Sunni and Shia radicals, and the religiously and politically motivated age-old rivalry between them? The roles of al-Qaeda, Saddam loyalists, and the Iranian theocracy? The bloodlust that had befallen the entire nation? Or the status of my relationship with religion?"

I never got back to her with an adequate reply.

By late August, I achieved a small but memorable milestone. I succeeded in "recruiting" a talented English-speaking Sudanese poet to start blogging about Sudan and other issues of importance to her. Her name was Chipster. She had been following my blog for three months and started hers in July. To me, it signaled the hopeful birth of a humble Sudanese blogosphere that could become a viable voice for young Sudanese wishing to speak for themselves to an international audience.

I was touched by the words of encouragement that Chipster e-mailed me. On her blog's sidebar she wrote, "I would like to make a difference in the world—not for the mere attainment of fame, glory, or an everlasting legacy. But to fulfill my duties as a human being; to be the voice of the oppressed and the minority; to reflect true Islam and to better serve humanity." She then finished with an acknowledgment: "Drima's blog has inspired me to start my own."

I didn't know what precisely inspired her or what it was I

did that was of value, but the more we e-mailed, the more I came to understand.

She told me she didn't really have issues with Western people since she had interacted with some in her life, but it was the Jews that she remained skeptical about. "I guess you stop generalizing when you actually interact with them," she said. "Sometimes I say that Allah made you announce your blog in Shamarat so I can come across it and get the opportunity to interact with the other mysterious world—the West—in order to better understand things and to expand my horizon, and believe me, I'm grateful." Chipster also commended me for trying to better represent Islam to non-Muslims, which was quite vindicating.

She came to see that Muslims and Arabs are the primary root cause of the backwardness and oppression happening in the region, and complained that if our religion had been implemented the right way, instead of exploited, we would be doing much better. I shared that sentiment, too—the desire to see true Islam prevail, even if I didn't know what this "true" Islam exactly entailed, but that didn't matter. It was based on personal preference.

Then over the following months, as my blogging evolved, Chipster began criticizing me out of a constructive and corrective desire that I heartily appreciated in her.

In an angry but well-intentioned e-mail, she was livid at how my tone toward Arab and Muslim misdeeds was becoming harsher, but turning softer when my target was Israel and the West.

And she was quite right. She called me out on my shift. While I was unabashedly critical of Israel's occupation and policies, I had become more aggressively outspoken against what I saw as the problem of anti-Semitism in the Muslim world and the widespread disempowering political culture of conspiracy theories. For that, I remained and always will remain vehemently unapologetic—even if many dualists continue to misinterpret and misrepresent such a stance as "treasonous." I won't budge. Regardless of the historic reasons and conflicts, such hatred of Jews—or anyone for that matter—is absolutely inexcusable. One can engage in scathing political criticism without resorting to the dehumanization of "the Other," even if or when the Other does that to us. We ought to be better. Moreover, the disempowering culture of conspiracy theories that breeds victimhood needs to be crushed.

The problematic issue that Chipster correctly highlighted in my blogging was something else. Bit by bit, I was becoming a lot angrier at the political lies, violence, and deceit of Arabia's tyrants and militants, than I was at Israel's and America's deadly misdeeds. I was concerned more with redeeming myself for my past sins of hating, than I was with the feelings of Arabs and Muslims who despised U.S. policies and Israeli injustice. I was driven more by a desire to show Jews and Westerners that only a minority of Muslims were hateful bigots, than by a desire to expose Israeli injustice against the Palestinians. And it all seeped into the tonality of my cocky sarcastic words, making them biased and tainted.

Truth be told, in unleashing my legitimate anger at all the unearthed lies and false Jewish conspiracy theories—the Arab dictator's Weapon of Mass Distraction of choice—I was actually unleashing my fury at part of my former and now disowned self. It was a messy process.

The hidden misleading political presuppositions and

assumptions implicit in what I did and believed previously were fast becoming increasingly visible to me. So much of what I held to be true in the political domain had fallen from place, and fallen from grace. And the fall was about to get deeper and more painful.

6

Infidelity

The sincere pursuit of Truth requires you to entertain the possibility that everything you believe to be "true" or "valid" may in fact be wrong. *Everything.* Your nationalism. Your religious beliefs. Your upbringing. Your unexamined convictions.

Your *story.*

That story you keep telling yourself about yourself and about the world. That core story you're so self-identified with and assume to be inviolably true.

"We're a great nation with a great history and culture."

"Our religious tradition and holy book is the truth. Theirs is rotten and corrupt."

"My God is awesome. Theirs isn't!"

All of that is open to reevaluation when it occurs in its various bigoted "us versus them" manifestations across the face of the earth. Every bit of it, and it can be painful. Because right beneath the surface of your unexplored presumptuous beliefs, you're probably going to discover things you'd rather just not deal with. It's just easier that way. But for how long?

"For how long, Amir?" the nagging voice inside my head

kept asking. By September 2006, I was beginning to feel fatigued from all the blog reading and blogging, but I couldn't stop. It was too late. My subversive thoughts and activities had already opened up a can of worms that had to be dealt with.

In uncovering many of Arabia's political lies and propaganda against Jews, I found some of them to be disturbingly intertwined with shocking religious edicts and textual references in the sacred books that I was not fully aware of.

Accusations by Imams quoting Qur'anic verses and claiming that the Jews are the descendants of pigs and apes. References to a Hadith that says Judgment Day will not come until Muslims fight the Jews; that every stone and tree with a Jew hiding behind will say, "Oh, Muslims, there's a Jew behind me. Come, and kill him." Fierce sermons asserting that the Jews are an eternally cursed people that God will reap eternal damnation upon.

In short, intensely hideous rhetoric with a religious basis.

It wasn't the first time I had necessarily heard such things, but this time the rhetoric landed on my ears differently. It deeply repulsed me, and the fact that it had any hint of religiosity infused with it horrified me.

Worse, the Middle-East Media Research Institute, MEMRI, a media propaganda organization started by a former Israeli Intelligence colonel, translated and subtitled the material into English and disseminated it on YouTube. They did it to highlight the dark side of religion's influence in the Muslim world in a stark and damaging one-sided manner, (while conveniently failing to highlight the hateful anti-Arab rhetoric sometimes spewed by Israeli media.)

I was dumbstruck. Is this really what Islam says about fellow human beings? Is this truly what my love stands for and advocates?

Accepting an obviously political lie as a lie is much easier than doubting the validity of a religiously or sacredly packaged "truth." The religious packaging adds an aura of sanctity, which consequently—thanks to our programming—triggers a sense of obedient reverence and a reluctance to question.

But this was too much to ignore, so I dug into the various interpretations. Specifically, I looked into the Qur'anic verses that supposedly said Jews were "turned" into pigs and apes (2:65, 5:60, and 7:166).

The interpretations varied. Some religious scholars were of the opinion that the verses did not refer to all Jewish people, but only a certain disobedient group that then died off. Others said that the group of Jews who were "turned into pigs and apes" reproduced and gave birth to descendants who inhabit the earth today in the form of, yes, you guessed it pigs and apes. Religious scholars with a more humanistic and reason-oriented inclination rejected a literalist reading. They said the verses refer only to certain Jews who disobeyed God and use the words "apes" and "pigs" in a metaphorical sense to describe certain qualities, whereby an ape is impulsive, and a pig is stubborn. Similarly to how in Arabic a man who's brave is sometimes called a lion, again, not in a literal sense, but metaphorically.

I appreciated the metaphorical reading by more reasonable scholars. However, I was still rattled by the zealousness and absurdity of the outspoken literalists, and that the Qur'an would contain any such descriptions at all in the midst of so many other beautiful verses in the first place. Verses about tolerance, compassion, and brotherhood, such as verse 13 from Surat al-Hujurat:

"O mankind! We created you from a single (pair) of a male and a female, and made you into nations and tribes, that ye may know each other (not that ye may despise each other). Verily the most honored of you in the sight of Allah is (he who is) the most righteous of you. And Allah has full knowledge and is well acquainted (with all things)."

How could tolerant verses like that exist within my beloved book together with other baffling passages? Why all this mental gymnastics to interpret tricky parts of the Qur'an? And who gets to decide which verse should be interpreted metaphorically or literally, and on what basis?

The more I sifted through pages and pages of Web sites about Islam, for it *and* against it, the more doubtful and shook up I became.

"What's wrong, Amir?" asked a seemingly insidious voice inside of me. "What's wrong?" it asked, again and again, inducing in my body subtle creeping sentiments of resentment and anxiety. Was I the one guilty of gradually becoming unfaithful to Islam as a result of my increasing confusion and weakened faith? Or had my Islam and its guardians been treacherously unfaithful to me all this time?

The infidelity—at times intense—felt shared on both sides, and the feeling grew as I slid into more guilt-ridden doubt, and as my anger toward my faith slowly fermented.

I wanted answers. I needed answers.

Answers to hose off and pour gushes of cold water onto the slowly burning flames that were beginning to simmer within me.

. . .

"There is no such thing as a peaceful Muslim. Peaceful Muslims are filthy scum who ran out of ammo. You're not gonna convince us with your *taqiyyah*, you fucking terrorist."

It was a viewpoint that permeated many blog comment sections that I frequented in the "American Rightosphere," where uncompromisingly rigid right-wing and neoconservative American bloggers regularly bashed Islam and criticized Bush for being too soft.

I began visiting those blogs because I wanted to learn more about American politics and what made political Americans tick. I wanted to defend Islam and show them that the extremists don't represent the faith; that "true" Islam is about peace; that Islam has a color-blind emphasis on the equality of all races and ethnicities; that the greatest form of jihad is the inner spiritual one and has nothing to do with warfare, and that the lower jihad that has to do with warfare has strict specific rules, which forbid the killing of noncombatants, women, children, and the elderly.

But no matter how hard I tried, my arguments were futile and amateurish. All I got in return most of the time was nothing but venomous hatred, anti-Islam talking points, and accusations of *taqiyyah*—a practice supported under some Islamic interpretations that justifies deception and concealing the truth when under threat.

In the American Rightosphere, *taqiyyah* took a sinister meaning and was frequently flung to smear and discredit well-meaning Muslims who attempted to clarify Islam's positions on controversial matters. If a Muslim desired to express something of a tolerant nature, he or she supposedly didn't sincerely mean it. It was just an act of *taqiyyah*—a deception to "advance the jihadist agenda to destroy freedom in the West." Under this guise, in the eyes of most right-wing congregants of those blogs, all Muslims were suspect and easy to dismiss.

I felt helpless and despaired in the face of the overwhelming hatred that was directed at me.

I knew the pain of racism. I knew the agony of bullying and abuse. I was more than familiar with their tastes. I had been stung by them and survived them years before, but I had no previous familiarity with this. No, not this. Not the attacks that were directed at my divine idealized beauty, the beauty that deep inside of me I still valued and treasured most: my Islam.

I couldn't bear to see my love attacked so rabidly and my Prophet insulted so casually. The poisonous words on my computer screen bewitched my university dorm room and gnawed at me in mockery. I felt demeaned.

Life on my university campus—located in the middle of nowhere, more than three hours away from Kuala Lumpur—was mind-numbingly boring on most days. The location was supposedly chosen to isolate students from KL's busy city life and to make them focused on academia instead. Under those circumstances most students spent an obscene amount of free time downloading and watching movies, and playing computer games, such as World of Warcraft. I, on the other hand, found myself blogging obsessively, watching movies, making music, and eventually reading books from the university library on entrepreneurship—books that I began borrowing after coming into contact with an initial book that set off the chain reaction.

That first book was called *The Cashflow Quadrant* by an American self-help author and financial literacy advocate named Robert Kiyosaki. I found it by accident on a friend's desk while hanging out on a weekend afternoon in his dorm room.

The book contained an eye-opening premise about the nature of money and financial freedom that can be summed up and explained in a basic simplified way using the Cashflow Quadrant diagram as follows:

On the left side of the Quadrant is where about 90 percent of people operate. You're either an "employee" and you have a job, or you're a "self-employed" individual and you own a job. In both cases, you exchange your time for money, and the amount of money you make is limited by how much you can charge every waking hour. Furthermore, by operating on the left side, you're basically pursuing what's called an "active income." Meaning, if you stop working, the money stops flowing.

Now, on the right side, that's where roughly 10 percent of people operate. You're either a "business owner" and you own an asset or a system in which people work for you, or you're an "investor" with money working for you. In both cases, your income is not limited by how much time you can exchange for money. There are no limits. You can grow your business and assets exponentially, and have them make money for you even while you sleep. In other words, it's "passive income" paradise.

I was instantly drawn in and finished the entire book in a few quick sittings.

"Why didn't anyone teach me about this before? Why aren't we armed with financial literacy and taught about the nature of money and financial freedom and independence? Why are so many of us so eager to study something mundane, graduate, and work for someone else to spend a lifetime trying to climb the 'corporate ladder'?"

With more reading, I'd come to find that the education system in its dominant form was designed for an industrial age to churn out smart compliant individuals to fill the workforce. It wasn't designed to bring out the best in people and encourage them to pursue their passions.

Again, it felt like another treachery by the guardians of the order. Society had deceived me with its baseless expectations and limiting conventions.

The seed was planted, and I knew I no longer wanted to spend my life working for someone else in cubicle hell doing something I had no real love for. My long-term plan would be to start an online business—maybe even become a full-time six-figure-a-year blogger like Darren Rowse of ProBlogger fame—and retire young, rich, and self-reliant, with plenty of free time to do things that mattered and made a difference.

In my view, it was the right and smart thing to do. There's nothing wrong with being an employee per se, but I abhorred the employee mindset that dictated that one should ultimately sacrifice his or her passion for a life-sucking job merely in order to make good money.

Islam also encouraged us to work hard and not to rely on others for handouts. In the Islamic tradition, there's a story about Prophet Muhammad—himself an entrepreneurial merchant who engaged in a lot of business before his prophethood—that demonstrates Islam's position on self-reliance. Once, a poor man came to the Prophet begging for alms. In response, the Prophet gave him money to feed his family and to buy an axe. He instructed him to use it to chop firewood, and sell it. The poor man did just that and was soon able to fulfill his needs from his own labor.

It's October 2006, and it's business as usual in the stridently anti-Islam, anti-Muslim portions of the American Rightosphere. Islam and Muslims: bad. So bad, in fact, that the question "Where are the moderate Muslims?" has to be repeated loudly, again and again to no avail. America, Western civilization, and Israel: good. So good, they're virtually incapable of doing any wrong unless the matter involves not being tough enough on Islam and Muslims, and of course, the Muslim's unpatriotic, soft, spineless, liberal, gay-loving friends, the Democrats.

Regular exposure to this caricature continued to frustrate me, but over time, it also expanded my view of things. It introduced me to many of the infamous heroes of the Rightosphere—within it and outside it in mainstream American media. Through blogs like Jihad Watch and Hot Air, which had very large followings, I came to learn about Ann Coulter, the fiery blond defender of the Christian Right. I came to know the opinions of benevolent radio personality Rush Limbaugh. I came to watch countless disturbing Fox News clips on YouTube featuring Sean Hannity and Bill O'Reilly. And not to forget, I also came to discover the jaw-dropping bad craziness of Christian fundamentalist Pat Robertson.

I came to clearly see that in the United States, there sure are a great many not "Jesus loves you" Christians, but "salvation through Jesus only, or else burn in hell" bible-thumping

Christians who are just as bigoted as their Muslim counter-parts, and have no shame in calling for the bombing of Mus-lims and the "enemies of freedom," and "opponents of Christianity," and casually excusing the deaths of innocents as collateral damage.

"There's no use in debating them," I dismissively con-cluded for a while, and eventually, the generalizing insults of much of the Rightosphere no longer provoked me like be-fore. I got used to it and could now read everything more calmly. My skin turned thicker.

But it wasn't all gloomy.

During my countless hours of surfing the blogosphere, I did come across numerous kind, open-minded conservatives from the Rightosphere. They were mainly traditional, family-oriented, Republican-voting, church-going friendly folks interested in discussing matters about Islam sincerely in good faith, and not for the sake of pompously "winning" an argument. Some of them made an obvious effort to ask their questions in a respectful tone, a gesture that I appreci-ated and which demonstrated their goodwill. We discussed polygamy and the status of women in Islam, controversial instances in the life of the Prophet and what they meant, Is-lamic law and secularism, and a myriad of other subjects.

I also took time to listen to their views about conservative political philosophy and classical liberalism, and to my sur-prise, I resonated with much of what they had to say. I learned about the ideals of limited government, free enter-prise, and the liberty of individuals. I tried to grasp some of the distinctions between conservatism and libertarianism, and with every gulp from this new cup of knowledge, my budding heretical and entrepreneurial spirit took a liking toward classical liberalism, and a disliking toward the welfare "nanny state."

However, questions on both sides remained unanswered.

I was not fully satisfied with arguments for unfettered capitalism and against socialism. If free-market capitalism worked so well as a wealth generator, then why was there still such noticeable poverty and homelessness in the United States? What about the welfare of the poor who can't find work? To assume that private enterprise can just magically "solve" these issues by creating jobs and providing good services is to basically assume that all enterprising individuals are motivated by compassion and not greed, which is obviously naive.

On my side, I left a discomforting number of legitimate questions unanswered as well. Chiefly among them were questions about Islam's teachings on war and peace, and the example of the Prophet when viewed through a contemporary lens.

I didn't know how to adequately answer them. Or perhaps I just wasn't ready.

"Hey, I just heard that the new batch of students from Sudan arrived earlier today," my roommate informed me.

I had just apathetically finished performing *zuhr*, the afternoon prayer—not really out of love—but mostly as a duty, a task that I felt I needed to get out of the way.

"*Wallahi tamaam*, where are they staying, so I can go and welcome them?" I inquired.

"They've settled down temporarily in different buildings. Some of them are on Hassan's floor, and the Southerners are with David right now at V4. I don't know where the rest are."

I changed my clothes and headed to V4 nearby from where I was staying at V5 on campus. On my way there, passing by the V4 cafeteria area, I spotted the new unmistakably Southern Sudanese students.

"*Salam, kafekum?* How are you?" I waved my hand and greeted them as I approached, but I didn't receive the response one would expect.

Their collective gaze of searing contempt rendered me invisible before them.

Sullied by dirty looks, I stood in the impoverished moment as an object of hate, an avatar onto which they projected all the injustices they've endured at the hands of tyrants originating from northern Sudan.

In their eyes, I was not Amir, a fellow Sudanese student in the university they've just joined. No, I was one of "them," one of those lighter brown-skinned "Arab Northerners," a *jallaba*, the embodiment of a monolithic evil and the source of tragedies.

One by one, they passed by me—a ghost in the middle of the walkway—initially with my palm stretched out to welcome them, and then as one trying to fully internalize and wrap my head around what had just happened.

When I told my Southern Sudanese friend Sokati about what took place, he shook his head and laughed in amusement and what I hoped was disappointment.

"Man, *wallahi* that sucks. I don't agree with what they did, and I think it's very unfortunate and really stupid. It's very sad to be honest," he said. "*Bas ya Amir,* I don't think you should take it personally. Really, man, you shouldn't. You have no idea what these guys have been through, and the kind of shit we Southerners have to deal with every day in Khartoum. Some of them may easily have lost a mother, or a father, or a brother, or a sister who got killed in the war, and may have even had their entire village burned down."

"Yeah, but what does that have to do with me? I mean, okay, some Northerners have done a lot of fucked up shit. To *everyone* in Sudan, by the way, including us Northerners— but why do I have to be held guilty for it? *Khalas*, get over it, we're not all bad people. Plus, I was clearly there to say hello and welcome them," I said.

"Listen, man, there's still a lot of shit happening, so it's easy for you to say 'get over it' when you're in a privileged position. Again, what they did is wrong, and I don't support it, but man, you're just going to have to accept it and let it be," said Sokati. "For some people there's just too much hatred and it's not easy. You have to give it time."

"Give it time. Aha, sure."

As the hands of the clock of Time ticked by, I've come to strongly suspect that among all the people of the world, a certain specimen of the Northern Sudanese is quite uniquely positioned to understand racism unlike most.

In Khartoum, the Northern Sudanese, especially one from the "elite" tribes, is privileged in every sense. Culturally, politically, militarily, socially, and financially. He's at the top of the strata, and often, he's oblivious to it and takes it for granted. Beyond the borders of Sudan however, in a country like Syria or Lebanon, the Northern Sudanese in the eyes of racists gets labeled with the Arabic epithet *abd*, a "slave." A "dirty" Arab breed or a non-Arab, tainted by the "impurity" of his "Africanness." A person who becomes the target of condescending prejudice and abuse merely because of the darker color of his skin.

Hence, by virtue of my mixed ethnic and cultural North-ern Sudanese heritage and the life I've lived, I began looking around me and seeing things through a more colorful lens. In the United States for example, I came to more intimately understand the interiority of what it's like to be black, white, or bi-racial, like Obama. White on black racism. Black on white resentment. Mixed bi-racial smiling faces and the some-times "competing loyalties."

In a nutshell, identity and its perils.

The year 2007 ushered itself online in rather gruesome victo-rious fashion right after what was perhaps the most celebrated death the liberal Arab blogosphere rejoiced in: the recorded execution of Saddam Hussein on December 30, 2006.

Videos on YouTube and LiveLeak went viral and were watched by millions. It was a historic widely televised occa-sion. To witness the humiliating end of the Arab world's most horrific dictator—one who killed hundreds of thou-sands and used chemical weapons against his own people, including innocent women and children—deeply satisfied a great deal of people, me included. While I now strongly cringe at my choice of words, I meant every one of them when I blogged that "Saddam Hussein got what he de-served and the fact the Iraqi government didn't skin him alive, spill acid on his face, slap him a thousand times, chop off his genitals, and then hang him, is actually a decent thing."

I never felt any remorse for Saddam. None whatsoever, which is one of the reasons why I was so angered by some of the vehemently anti-American Arabs and Muslims who blogged sad "obituaries" for Saddam, "the fallen hero," the "martyr." Their anti-Americanism—in many ways easily understandable given the destruction of Iraq—was so unfathomably intense to the point of overshadowing and glossing over Saddam's murderous rampage and war crimes, cheapening in the process the blood of the Muslims and Arabs they claimed to defend.

It was a sad, frustrating affair.

As 2007 rolled in, I never really gave my formal education the attention it required. I was too busy pursuing my own self-directed informal education on history, sociology, entrepreneurship, social media, and politics. I was too busy blogging, collaborating with other Middle Eastern and African bloggers on advocacy projects, and trying to spawn a bigger Sudanese blogosphere.

I joined Bahraini blogger Esra'a Al-Shafei at her invitation as an initial partner to start Mideast Youth, a group blog site dedicated to giving a voice to progressives and minorities, and spreading democratic ideals. I helped craft the new mission statement and recruit suitable bloggers from around the region. Together, we took steps to welcome Iranians, Baha'is, Kurds, Sunnis, Shia, and, quite controversially, even leftist Israelis. The project took off, but a short while later, I had to bail out as a partner because of time commitments. I stretched myself way too thin. Esra'a however persevered and years later went on to win numerous awards and recognitions for her commendable work and creative dissidence.

On my side, as more blood spilled in Darfur, I led an online initiative in partnership with Mideast Youth and a site called Good Neighbors to spread awareness about the ethnic cleansing in the western region of Sudan and to call more attention to it in a nuanced manner. The result was the Web site Darfur Awareness with the provocative slogan "200,000 Dead and Raped Sudanese Matter." We used the platform to post updates about the conflict, and to distribute digital graphic banners for bloggers to display on their sidebars, and while the reach of the Web site wasn't huge by any significant measure, the project did help boost awareness among roughly forty thousand folks at the very most. By online standards, it's a small number, but in the real world, it could fill a stadium, a thought that satisfied me and helped shut up my inner critic.

On another front, I joined Global Voices Online, a premiere community of activists and citizen journalists, after receiving an invitation to become their volunteer Sudan author writing round-ups of the activity in the small but growing Sudanese blogosphere. Accepting that invitation would turn out to be one of the best decisions I made in my life, because over time, GVO—cofounded by Ethan Zuckerman and Rebecca MacKinnon in 2005 at Harvard University's Berkman Center for Internet and Society—would end up connecting me to a number of individuals who'd profoundly impact my social and political awakening.

In the meantime, I also continued updating my blog with rants, curses, and sober analysis, which led to a growing regular daily readership in the few hundreds and a Weblog Award nomination. I also remember having a brief e-mail exchange with the UN Secretary General's special envoy to Sudan at the time, Dutch diplomat Jan Pronk, whose work I appreciated, and later finding out that some UN staff were following my blog.

But more memorably though, around that time, I woke up to a painful, treacherous infidelity that left me seething with rage. It didn't happen instantaneously. It took time, but when it finally dawned upon me, I felt crushed under the revelation's weight and immensity.

Often on the Internet, the anonymity I hid behind gave me free reign to criticize whoever and whatever I wanted, whenever I wanted, the way I wanted. And as I got more comfortable with this newfound freedom, I took full advantage of it, engaging sometimes in rhetorical styles that brought out the worst in me. But most of the time, the opportunity to speak freely and anonymously enabled me to shed my limiting social conditioning around taboo matters. It allowed me to build my confidence and gradually find my voice.

In response, a few readers found some of my material and style objectionable. My criticism of disempowering conspiracy theories and my attempts to humanize the diversity of Jews—Ashkenazi, Sephardic, liberal, socialist, secular, orthodox—especially didn't sit well with them. And for that, I received hate mail and attempts at intimidation. It wasn't serious, but I did feel the pressure.

"How many more like them are out there reading my blog and getting pissed off?" was a constant question that I contemplated with unease.

I understood where my critics were coming from. I empathized with them, but I deeply resented their tactics and inability to engage in reasoned debate. Instead, they went by the Arab tyrant's propaganda manual. It goes like this: when an opponent of yours says something you don't like, don't bother debating the subject matter, rather smear him with the epithets "CIA agent," "Zionist," "traitor," and "apostate," or at the very least, imply he's one.

In some real-life settings, when one makes such politically motivated accusations against another, one essentially advocates the killing of the target of these accusations. After all, the punishment for treason and apostasy in numerous Muslim countries is death.

The subtle intent inherent within the tenaciously critical messages I received—whether their authors meant them or not—was not lost on me. It angered me. My crime? Having a different opinion that repulsed some unforgiving mortal souls.

But I hardly budged and I continued with my regular scheduled programming, eventually stumbling on a philosophical quote that left a strong impression on me. So strong in fact, it was a crucial turning point after it had magnanimously settled in.

Those mind-transforming words on my screen were, "I disapprove of what you say, but I will defend to the death your right to say it," supposedly said by a French philosopher named Voltaire. I stopped and read the quote a few more times. "I disapprove of what you say, but I will defend to the death your right to say it." Again, slowly. "I disapprove of what you say . . . but I will . . . defend . . . to the death . . . your right . . . to say it."

Huh.

The quote dissipated something. It lifted a cloud of smoke, and injected an alkaline idea-virus deep into the acidity of my consciousness. And little by little, that alkaline notion would come to neutralize aspects of my inner reality, leading to a pivotal culmination: my close reading and inspection of the Universal Declaration of Human Rights.

Article 1: All human beings are born free and equal in dignity and rights. They are endowed with reason and conscience and should act towards one another in a spirit of brotherhood.

Article 18: Everyone has the right to freedom of thought, conscience and religion; this right includes freedom to change his religion or belief, and freedom, either alone or in community with others and in public or private, to manifest his religion or belief in teaching, practice, worship and observance.

Article 19: Everyone has the right to freedom of opinion and expression; this right includes freedom to hold opinions without interference and to seek, receive and impart information and ideas through any media and regardless of frontiers.

Article by article, I reflected upon the illuminating text. Upon the inalienable rights made alien in my heart and mind by the guardians of the order. Made absent from the make-up of my valued convictions. Foreign. Far away. "There," not "here." Concepts that I formerly felt were vague privileges, that some were fortunate enough to enjoy but others didn't and couldn't, because "that's just how things go." Because "that's just the way it is."

Because maybe some of us are just destined to be forever destitute and hopeless. And perhaps we are. Perhaps as long as we're kept ignorant of these rights, as long as they're kept away from us and prevented from taking root in our souls, then we *will* remain destitute and hopeless—so hopeless, we'll be relegated to the dustbin of history.

"Why have I not learned anything about this monumental document during my childhood school days? Why have I not been taught about its significance by the various guardians of Islam I studied under?" I questioned and wrested internally. "Why haven't I heard it being discussed at home by family? So all this time I had rights? Rights that are rightfully mine? Rights that were stolen from me? Rights that I was treacherously denied? Why?"

Indeed, in the name of all that is holy and sacred, why?

Why, why, *why*?

No, human rights are *not* privileges. They're *not* meant for "some." They're meant for *everyone*—even that young unsuspecting twenty-year-old me. Freedom of speech, freedom of religion, freedom *from* religion. The whole list. Every single one of them is my right, and therein laid the seed of the conflict that would soon blossom and trigger a full-blown confrontation between myself and that which I was too afraid to confront before: the troubling aspects of my no-longer-idealized beauty, my Islam.

For within the text of the Universal Declaration of Human Rights, freedom of thought was my right. Freedom of speech was my right. And even *disbelief* was my right, but not my right in the Islamic tradition I knew. Not according to Islamic law as I was familiar with it. Not as too many Muslims believe it, for too many believe in the imposition of death for blasphemy. Death for apostasy. Stoning for adultery. The amputation of hands for thievery. Extremely harsh and bloody punishments in the context of today's modernity. Special tax and second-class status for the non-Muslim *dhimmi*. "Unjust, undemocratic, backward tyranny," I internally declared in rage and agony.

My Islam, my romanticized love, my beauty, she had fallen from her idealized place, and fallen from grace. Lame, simplistic declarations that she is "a religion of peace" were no longer going to suffice. She and her guardians had lied to me. "But it can't be true!" I wrestled still. The culture she and her practitioners created was after all a great civilization that gave the world so much innovation and progress in the form of science, architecture, and art. So what happened? What went wrong? How did she really lose her virtue? How did she stagnate to her current sad, depressing, ugly state?

Was it truly because of Muslim moral decadence and the infidels as I had learned in my early formative years? Or was it something else?

PART III

The Painful Heartbreak

7

How She Really Lost
Her Virtue

He had a calm yet serious look in his eyes that hinted at tranquility and defiance. Dressed in white robes and garments, were it not for his bulkier stature and white turban, he would have borne a bit of resemblance to India's nonviolent resistance movement leader Mahatma Gandhi. Yet even if he didn't resemble Gandhi in appearance, he certainly did in temperament and conduct.

I took another look at his picture on my computer screen and clicked on to the next page. The more I read about him, about this man whom many came to call "Sudan's Gandhi," the more intrigued I became. Born in Northern Sudan around 1909, Ustaz Mahmoud Mohammed Taha was a Sudanese Islamic reformer who mobilized a movement in Sudan for religious change. He called for social justice, equality between men and women, and equal citizenship status for Muslims and non-Muslims. By early 2007, I had been immersed in his views online for a few months, and found them very appealing.

Taha provided hope. He and his student Abdullahi

An-Na'im, whom we'll come to later, opened me up to new perspectives that presented a path for reconciling the conflicts that troubled my relationship with Islam. In Taha's view, Islam in its original form had gotten corrupted and Muslims needed to reread the Qur'an in light of a crucial distinction between two categories of verses it contained— Meccan verses and Medina verses.

According to the Islamic tradition, the Qur'an was revealed to Prophet Muhammad during a nearly twenty-three-year period starting from 610 CE, when he was at the age of forty, to his death in 632. The revelation came down through the angel Gabriel in two stages, the first of which began in Mecca. During those earlier days, the revelation of the Qur'an was characterized by verses that encouraged peace, compassion, and tolerance. At the time, the Prophet's nascent community of followers was still small but growing, and as it grew and voiced calls for social justice, it caused concern among the oppressive and brutal ruling tribal polytheists of Mecca who rejected the message of Islam.

And so for years, Muhammad and his followers were mocked, ridiculed and at the peak of hostilities, boycotted and severely persecuted by their opponents.

Some of the Prophet's earliest and unprivileged followers from nonprominent families were also tortured to death by Abu Jahl—a particularly hostile Meccan pagan and bitter enemy of Muhammad—in an attempt to make them renounce their newfound monotheistic faith and discourage others from adopting it. The conditions, endured by the community for over a decade, were harsh and ugly to say the least.

And despite that, during this entire difficult Meccan phase, the Prophet responded with peace, patience, and restraint and acted in accordance with Qur'anic revelation. He preached the ideals and more importantly embodied them in his dealings with his opponents in Mecca.

For instance, in 23:96 the Qur'an commanded Muhammad to "Repel evil with that which is best," and in 16:125 to "Invite (all) to the way of thy Lord with wisdom and beautiful preaching; and argue with them in ways that are best and most gracious." Then in 16:126 the Qur'an goes on to say that "if ye show patience, that is indeed the best (course) for those who are patient."

As evidenced by the above verses—the like of which there's many in the Qur'an—Islam throughout the Meccan period was essentially pacifist in nature. Critics claim that was the case only because the Prophet had no other choice but to be pacifist. He was powerless and was in no position to engage in violence, they say.

In light of later Qur'anic verses, one will clearly see that this isn't true and that instead an affirmation of the primacy of peace was the critical reason. This brings us to the Medina phase of Qur'anic revelation that followed the Meccan period.

After the situation in Mecca became unbearable, the Prophet emigrated from Mecca to Medina and joined the Muslim community there where it grew and prospered. His emigration was such a significant event, that it came to mark the beginning of the Islamic lunar calendar.

Over at Medina, the Prophet established a charter that saw bonds of neighborly relations form among Muslims and non-Muslims. The community grew in influence under his political and religious leadership—a differentiation in roles that is important to make, and which too many Muslims fail to grasp. Mecca's ruling elite wasn't pleased with this development, which led to events that set up conditions for violent confrontation.

As the battles drew closer, the Prophet continued receiving regular Qur'anic revelation as told by the Islamic tradition. During this post-emigration phase, the revelation came to be characterized by verses that were now very different in tone and content compared to the earlier tolerant Meccan verses. These new war-related Medina verses were not revealed all at once, but instead came in stages.

First, they granted Muslims permission to fight the unbelievers who persecuted them as the Qur'an in 22:39 proclaims: "To those against whom war is made, permission is given (to fight), because they are wronged, and verily, God is most powerful for their aid."

Secondly, after permission was granted to Muslims to fight, another verse was revealed to the Prophet that dictated the defensive fighting must be conducted within certain rules and limits described in 2:190 to 2:194 as follows:

Fight in the cause of God those who fight you, but do not transgress limits; for God loveth not transgressors. And slay them wherever ye catch them, and turn them out from where they have turned you out; for tumult and oppression are worse than slaughter; But fight them not at the Sacred Mosque, unless they (first) fight you there; but if they fight you, slay them. Such is the reward of those who suppress faith. But if they cease, God is oft-forgiving, most merciful. And fight them on until there is no more tumult or oppression, and there prevail justice and faith in God; but if they cease, let

there be no hostility except to those who practice oppression. If then any one transgresses the prohibition
against you, transgress ye likewise against him. But fear
God, and know that God is with those who restrain
themselves.

Following the intensification of the hostile situation between Mecca and Medina, the verses no longer merely granted
Muslims permission to engage in war, but unequivocally
prescribed it to them as a religious duty as clearly instructed
in 2:216 and 2:217, where the Qur'an says "Fighting is prescribed for you, and ye dislike it. But it is possible that ye
dislike a thing which is good for you, and that ye love a thing
which is bad for you. But God knoweth, and ye know not."

In effect, the verses enjoined Muslims to wage militaristic
jihad against the unbelievers of Mecca, albeit conditionally
and under certain circumstances.

Ultimately, the battles between the Muslims and Meccan
pagans came to a close with a Muslim victory and takeover
of Mecca. The Muslim army led by Muhammad could have
vengefully massacred the pagans of Mecca but didn't, as that
would have been a violation of Qur'anic commandments and
limits.

And herein is where all the "fun" begins.

If things are as clear and straightforward as I had explained
above, then why is there so much turmoil? One may wonder
how can there be so much senseless violence in the name of
Islam, then? One may also legitimately question and wonder
about the expansionary conquests undertaken by Muslim
armies after the Prophet's death, and their sometimes offensive, not defensive, nature.

Alas, in reality things are not as simple as explained in
the preceding passages. Over the decades and centuries after
Prophet Muhammad's passing, Muslim scholars developed a
complex body of religious literature consisting of competing
interpretations of the Qur'an and the Prophet's sayings and
conduct. Eventually, the view that prevailed dictated that
the Medina verses on jihad abrogated and repealed earlier
tolerant Meccan verses. This was not some random arbitrary
act. Rather it was based on the Qur'anic principle of abrogation, itself mentioned in the Qur'an in verse 16:101 for example, which says: "When we substitute one revelation for
another,—and God knows best what He reveals (in stages)—
they say, 'Thou are but a forger' but most of them understand not."

And this of course brings up the million-dollar question:
who among the religious scholars gets to decide the verses
that abrogate and that get abrogated? How, why, and on what
basis?

The intricacies involved in the matter are too long and
complicated to break down in this book, but at the risk of
oversimplifying things, one can safely say that the pro-
abrogation perspective—while contended by other scholars—
prevailed in matters of jihad at the end of the day because
it was politically useful. Since then, it has become the rather
accepted consensus among dominant and domineering Muslim scholars.

And it is precisely this type of politically motivated
consensus that Ustaz Mahmoud Mohammed Taha, the Sudanese Gandhi, was mobilizing his nonviolent religious reform
movement against. Specifically, he advocated for a new Sharia
based on Meccan verses—a stance that many came to find

controversial because in their view, Taha appeared to be dismissing the rest of the Qur'an consisting of Medina verses.

Still, while Taha's movement was relatively small, it was loyal and very dedicated, and its ideas seem to have threatened the order of things. Consequently, Sudan's military regime, led at the time by the opportunistic dictator Jaafar al-Nimeiry, with alleged collaboration from cunning elements of the Sudanese Muslim Brotherhood, chiefly among them Hassan al-Turabi—yes, that same Turabi—conspired to bring Taha down, now an aging man in his seventies.

The despots made their move in response to a publication authored by Taha that opposed the implementation of the government's version of the Sharia. For authoring it and distributing it, they accused him of apostasy and sedition, and ruthlessly pursued their plans in a matter of days.

On the morning of January 18, 1985, after refusing to recant his beliefs, Taha was brought out for his scheduled hanging. He was publicly executed to the cheers of a crowd of Muslim Brotherhood supporters. His body was then flown by helicopter and secretly buried in a remote location unknown to his family and the public until this day.

Four months later, appalled Sudanese angry at their dictatorial government's abuses and mismanagement took to the streets in a revolution that overthrew Nimeiry's regime. Democratic rule was soon restored, only to be deposed again in 1989 by al-Turabi's National Islamic Front.

In a detailed article published on September 11, 2006, in *The New Yorker*, George Packer called Taha "the moderate martyr." But he wasn't. He was more than a moderate, for moderate is a relative term, used to inadequately describe one in contrast with worse company. In Taha's case, while some

of his ideas were awkward and inane, his message is ultimately so full of humanity, it puts him nowhere near the
ruthless dictator and power-hungry Islamists who murdered
him.

In reading Taha's story and coming to learn more about the
contested nature of Qur'anic interpretation, I started to become aware of the complexities involved in "Islamdom," and
how the majority of Muslims aren't even aware of these
complexities. Most don't even read the Qur'an closely, let
alone read it through a lens that contextualizes verses appropriately. Instead, they entrust themselves to religious leaders
claiming guidance from God, and preaching archaic doctrines frozen in time. The episode woke me up to my pitiful
religiosity.

Sure, I now understood the difference between the Medina
verses and Meccan verses. Sure, I came to see how militant Islamists and jihadists subscribe to the views of pro-abrogation
scholars and the doctrine that divides the world into two hostile domains: the Abode of Islam versus the Abode of War, but
dozens of troubling questions remained. Where did true Islam stand in regard to other matters? Matters such as apostasy, women's rights, and free intellectual inquiry?

Clearly, I had more to investigate and discover. And many
of the answers would come to arrive either in the form of
more questions or insightful contentious debates in a new
virtual playground that came to have an incisive effect on
my worsening relationship with my faith: the American
Muslim blogosphere, or in one word, the "Islamosphere."

I am unable to recall how exactly I came across the Islamosphere. But I do vividly remember blogging about and

becoming addicted to one particular American Muslim blog written and maintained by the Pakistani-born blogger-turned-author Ali Eteraz.

Ali's written demeanor was that of someone who grew up as a third-culture kid. He was born in Pakistan, had lived in different settings, and finally ended up immigrating with his family to America. Like mine, his was a journey to belong and to reconcile the perhaps irreconcilable, a journey in which his relationship with Islam came under scrutiny. And in his anecdotes and stories, I recognized a lot of myself.

With his witty commentary, and blog post titles like "Theological Diss of the Day," Ali's blog quickly became endearing.

Initially, before I began to appreciate his writings, I had attacked his views during my first online visits for his espousal of secularism and total separation of Islam and the state. I still strongly felt that Sharia must have a place in a Muslim country.

"The solution isn't to get rid of our divine Sharia, but rather it is to implement a moderate version fit for today's world, the correct Sharia that represents true Islam, protects morality but also allows people their freedoms," I had thought and decided, even though I couldn't really elaborate the valid basis for this moderate correct Sharia I aspired to see.

I had never met Ali Eteraz in person or known him in real life. But by reading anything I could find by him, I felt like I had found an intellectual older brother treading the path ahead of me. Someone whom I understood, and more important, made me feel understood.

Just as The Big Pharaoh had introduced me to the liberal Arab blogosphere, Ali was my gateway to a plethora of

American Muslim bloggers in the Islamosphere. There were
the Salafis like Umar Lee, the Shia like Aziz Poonawalla, the
African Americans like Tariq Nelson, the traditionalists, the
modernists, the Sufis, the secularists, and even a few atheists
who considered themselves cultural Muslims. Through
them, I became familiar with distinctions and diversities
that were not part of my Islamic consciousness.

Every group that identified with Islam had its own approach and theological reasoning, and all of them engaged in
open debates about the religion in a frank way that was much
less dogmatic than anything I had ever witnessed. Theirs was
an Islam that, for the most part, affirmed the values of the
American constitution, an Islam of openness and possibilities
that perhaps held potential to salvage my relationship with
my faith if it was to ever recover.

But there were still obstacles on the path to recovery and
discovery, and the most immediate were Sharia and secularism. Ustaz Ashraf's echoing voice from my Qatar neighborhood mosque still haunted me, and so did Raheem's from that
second abhorrent international school I attended in Malaysia.

"In the West, women walk around naked, inviting all kinds
of obscene stares. They're hardly covered, and they call this
freedom! Freedom! God's Sharia prevents this. It restores
dignity and respect to a woman. It gives her freedom but it
also preserves her honor."

"The infidels must be guided to the truth, and Sharia has
to spread. This is why jihad is important."

The fear was ever-present, lurking quietly at the back of
my mind. "With secularism in place, Islamdom would be
overrun by legalized alcohol, porn, drugs, strip clubs, and

debauchery!" What was I, Amir—Arabic for "prince," and "leader of the faithful"—what was I to think and do?

One fateful evening in 2007, as I was treading through the Islamosphere, my attention shifted back to the Sudanese Muslim scholar Abdullahi An-Na'im.

An-Na'im was a student of Ustaz Mahmoud Mohammed Taha who left Sudan after Taha's execution. When I learned of him, he was a professor at Emory University in the United States, coincidentally the same place where the American Pakistani blogger Ali Eteraz had studied in and got to know An-Na'im. There, reveling in the intellectual academic freedom of his educational institute, An-Na'im freely pursued research on Islam, secularism, and human rights, and worked on a book about the future of Sharia.

I got in touch with An-Na'im and downloaded some of his scholarly work on the subject. What I found was a bittersweet truth that would take time to fully diffuse into my being.

Indeed, the Sharia we Muslims speak of today is very different from the Sharia that existed during the time of the Prophet. The four dominant Sunni Islamic schools of thought—Hanbali, Maliki, Shafi'i, and Hanafi—did not even exist during Muhammad's reign. Like the contested doctrine of Qur'anic abrogation, the schools of thought were all developed centuries later after the Prophet's death by religious scholars and men. Mere fallible bearded *men*, rarely women in case you haven't noticed. And it was their far-too-often overlooked fallibility that An-Na'im emphasized for me. Sharia—in practice at least—cannot and should not be considered divine, because its interpretation, formulation, and application will always inevitably be the effort of fallible men prone to mistakes and the influence of their cultural, political, and social environments.

The conclusion I drew was straightforward. "The Sharia as a divine project is a lie," I silently declared. "Sharia in Iran, Sharia in the Maliki school of thought, Sharia on the moon— *any* Sharia. The supposed and far-too-often assumed divinity of them all is and always will be a lie. By pure virtue of being interpreted and applied by men, Sharia in practice ceases to be divine."

As for secularism, and Islam's stance on apostasy and free intellectual inquiry, in the words of Abdullahi An-Na'im, "If I don't have the freedom to disbelieve, I cannot believe." Whether or not it contradicted the religious literature of the Islamic tradition, An-Na'im's one-sentence statement of wisdom did it for me. It was bulletproof. It gave me the answer my heart was desperately seeking. It also made me rethink the notion of sin, and how the policing of morality can and does lead to a society rife with hypocrisy and hollow acts of goodness. Finally, as An-Na'im would come to write in his uplifting book, *Islam and the Secular State*, "In order to be a Muslim by conviction and free choice, which is the only way one can be a Muslim, I need a secular state," meaning "one that is neutral regarding religious doctrine," and "that facilitates the possibility of religious piety out of honest conviction." Apparently and contrary to popular opinion, "throughout the history of Islam, Islam and the state have normally been separate." This does not entail an authoritarian model like Ataturk's Turkey, for that is a *secularist* state, one that regulates religion and forces Muslim women to take off their hair cover, and is as such a violation of liberty. An-Na'im makes great nuanced effort in clarifying and explaining the important, critical distinctions.

Many journeys in and out of the Islamosphere later, I painfully and inevitably concluded that my incoherent and formerly fiercely passionate, ardently stupid, romanticized conception of Islam all along wasn't anywhere near the best or most accurate. It was just one of various man-made politicized, culturally contaminated interpretations of the sacred texts that I was taught to parrot, but never to think about critically.

Somehow, finally accepting this truth felt good. It felt emancipating because it freed me from remaining beholden to the suffocating, dark, stinking dungeons of subordinating dogmatism. I could now breathe more easily.

Even though I had discovered a great deal about Islamdom— that she's not as simple as the majority of Muslims assume her to be; that she has a complex history; that she contained many difficult-to-face truths that are hard to swallow by any contemporary lover of hers, especially the fanatical kind—I still hadn't arrived at the answer to the key overarching question.

How did she *really* lose her virtue?

Yes, I internalized how after the death of Prophet Muhammad, culture and politics seeped into the post-Qur'anic tradition of Islamdom including the Hadith, making it pregnant with sometimes alarming content offensive to the modern sensibilities of a twenty-first-century globalized world beyond the desert dwellings of seventh-century Arabia.

But how did Islamdom rise and become such a great

civilization? A civilization that gave us words and inventions like algebra and algorithm, and invaluable advances in optics, astronomy, and medicine? And not to forget, breathtaking architectural feats like the Alhambra Palace in modern-day Granada, Spain? How did she rise to such achievements? And more importantly, what *really* made her fall? What was the special virtue she lost, that perhaps we could bring back to revitalize her and revive her again to her former stature?

The answer would soon arrive in simplistic form. But as I searched and waited, the doubt crept deeper, and my faith got weaker.

By June 2007, I was fast approaching the end of my eight-month corporate internship in Kuala Lumpur at the Asia-Pacific headquarters of a Fortune 500 global telecommunications company as part of my university degree.

As a market researcher and database analyst, I was tasked with the enjoyable responsibility of assessing the wireless telecom infrastructure and the competition in Southeast Asia to help my bosses determine which countries held the most potential for the conglomerate's expansion. And as I dug into the data and reports, I became amazed by how wireless telecom technology had spread so fast, and was set to grow even faster in places like India and Africa. The costs of mobile phones and telecom infrastructure were headed downward, while bandwidth capacity was headed upward.

"Damn, this could change everything," I thought. The implications were huge. What would it mean if more and more citizens had easy access to free-flowing information? How would Islam change if more Muslims discovered modernist interpretations of their religion and learned about human rights? How can one spread such content wider and further? Those were questions that spellbound my attention and imagination for days and weeks on end. Questions that compelled me to return to university in August 2007 for my final year to major in a field called knowledge management, and research how social media can be used to revolutionize it.

My love for learning about science and technology—long withered many years earlier by the challenge and trauma of suddenly moving to a new English-language schooling system—returned with full force and fueled my voracious appetite for new knowledge. Knowledge of subjects that were now no longer compartmentalized in my head, but excitingly interrelated.

I spent hours reading blogs like TechCrunch, eating up the writings of venture capitalist Paul Graham, and learning more about entrepreneurship. But away from the Internet and the books, and within the confines of my hostel room, my Muslim roommate would repeatedly say to me, "Man, something is not right.

"Amir, I'm beginning to notice that you don't perform your prayers like you used to. *Ya zoul wallahi*, something is not right, *fe shino*, what's up?"

Sensing he wanted a convincing answer, I reluctantly said, "Nothing. I just forget to sometimes."

"What do you mean you forget? You see me praying in front of you and you hear the *azaan*, what more than this do you want? Seriously, what's the matter with you these days?"

His persistency wore my patience thin and made me burst out, "You really want to know? You really want me to answer? *Khalas*, no problem, download *The Matrix* from the network, and watch it. Watch it first, pay attention to what happens to Neo, and then we'll talk! Until you watch it, don't ever ask me any of those questions again."

The outer layers of my Islam were beginning to show major cracks. Enough to weaken other layers beneath and expose them to the elements.

Again, my chest felt heavier. Perhaps it was Satan and his whispers again, or perhaps I just needed to get more sleep. In need of some consolation, I mentioned my predicament passingly in a brief e-mail to an American Jewish cyber friend and psychologist named Howie who read and commented on my blog regularly. The anonymity made it easier.

"I think you will have lots of problems with feeling shitty because you seek the truth, which is gray, elusive, inconclusive, shifting, and threatens the way we see the world," he said.

"Funny," I thought. "Seeking it has already threatened my world. The damage is done."

"You are psychologically incapable of closing your eyes, Drima," said Howie in his e-mail. "Therefore, you're gonna suffer lots of cognitive dissonance and sadness and confusion and also have a chance to be something great."

"So much for a consolation, Howie. Thanks," I said to myself sarcastically as I read his e-mail, but something caught my attention.

"What's cognitive dissonance?"

Wikipedia defined it as a "discomfort caused by holding conflicting cognitions," and explained that being in a state of dissonance can lead one to experience feelings of dread, guilt, and embarrassment—all emotions I've felt quite intensely and struggled with frequently. But in ustaz Ashraf's fearful, irrational universe, he had a one-word explanation that scarred me throughout my whole cursed life: Satan.

I worried and succumbed to the horrifying terrors of Hell and Satan far too often in a way I wish upon no one, when all along there was a simpler, rational, scientific explanation to what I was experiencing when I doubted and questioned. An explanation called cognitive dissonance.

Another lie. Another deception. Another treacherous infidelity.

A part of me wanted to erupt in a volcanic burst, but my heart was so tired and emotionally drained out from my relationship with Islam and her guardians, the anger registered only as a blip on my radar.

Rejuvenated after much sleep, I woke up the next day in a better state. At last, Satan's so-called whispers of doubt would have no hold over me anymore. I'd now have more options. I could now think my way into new forbidden territory without feeling deeply guilty or disloyal. Thus began my gradual foray into the beautiful heretical world of free thought and guiltless doubt.

On August 30, 2007, five days after my twenty-first birthday, I received an e-mail that contained the following: "Please find attached an invitation for our October 22–23, 2007, conference, Overcoming Extremism: Protecting Civilians from Terrorist Violence. We would be delighted if you would join us as a participant for the two-day event in Washington, D.C."

It wasn't the first all-expenses-covered conference invitation I had received. Global Voices Online had extended one to me to attend their 2006 Summit in New Delhi, focused on citizen journalism and online free-speech issues, but I couldn't make it because I had exams.

This, however, was an invitation to what I felt was a different kind of conference, one that brought about a feeling of slight discomfort.

"Extremism? Terrorism? What does this have to do with me?"

Among the attendees were a public list of big-name participants, including Dr. Hany El Banna, president, Islamic Relief Worldwide, Phillip Bennett, managing editor, *The Washington Post*, Irene Khan, Secretary General, Amnesty International, Aryeh Neier, president, The Open Society Institute, Sir David Veness, former head of counter-terrorism at Scotland Yard, and John Zogby, president, Zogby International.

I did what any cautious person would do and Googled some background information on the organizers and the speakers. Once I satisfied myself, as well as dodged and addressed my father's questions, I made up my mind. "I'm going."

After a week with my brother in Chicago, I arrived at Dulles International Airport in Washington, D.C., on October 20, 2007, and checked into my room at L'Enfant Plaza Hotel.

America and I were back together again, and this time, she and I would witness our complicated relationship evolving to newer heights.

That evening I was sitting downstairs at the hotel lobby, unaware as I'd soon discover, that the Arab guy waiting nearby was Lebanese blogger Mustapha of Beirut Spring, "Godfather of the Lebanese blogosphere," who was inspired to start blogging after the assassination of the former Prime Minister of Lebanon, Rafic Hariri. A few minutes later, a large Arab-looking guy in his mid-twenties emerged out of the elevator. Our eyes met, and we exchanged intrigued looks.

"Could that be him? It must be," I thought

"Drima?" he asked, after taking a few quick strides and sitting down across from me.

"*Aiywa*, yeah, and you're Sandmonkey?" I asked with a smile.

I was already expecting his presence after reading on his blog that he'd be traveling to D.C. for a conference and confirming the details with him over e-mail. Having only seen a picture he blogged of himself wearing a costume mask to hide his identity, I had noticed that he was large, and had big hairy fingers. It would be hard to mistake him.

"Yup, that's me. I am the Egyptian Sandmonkey," he replied with a deep chuckle.

"The Sandmonkey, *akheeran*, we finally meet," I said as we shook hands.

After dinner with Mustapha of Beirut Spring and two staff members from the conference organizer, Sandmonkey and I headed out to the Adams Morgan neighborhood to smoke some shisha, a water pipe for fruit-flavored tobacco, otherwise known as hookah in North America.

Sitting face-to-face in laughter, it felt like we had known each other for years, and not just three hours. Like the shisha smoke we exhaled into D.C.'s cold wind, the year and a half we had known about each other through our blogs had dissipated fast and gracefully.

"What made you start blogging?" I asked him.

"It's a long story," he said, and proceeded to tell me about

how he almost got killed in a terrorist attack that blew up an
Egyptian resort he was vacationing at. "It was close, and by
that point, *khalas*, I had enough. I had to say something
about all the crap I was noticing, you know, and all these
religious nut jobs."

That was Sandmonkey's turning point, and the start of
his journey, conscious or unconscious, as one of Egypt's most
outspoken and visible activists.

I thanked him for poking holes in all the disempowering
United States and Israel–related conspiracy theories I believed
before and for helping me see beyond them. "Seriously, thank
you, man, your blog really helped."

"*Rabbina yikhalleek*, I'm glad it did something."

I took another breath, and exhaled more grape-flavored
smoke. "Aren't you afraid you might get caught, and something bad might happen to you? I mean, you say a lot of
crazy stuff about the government and Mubarak. What if you
get arrested?" I asked in bewilderment.

Eight months earlier in February, the Egyptian blogger
Kareem Amer, who blogged under his real name and identity, was sentenced to four years in jail for the "crimes" of
publishing what the court considered blasphemous writings
against Islam, and for insulting the Egyptian president,
Hosni Mubarak. The authorities wanted to make an example out of him to deter the others.

"You just don't think about it, and don't be too reckless."
replied Sandmonkey.

On the morning of Monday, October 22, 2007, I strolled
into the Ronald Reagan Building and International Trade

Center for the start of the conference where I was met by other participants and prodemocracy Arab dissidents.

As I sat with Sandmonkey for tea and bagels, he suddenly pointed out, "Dude, Irshad Manji is here. Look, she's right there."

The first time I discovered Irshad Manji, the Muslim feminist and self-identified reformist, was when I was reading a strongly critical article that painted her as a sell-out and an opportunist. Typically, those were the kinds of articles I continued coming across about her. Then one evening I decided to have a look at her Web site just to give her the benefit of the doubt. Standing happily in pictures together with Salman Rushdie and Ayaan Hirsi Ali isn't exactly going to win you many Muslim friends. My mind was made up and I chose to dislike her. This lasted for a while until the American Pakistani blogger Ali Eteraz caught my attention with his negative-turned-positive coverage of Irshad's efforts. So I decided to take another look at her.

It became clear to me that she was conducting a shift in strategy and very possibly also experiencing a change in heart. In the last update on her Muslim-Refusenik Web site, she wrote, "This will be my final update on muslim-refusenik. com. I'm about to launch my new site, which will stand for Muslim reform and moral courage rather than merely against all that troubles Islam today. I'll also be blogging, posting more free-of-charge translations to defy the censors, and making it easier to use and distribute my content wherever you are in this world."

I was pleased to read about this shift. Irshad had angered many Muslims with her controversial book *The Trouble with*

Islam Today, which laments that the trouble with Islam is Muslims themselves, and claims that unlike other religions, in Islam, literalism is mainstream. In the book, Irshad also affirms the importance of thinking for one's self and encourages the practice of *ijtihad*, Islam's dented tradition of critical thinking, which was a positive call.

Nevertheless, her approach and the fact that she openly acknowledged being a lesbian Muslim woman compounded her problems severely.

Given what I had read about her, I was surprised to see her enter the building alone. I had learned that she installed bulletproof windows at her home and started traveling with bodyguards because of some death threats she had received.

I didn't want to miss her and so I hurriedly approached with a bagel-filled mouth, a cup of tea in one hand and a half-eaten bagel in the other. Not surprisingly, I couldn't utter much immediately. She grabbed a light breakfast and we sat down alone.

I had questions I wanted to ask her and confront her with. I disregarded her sexual orientation and explained to her that while there were certainly various areas of disagreement, I strongly supported the overall goal of Project Ijtihad, which encouraged Muslims to think critically, but I was critical toward what I felt was her highly subjective and personal approach to Islam's reinterpretation. "Where's the methodology?" I wondered. Unable to resist commenting, I also told her, "I'm surprised you came in alone without a bodyguard."

She took in what I said, and nodded her head back and forth. "If I encourage others to speak up while I myself keep protection then it's very hypocritical of me," she replied. "Others can't afford the same luxury. That's when I decided after much thinking that I'd rather not have any bodyguards. If I get hurt, then I get hurt. If I die, so be it."

I admired that.

The first session of the conference began with a speech by the Secretary General of Amnesty International, Irene Khan, in which she spoke about the increasing number of terrorist attacks carried out against civilians, and the importance of defending human rights.

At the start of the Q&A session, a passionate Lebanese professor questioned her over why "American and Israeli state-sponsored terrorism" wasn't included in her speech, followed by an Israeli who attacked the Secretary General for "doing the propaganda work of Hamas" by what he saw as "drawing a symmetry between what Israel does and what terrorist organizations such as Hamas do." It was a perfect demonstration of the land-mine-infested topical terrain that is the emotionally charged Israeli-Arab conflict. Step in, even with innocent, carefully worded remarks, and something is bound to explode.

After the break, the participants and audience had to pick one of three workshops, which were unfortunately held at the same time, "The Evolution of Terrorist Tactics," "The Changing Media Landscape," or "Community Responses." Only then it became very clear to me why bloggers were invited to the event and why my presence was relevant.

The conference was divided into three themes focused on security issues, human rights, and new media, and we, the bloggers, were expected to share our views on new media–related issues based on our knowledge and experience.

Nonetheless, I accompanied some of the other participants to attend the workshop "The Evolution of Terrorist Tactics" since it's the subject we had the least knowledge about. What I witnessed there sent me into a whirlwind of worry. I was young and unprepared for it. Present in the large room were many U.S. military personnel and a high-ranking decorated official from the Pentagon who spoke with other panelists about the dangers posed by terrorist organizations.

The presence of those Pentagon officials triggered a sudden anxiety within me. It was a wake-up call for the naive, inexperienced twenty-one-year-old me. "What the hell did you get yourself into, Amir?" a voice inside admonished me. "This blogging shit is not a game. What are you even doing here? This is not what you signed up for. It's not a joke. This is serious stuff *ya zoul*."

Around me, attendees and participants, including Arab journalists, sat back taking notes and listened calmly as if nothing of a concerning nature was happening.

On the morning of the second day of the conference, I met Mohammed Fadhil, the Iraqi blogger behind Iraq the Model, which famously supported the invasion of Iraq and the toppling of Saddam Hussein. It was rumored to be widely read by White House officials. President George W. Bush himself cited the blog in a speech in support of his policies and received Mohammed and his brother at the White House on one occasion. It was evidence of the influence blogs could have on policymakers.

I greeted Mohammed and introduced myself. While I had blogged about my support at the time for the war against al-Qaeda and the Taliban in Afghanistan because I viewed it to be unfortunate but necessary, I was critical of the war in Iraq, and so I asked Mohammed about the situation.

"How do people feel about the U.S. military presence? The majority of Iraqis obviously don't share your views and want them out."

"If you ask the people if they want the Americans to stay, they of course say no, but most people don't want them to leave straight away, because they know it will create problems. They say we want them to leave, but not right now, only after things are more stable."

"I guess that makes sense. . . . By the way, is your name really Mohammed Fadhil, as in that's your real name? The same one you use on your blog?"

"Yes. Don't believe me? Here, look at my passport."

"*Damn*, it really is your name. *Wallahi inta majnoon*, you're insane! They can find you and hunt you down. Aren't you even worried about that?"

"*Ya Amir*, you don't even want to know the kind of things Saddam has done to us. The killing. The torture. The rape. The mutilations. With him gone, I'm optimistic about the future. It won't be easy, but I'm optimistic. Iraq will be better."

What struck me the most about Mohammed as he relayed his stories and puffed his cigarette, was his laid-back attitude and wide smile. I may not have agreed with him about the justifications for the war or the positive aspects of its outcomes, but I certainly empathized with his predicaments, found his almost reckless bravery admirable, and wished him the best.

In a few hours, we reached the last session of the conference, which was a panel consisting of victims of terrorism. There were four of them: an Irish man who lost his son during The Troubles, a Kenyan from the U.S. embassy bombing in Nairobi, a Russian from the Beslan school siege, and Ashraf al-Khaled, also known as "the Groom of Jordan," who lost his father and father-in-law when his wedding was hit in the Amman hotel bombings. Hearing them all speak and seeing them in person made their stories more real, raw, and impactful.

Also, sometime on that same day, for the first time I knowingly shook hands with a friendly Jewish man wearing a yarmulke, and had a short, funny conversation with him. I also thanked the liberal American Jewish director Ari Sandel for his Oscar-winning short film, *West Bank Story*, which promoted a message of peace between Israelis and Palestinians. It was screened during the conference and found a very receptive audience.

Coincidentally, at night, while sitting alone for a quick dinner at the hotel, I was joined by the Groom of Jordan himself, who told me more stories, and inspired me with his calm and content demeanor, despite the tragedy he experienced.

In the morning, I finally had time to explore D.C. properly and take pictures. I left the hotel with the conversations of the previous days replaying in my mind: Sandmonkey's blunt, politically incorrect blogging and seeming lack of concern for the potential consequences. Irshad Manji's perspective on having bodyguards and her remark that "courage is not the absence of fear. Courage is the recognition that some things are more important than fear." Mohammed Fadhil using his real name while blogging controversial views in the middle of a volatile Iraq. The Al Azhar educated Dr. Hany El Banna, president of Islamic Relief Worldwide, and his decision to set up a large charity organization to perform the daunting task of helping alleviate poverty. The words of an exiled Arab prodemocracy dissident who dismissed death threats because "the probability of a threatener acting on a death threat most probably isn't higher than the probability of dying in a car accident anyway, unless you're a target they really want badly."

Tales of hope and sorrow, despair and assertiveness, loss and pragmatic optimism. There was no being immune to their influence on one's heart and mind.

"But is all this activism really worth it?"

Arriving nearby Union Station, my thoughts shifted back to my surroundings. I couldn't help but experience Washington through a crumbling lens of preconceived notions. The "belly of the beast," the "major kitchen of world politics," the "big bully." One would expect it to feel shady, even wicked, but it was, dare I say, tranquil and beautiful, and full of friendly people.

It was hard to fathom that such a nice, normal place had the capacity to make all of those influential decisions that sent regular shockwaves across the planet. Shockwaves sometimes devastatingly ominous, and sometimes bearing blessings. But again, America is who she is.

Standing at the Washington Monument, I drew in a deep breath of cold air, and held my chest out in gradual acceptance, savoring the paradox of the moment.

America and I would never be the same again.

. . .

"How did Islamdom *really* lose her virtue?"

The question still persisted, and in doing so, at last handsomely paid off and introduced me to a new set of heroes cooler than the action figures of my childhood. These new heroes of mine were called the Mu'tazila.

The Mu'tazila were an early group of Muslim philosophers and theologians who emerged during the formative years of Islam, and gained ascendency over another group of Muslim theologians called the Ash'ariyya, whom they were engaged with in a spirited war of ideas on numerous issues, including the ontological nature of the Qur'an.

I saw the various battles I read about in black-and-white, and in my eyes, they resembled an almost epic manichean fight and cosmic exchange of blows and stunts.

Here's how it basically went. The Mu'tazila, also sometimes referred to as the Rationalists, held philosophy in high esteem, emphasized free will, and believed that the interpretation of the Qur'an and the Hadith are subordinate to human reason. They also believed that all theological propositions must conform to the principles of rational thought, and if for instance a certain Qur'anic verse didn't, then it had to be interpreted allegorically. The Ash'ariyya, known as the Traditionalists, on the other hand, didn't have as much appreciation for philosophy, and instead emphasized predestination, were more literalist in their interpretations of the Qur'an, and insisted that reason should be subordinate and subservient to revelation—a stance I found appalling.

Thus, by virtue of their positions, the Mu'tazila and Ash'ariyya found themselves at each other's throat, each determined to have their views prevail over the other's. But it gets better, because Team Mu'tazila and Team Ash'ariyya each also had their changing political backers and patrons.

In the ninth century, al-Ma'mun, the Caliph leader of Baghdad at the time, declared the Mu'tazila creed as the religion of the state, and persecuted the Ash'ariyya. A few years later, the political situation changed dramatically, and a new leader, al-Mutawakkil, took over and reversed al-Ma'mun's policy, favoring the Ash'ariyya instead.

The Ash'ariyya's views on predestination, that everything that happens is supposedly "God's will," would later prove to be politically useful in getting the masses to accept their rulers—whether just or unjust, kind or oppressive—also as part of "God's will," and therefore to be obeyed. The Ash'ariyya prevailed with a vengeance. Luckily, the Mu'tazila's views had already spread to other parts of Islamdom, where they flourished and contributed significantly to the rise of the Islamic Golden Age—a period of science, progress, and discovery, which affirmed independent reasoning and empiricism.

Not so luckily, the Mu'tazila as a distinct movement came to an end, and the Ash'ariyya became the orthodox theology dominant until this day. One person I came to despise for his role in defeating Mu'tazila-oriented ideas, and spreading the shackling dogmatism of the Ash'ariyya, is the revered traditionalist Muslim theologian al-Ghazali. The one person I came to admire most was al-Ghazali's opponent, the Spanish-Arab Andalusian Muslim philosopher Ibn Rushd, defender of Aristotelian philosophy, known in the West as Averroes, and notably respected for helping inspire Western

Europe with the foundational ideas for modern secular thought.

I was high on historical revelations, but frustrated by the fall and devastation.

"If only the Mu'tazila had survived. If only they had won. If only that idiotic moron al-Mutawakkil didn't screw things up. If only al-Ghazali and his ilk had been defeated. If only Ibn Rushd had prevailed! If only," I grieved in despair.

So how did Islamdom really lose her virtue?

Simply, she forgot the importance of reason. *That's* how she really lost her virtue. It wasn't because of moral decadence. It wasn't because of the infidels. No, it was because of one main reason, and that was forsaking Reason. Never mind the other factors. Never mind the Mongol invasion that sacked Baghdad in the thirteenth century. Never mind that the story is actually more complex than that. It didn't matter to me. I saw one thing, and one thing only: the decline of reason.

We had to re-establish philosophy, so we could liberate the Muslim mind from the shackles of dogma, so we could re-establish a Muslim culture of science, so we could rise again.

We had to bring back Reason.

As for the traditionalists of today, they love to brag about Islamdom's Golden Age achievements. They love to gloat about her past glory and relative harmonious openness. They love to point out her former advancement of herself and the world through her sciences and innovations. And yet, those same traditionalists persistently attack the very intellectual foundations and factors that made Islamdom rise to her greatness in the first place: the firm emphasis on reason and empiricism. Not dogmatism, blind reverence, and unexamined faith.

Sitting in my chair, the idiocy of it all was unbearable. "Despicable," I cursed the traditionalists under my breath. "Absolutely despicable."

8

Infatuated with Atheism

It was a dark and humid December night close to 12:00 A.M. I stepped outside and walked up the hill. I could still hear the growing excitement of the small crowd I left behind at the party as they anticipated the countdown. Holding the metallic object in the grip of my hand, I too anticipated the ticks of the hands of Time. My grip tightened. "This is it, Amir. It ends here. *Enough*," whispered the dull breeze. Drips of sweat forming on my forehead, I smiled in delicate sorrow and giddy suspense, and felt my heart racing faster. "Ten, nine, eight, seven, six, five . . . ," roared the crowd in the distance, its collective voice carrying with it the memory of my first blog post, and the month-old memory of the Sudanese teddy bear crisis.

Ah, yes. That wonderful Sudanese teddy bear crisis. The government-appointed guardians of Islam in Khartoum had instigated a stupendously stupid and embarrassing spectacle involving a British English teacher named Gillian Gibbons who allowed her young class students to choose "Muhammad" as the name of a teddy bear. The child who picked the name had decided to name the teddy bear after himself, a totally innocent and legitimate act, but someone within the school, allegedly holding a grudge toward Gibbons, found out and decided this was an "insult to Islam."

By the time news of this "grave insult" traveled beyond the British international school's walls, the hard-liners were already implementing their exploitation plans. On November 30, 2007, about ten thousand demonstrators descended into the streets of Khartoum, some brandishing swords, demanding the execution of the arrested poor teacher. Soon, the furor was all over global news networks, making my people and Khartoum look utterly ridiculous.

In reaction to the stupidity, I rallied some Sudanese bloggers to express their condemnations. Next, I let out my snarky Drima and blogged about how the "whole thing is just so unbelievably pathetic. Clearly it's an honest and innocent mistake. Oh no, how stupid can I be, she's a white British infidel so it must be a freaking Zionist crUSAde and Jewish conspiracy."

Upon learning of the hard-liners' calls for demonstrations after Friday prayers, I sarcastically wrote about how it's going to be "fun."

"Damn, I'm so jealous, I wish I could join them. There will be shouting, and screaming, and jumping, and a big crowd of furious people. Seriously, what's there not to like? The only thing missing is a heavy metal band. Now *that* would be cool. We'll make a mosh pit, head bang together, and proclaim 'down with the infidel teacher.' Oh, and then we'll start burning some American flags!"

Almost instantaneously, my blogging caught the attention of the BBC and an article entitled "Bloggers condemn Sudan for arrest" was published with a link to my blog, and quotes of what I had said. That, and other publicity, sent my blog traffic to its peak of nearly ten thousand hits a day. I had now been thrown into the brewing media storm.

Sadly, many visitors had clearly neither read the BBC's article nor my blog post, because while I did receive much thanks from British citizens who came to understand the event for what it was, I also received some intense hate mail from British citizens angry at Islam and the treatment of their fellow countrywoman. I replied to them to clarify the situation in a final attempt to defend my faith. But looking back, perhaps what I was really seeking to defend by then wasn't my Islam anymore. Rather, it was my identity as a Sudanese, and as a Muslim. Because truthfully, my Islam was already crumbling, and our relationship was hanging on by a thread.

And so while the outside world may have seen me as a defender, inside, I was in shambles and disarray.

Funny thing is, I never set on a quest to fall out of love and into animosity with Islam when I first ventured into the blogosphere. Quite the opposite. But sometimes, things don't turn out the way you'd expect. For in seeking to chip away at my old suspect convictions, my faith somehow found herself at the receiving end of my chisel, and slowly but surely, I unshackled the fieriness of my newfound and rediscovered love—my Reason—freeing her from the overbearing dogmatism under which she has been subordinated for far too long, and far too painfully for my heart and mind to continue to bear.

Islam means "submission," they say. Submission to what?

Ah, well yes, to the will of God, one I've known too often throughout my life in fearful terms that demanded unquestioning submission and yielding to His supreme authority. Or else!

Fortunately, or unfortunately depending on where you stand, by the seconds-away, quickly-approaching dawn of 2008, I had reached a point where I simply, absolutely, and irrevocably refused to live under such submission anymore. Even the silly veiled death threats I occasionally received online and potential negative real-life ramifications were not going to stop me

"If there really is a God, there is no way in Hell I'm going to continue believing in Him out of fear of Hell. Enough," I determined.

As Thomas Jefferson apparently once said, "Question with boldness even the existence of a God, because, if there be one, he must more approve of the homage of reason, than that of blind-folded fear."

". . . six, five, four, three, two, one," continued the happy chants at the distant party pad as I held on to the metallic object I carried. "Happy new year!"

I loosened my grip, pulled the can opener, and in an act of asserting my awakened will, I chugged down a few small gulps of warm beer. It was the first time I had ever drank alcohol.

"So this is what my friends have been bugging me to drink and try all these years?"

The taste was disgusting.

Beyond the entities of religion—physical or intangible—one will still confront the confining repressive norms elsewhere. They're inescapable.

Submission. Subordination. Subservience. Three words with meanings that infuriate me beyond words. Three words with meanings you'll still very probably find forced upon you by entities like governments, schools, bullies, community, family, and of course, the workplace.

Given how much time we spend in the modern workplace—around forty hours a week (if you're lucky)—I strongly felt that it is of paramount importance that we, as creative beings, strive to do what our hearts desire. To do work that matters. To do it fiercely and with devotion, rather than accept a livelihood we resent, or work under abusive authoritarian bosses worthy of facing dissent.

Faced with two prospective job opportunities at Fortune 500 companies, I had to make a decision. Higher pay and a high probability of cubicle hell at one of two corporate giants, or the third choice—an opportunity with a small Silicon Valley style tech-start-up and incubator that had just appeared out of the blue.

To make my decision before graduating university, I decided to take a one-month internship during my holidays at the unconventional start-up company, which had relocated from New York and San Francisco to the emerging and less costly scene in Kuala Lumpur.

The company provided an open environment and liberal work culture unlike anything else I could find in KL. It had a flat decentralized organizational hierarchy, and reveled in an upbeat, fast-paced, irreverent entrepreneurial energy that knew no limits. It employed a small diverse team from all over the world, and invested in their growth. Moreover, its cofounders—one, a former Boston Group consultant and high-profile eBay executive, and the other, a passionate meditation instructor who had a short stint at Microsoft—worked directly with team members and mentored them for bigger visions and projects.

What was there not to like?

Without any hesitation, I delved right in after smoothly passing my interview, and worked with a specific agenda in mind: acquiring in thirty days as much knowledge about digital marketing and copywriting as humanly possible. Why? First, so I could build my own well-marketed online business sometime in the future, and second, so I could apply what I'd learn for the purpose of digital activism and human rights advocacy.

With the online business, I'd be able to break free and achieve what a friend once described to me as the "Four Freedoms." Location Freedom: the freedom to work online from anywhere in the world. Inner Freedom: the freedom to do work you're passionate about and be fully self-expressed. Time Freedom: the freedom to have flexible working hours. Financial Freedom: the freedom to not have to worry about money.

With digital activism and human rights advocacy through the open Internet, I'd be able to spread empowering knowledge, and awaken the slumbering and oppressed.

Thus, within one month of joining, I thankfully managed to learn multiples more than I did during my preceding eight-month corporate internship.

There, in the midst of brainstorms and innovation meetings, I witnessed first-hand the beautiful power of reason as she danced and moved—gracefully, elegantly, confidently toward the betterment of humanity—swayed and counter-swayed, not by outbursts and boasting, but mostly by reasonable argument and counter-argument, bringing forth the best of ideas, ones that were quite easily replaceable whenever solid new evidence emerged and better ideas came to light.

I also learned to probe the effects of my own cultural conditioning more closely after discovering that one of my colleagues—a friendly, kind, and helpful guy named Jay—was gay. For weeks, I had no idea. He wasn't soft, or effeminate. In other words, he had none of the noticeable characteristics I associated with being gay.

"So what are you going to do now after this discovery, Amir? Despise Jay? Stop befriending him because of his sexual orientation? You know that's just absurd. Maybe it's time you truly considered that neuro-scientific research you read about recently that says some people are actually born gay," I thought. "Which one is it going to be, Amir? Which one are you going to consider more? Reason or tradition?"

In mid-January 2008, I returned to university to complete my final semester, and in the process of researching my knowledge management thesis, I dug deep into a precious gold mine of life-changing philosophical insights. The kind I had been struggling to grasp all my life quite desperately. The tool of philosophical tools for anyone seeking a way of discerning truth from falsehood, and facts from delusions.

I had finally found it: epistemology, the philosophy of knowledge.

My foremost, most fundamental heart-aching inquiry was there. It was all there! Finally articulated in a relieving, fog-clearing language. "What is knowledge? How is knowledge acquired? To what extent is it possible for a given subject or entity to be known?"

Whenever my school teachers' lessons had conflicted with what my parents had shared, whenever I wondered about the existence or nonexistence of Heaven and Hell, whenever I contemplated the validity of different approaches to Qur'anic interpretation and whether or not they constituted cherry-picking according to personal taste, all along, the mental challenges and questions I had been struggling with were essentially questions of an epistemic nature.

Whose knowledge is more accurate? Who's right? Who's wrong? What makes them right or wrong? How did they acquire that knowledge to begin with and what makes them confident of its validity? Who and what am I supposed to believe or trust anymore?

One particular issue that deeply troubled me was the interpretation of the controversial supposed "wife-beating commandment" in the Qur'an in 4:34, which in the Yusuf Ali English translation is spelt out as follows: "As to those women on whose part ye fear disloyalty and ill-conduct, admonish them (first), (Next), refuse to share their beds, (And last) beat them (lightly); but if they return to obedience, seek not against them Means (of annoyance): For Allah is Most High, great (above you all)."

Again, and again, I came across too many traditionalist Islamic scholars in articles and on YouTube who felt no shame in asserting that the verse recommends the beating of disobedient wives to discipline them, albeit lightly in order not to cause injury. How cute. As if such enormous generosity should count as some consolation. Worse, other English translations of the message of the Qur'an by individuals like M. H. Shakir, Muhsin Khan, and Mahmoud Ghali also used the words "beat," "hit," or "strike."

Needless to say, I was again repulsed and horrified. This wasn't content from a particular man-made Islamic school of thought. This wasn't from Islam's second sacred source, the Hadith. No, this was in the Qur'an, Islam's most sacred core, God's eternal perfect message to humanity. And as far as I saw it, the root word in the original Arabic, "daraba," at least when commonly used by modern-day Arabic speakers, did certainly mean beat.

There was no way around this. Or was there? Thankfully, I discovered there is, because according to Laleh Bakhtiar, an American Muslim professor, the word has an alternative meaning in Arabic, which is "to go away," or "to travel."

While the majority of traditionalist scholars will disagree with her, I appreciated her feminist perspective, and those of scholars like Amina Wadud, but once more, "Isn't that cherry-picking?" I asked myself.

On one hand, Laleh Bakhtiar had a valid point, because in the same chapter the controversial wife-beating commandment is mentioned, verse 4:101 mentions a variation of the root word "daraba," in a context that clearly makes it mean "to travel." In fact, it's translated that way in numerous English translations of the message of the Qur'an, including Yusuf Ali's.

On the other hand, the majority of traditionalist scholars, throughout the years, still held on to the wife-beating meaning of the notorious wife-beating verse.

So again, who's right, and who's wrong?

I wondered, "If Laleh Bakhtiar can tweak the meaning of the word just like that, then what stops others from doing the same to other words?"

Sure, wife abuse happens all over the world, including in the West, where it's usually accompanied by alcohol abuse. Yes, such content is not unique to Islam, because you can certainly find similar commands in the Torah and the Bible, too. (Stoning disobedient sons to death anyone? Yup, Deuteronomy 21:19-21.)

And yes, a great deal of many Islamic scholars take great effort in relaying stories about how the Prophet Muhammad used to treat his wives kindly, and how he encouraged compassion and love toward one's spouse. Sure, these Islamic scholars always love to point out how Islam gave the women of seventh-century Arabia more respect, dignity, and expanded rights than they had. And that's all nice and wonderful.

Unfortunately, in my doubtful heart, none of that changed the fact I came to accept: that the verse in question seemed pretty straightforward. There was no "Medina versus Mecca" historical contextualization required here. This time, the interpretative disagreements took on a linguistic dimension. But the traditionalist consensus seemed clear.

How does one truthfully navigate that?

Eventually, after much reading and thinking, I became increasingly dissatisfied with what I felt were highly subjective and personalized attempts at reinterpreting Islam's sacred texts for the twenty-first century. Not only that, but the tolerant, and compassionate rereadings were themselves a product of reason, brought into the world by rationalist minds attempting to upgrade their religious traditions and heritage to adapt them to the modern world's moral sensibilities.

"More reason for me to love and adore reason," I thought.

Moreover, "If Islam can be interpreted as we please, then it can't be a religion with clear instructions regarding what's morally right or wrong, and how to live our lives righteously and ideally. We'll just be able to reinvent too many aspects as we wish," assessed my inner skeptic.

I found the relativism unacceptable, pouring more fuel onto my simmering insides. "We need an objective framework and methodology!" my heart and mind demanded. And that's where reason's epistemology came in, presenting itself magnanimously as my potential salvation.

By February 2008, my steep downhill slide of doubt had been continuing unabated with no end in sight. I had no one to talk to. No one to console me. No one who understood me intimately enough to comfort me.

My heart was hurting, and starting to sometimes cry tears of blood.

So I did the only thing I felt I could to release my accumulating sadness and grief. I strummed my guitars, but the melodies failed to uplift. I attempted to blog, but felt those who knew my real identity wouldn't take matters lightly as I went adrift. Hence, with familiar options unavailable, I began writing privately to myself in an attempt to heal and cause a positive shift.

And as I began to type, my words of doubt appeared on the screen, staring sternly right back at me, demanding they be fully internalized and acknowledged. Demanding they be recognized!

Thus, on a rather subdued evening of defiance and distress, I wrote, "Picture this. Jasmine, a little four-year-old girl, sleeps at night with her large pink teddy bear by her side. She cuddles with it. Sometimes she even talks to it. At times she wakes up in the morning with the teddy bear still wrapped in her arms. And when she leaves her house, she brings it along and places it nearby in the family car's backseat right next to her. Clearly, the teddy bear gives Jasmine comfort and provides her with a sense of security. Clearly, she loves it, but no matter how much she loves it, the teddy bear can't love her back. No matter how much she cares for it, the teddy bear can't care back. It's not a real person. It's merely a stuffed toy.

"And now here comes my provocative question," I warned. "What if religion is a teddy bear? What if it's just a human creation and a figment of our imagination? After all, you do often hear religionists defending religion by claiming that it provides people with a sense of purpose, and that it gives them comfort, something which is largely true. But so what, I say to that. Just because something makes you feel good doesn't mean it's necessarily based on the truth. So again, I ask, what if religion is merely a teddy bear?

"Screw comfort," my angry voices pushed back. I wanted truth. I wanted *the* truth. But soon, I became convinced that too many central religious questions lacked the clear satisfactory rational answers I desired.

"Does God exist?" If yes, then what kind of God: deistic, theistic, pantheistic? And if He does, then "what qualities does He possess?" I didn't know, and decided there was probably no way to know the answers to such questions. Despite that, part of me still had faith in the existence of a divine deity.

By the time May 2008 had come and gone, I was in tatters. My agnostic theism gave way to a sad, despaired, and unstable agnosticism, only to then have my attention grabbed by the neck by yet another new set of heroes: the Four Horsemen of the New Atheism—Sam Harris, Daniel Dennett, Christopher Hitchens, and Richard Dawkins.

Together with Hitchens, Dawkins—a world-renowned evolutionary biologist—was perhaps the "nastiest" of them in demeanor, writing in his massive bestselling book, *The God Delusion*, the following: "The God of the Old Testament is arguably the most unpleasant character in all fiction: jealous and proud of it; a petty, unjust, unforgiving control freak; a vindictive, bloodthirsty ethnic cleanser; a misogynistic, homophobic, racist, infanticidal, genocidal, filicidal, pestilential, megalomaniacal, sadomasochistic, capriciously malevolent bully."

With such strongly worded criticism, and book titles such as Hitchens' *God is Not Great: How Religion Poisons Everything*, the Four Horsemen of the New Atheism were a force to reckon with, a force that could not be ignored.

Fiercely anti-theistic and blunt, they unleashed their wrath at the dragons of religious dogmatism with the mighty sword of reason, slaying the beastly creatures down mercilessly without an iota of political correctness. And if that didn't suffice, they gloriously brought out the artilleries of science and awesomely blew up the facade of the house of religion, one bombshell at a time. Rightfully, vengefully, skillfully, they reloaded and just kept on pounding, without pausing for a single breath.

In my eyes at the time, they were the twenty-first centu-ry's heroes of reason, my new love with whom I had been regularly spending hours in mind-nourishing online dates, watching YouTube videos of her advocates and defenders, thus growing greatly fond of them. Thus becoming deeply infatuated with atheism as we shared a common enemy. Thus growing in my animosity toward religion—*all* religions—including my former love, my Islam.

And as the 2008 U.S. presidential election heated up, the exchanged rhetoric would come to prove me right. Accusa-tions that Obama is a secret Muslim. Proclamations by Mc-Cain's Christian spiritual advisor, Rod Parsley, that "Islam is an anti-Christ religion that intends, through violence, to conquer the world," that apparently "America was founded, in part, with the intention of seeing this false religion de-stroyed," and that "Muhammad received revelations from demon spirits, not from the living God."

As if Christendom's Crusades and the Inquisition were all lovey-dovey incidents, and Western colonialism has nothing to answer for.

Sick of the idiocy, at last I accepted what should have been the obvious. Organized religion, similarly to politics, divides us into "believers" and "nonbelievers," and the "to-be saved" and "to-be punished" by the "correct" God of our choosing.

Worse, it then sets us out against each other, at best, in-fected by suspicion of "the Other," and at worst, full of hatred and contempt in our hearts toward fellow human beings.

At least you could much more easily question politics. Not so with religion in general, again, thanks to its larger-than-life reverential status and sanctity in most societies—sanctity unworthy of respect or adoration. Sanctity and superstitions that had to be destroyed, and whipped off the face of the earth.

We stepped out onto the expansive outdoor balcony on a late July night to take a break during the intermission of the orchestra show. Upon hearing me speaking French-accented English with my friends, she strode toward me gracefully and elegantly, her hips rhythmically swaying from side-to-side with each step, and said something to me in what was clearly French.

"*Oui*," I replied.

Visibly delighted, she went on.

"*Oui, oui.*"

And on, and on.

"*Oui*," I replied again, to which she finally stopped, and in heavily French-accented English confusedly said, "Wait, you don't speak French, do you?"

I chuckled. "No, I actually have no idea what you were saying, but I'm guessing you thought I speak French when you heard me jokingly impersonating how French people speak English.

"Amir by the way," I said, smiling, with my hand extended.

"And I'm Doubt." She shook my hand. "You're quite sly and mischievous, aren't you?"

Beautiful, blond, and with big, round, penetrating blue eyes, I admired her form for a few seconds as she spoke. "Sly and mischievous?" I asked with a wider mischievous smile. "Sometimes, I guess. And you? Ah, you're probably one of those young idealistic girls here in KL for a few months on an internship, working in an NGO or something, thinking you can save the world. You're probably feeling like you miss home, and the familiarity of French culture. I'm guessing you're tired of Asia, which is why when you heard me speak with a French accent, you thought I was French or something, and got all excited."

Looking at me suspiciously, she said, "What are you? Psychic?"

"No, your friend over there knows my friend, and I heard them mention earlier that you work at an inter-faith NGO."

"Ha, you really are sly," she said with an adorable laugh.

"Okay, maybe I am, NGO girl."

"Yes, I'm a totally angelic NGO girl, who's going to save the world, and help bring peace to all of humanity, until we're all big happy Care Bears dancing in sunshine."

Laughing at her exaggerated dance movements, I looked straight into her eyes, and said, "Look at you! You're quite sarcastic, aren't you? Well, hey, to be honest, I actually think it's cool that you're here working with an inter-faith NGO, and you know, trying to bring about change, and understand stuff."

She smiled. It was as if she felt understood.

Our attraction to each other was instant.

"I'm still struggling to understand Immanuel Kant's *Critique of Pure Reason*. It's one headache of a read, but at least I'm starting to grasp the main ideas. I mean, I really appreciate how he spends so much time and effort defining the terms before making his argument. People ought to do that more often: define the terms they use. God, faith, religion, knowledge, evidence—I mean seriously, we all use these terms assuming everyone shares our definition of them, when that's so not the case," I ranted.

"I agree," replied Doubt calmly, after taking another shot of fresh fruit juice through her straw.

I waved to the waiter. *"Boss, ada tandoori chicken?* Do you have tandoori chicken? *Okay, satu tandoori, dan satu fresh oren tapi kurang ice, boleh?* One tandoori, and one fresh orange juice, but with less ice, okay?"

"Boleh lah, yes, can," responded the Malaysian Indian waiter, and shook his head from side-to-side, noting down my order.

"Doubt, oh Doubt, the *mamak* is a must-have unique Malaysian experience for anyone visiting. It's one of the things I really love about this country," I commented.

"What are you trying to achieve with your reading?" she asked.

I sighed. "I just want the truth. I'm so sick and tired of not knowing it—what is it? I mean, don't *you* wanna know what the truth is?" I asked challengingly.

Taking another shot of juice, lost in subtle mysterious thoughts, she calmly dropped the provocative statement. "There's no such thing as truth."

I didn't know how to react. I envied Doubt's content answer, but I was also repulsed by it.

"Oh, here we go. Everything is all just relative, right? There's no objective truth, right? There's no meaning or purpose in life. There's no right and wrong. Okay, so let's say a woman gets stoned to death in Saudi Arabia, isn't that wrong? Isn't that repulsive? Or are you going to tell me, 'Oh, it's their culture'?"

"Of course it's wrong! But that's my perspective. To them,

they don't think they're wrong, they think it's normal. So how can you say it's objectively wrong?"

"It's an ugly fucked-up practice that should stop. The world has changed, and people have moved on. There should be no place for this kind of shit anymore."

"Yes, okay, I agree, but on what basis is it *objectively* wrong?" asked Doubt defensively.

The waiter returned with my order, and placed it on the table. Thirsty from talking so much, I drank my blended orange juice in big gulps and took a deep breath before speaking calmly.

"So is this why you don't like to plan, and why you're afraid of commitments? If there's no way to know truth, then why bother about the future? That seems to be your philosophy. 'Just go with the flow.' That's the idea, right?"

"Yup, basically, yeah." Doubt nodded, moving her fingers through strands of her golden hair.

"But wouldn't you want to plan your career, for instance, come up with your goals, and work toward them? You should," I said.

"I know, I know, you're right. I should, but I'm just not ready. I'm not as passionate as you, so you, mister Amir, *you* can go ahead and chase your dreams."

"I don't get it. How are you so content with not knowing the truth? With not having some basic freaking plans?"

"I'm not like you. I'm fine with uncertainty."

I had an uneasy relationship with my shifting agnosticism while in Doubt's company. I wanted to be content with not knowing like she seemed to be. I wanted to know like Hitchens and Dawkins knew, because the uncertainty of not knowing felt excruciating. It felt miserable. I wanted to be free of my unstable agnosticism and the mental pendulum that sometimes still swung between belief and disbelief. I wanted to settle for a final position.

Thankfully, on the lovingly intoxicating side of things, in expressing my tormented soul to Doubt, I finally at least had found someone to talk to. Someone to console me. Someone who understood me intimately enough to comfort me.

"Man, so who's the gorgeous French babe? How did you meet her?" asked my Venezuelan friend, Eric, insistently.

"No, no. It's not what you think. She's just a friend, man," I said, brushing aside what Eric was insinuating.

"Dude! I'm not blind. I can easily see the chemistry. She likes you man, and I can clearly see you like her, too. You two got it going on. So stop being a pussy. Come on, make your move. Tonight is your night."

"No, man. *No*, nothing is happening tonight. She mentioned she misses dancing salsa, so I decided to surprise her and bring her here to Q-bar. Now let's get us some fun VIP treatment."

"All right *mi amigo*, welcome, make yourself comfortable. Let's get you some drinks."

"I'll have some gin, please," Doubt told the waiter, taking a seat with us outdoors after returning from the washroom. "And I'll just have a Coke," I said, to which Eric responded with a "What the?" look on his face, accompanied by the loud festive sounds of live Latin music playing inside. Soon, we were joined by my close friend, Ali, who settled right in and started cracking jokes, while exchanging looks with Eric, as if hatching a plot.

Once finished with our drinks, I reluctantly invited Doubt for a dance inside. She was fast, and skilled with her moves, and I, not used to salsa, did my best to follow the rhythm.

Minutes into the dancing, Ali approached us with objects in our face. "Hey guys, have some tequila shots," he shouted while the music blared in the background. "Just have them quickly right here, and I'll take the shot glasses back." Without thinking much, I licked the salt off the brim, shot the burning liquid down my throat, and sucked the small piece of lemon dry. Doubt did the same, and we continued dancing.

Minutes later, Ali returned, yet again with more shots.

And again, this time to the raï tunes of Cheb Khalid's song, Abdel Kader flooding the room from the DJ's speakers.

On the dance floor, with sensuous music permeating, and tequila and anxiety coursing through my veins, I hesitantly drew Doubt's body closer to mine, and exhaled down her sweaty moist neck, unaware of the ethnic-cultural hybridity of the moment.

We danced. We swayed. We embraced.

We did all three at once in the midst of a sovereign dominion of our making—a seamless integration of leftist French idealism and secular humanism, merged with Afro-Arab Averroism and hospitable egalitarianism.

But the barriers of my conditioning held me back, denying me from the erotic frenzy I longed to fully taste, denying her desire to cast me into sensual daze.

Eyes closed, internally wrestling, aching, dying—she must have sensed it. Then in a split-second of an instant when I wasn't paying attention, she nudged my barriers over the cliff to their gruesome death, and gently locked her lips with mine—slowly curling her wet salty tongue inside my mouth in sync with the melodies, thus freezing time.

We must have triggered the enraged, appalled, horrified shouts of the hardline, right-wing Jean-Marie Le Pens and Sayyid Qutbs of the world on both sides.

Score.

Gazing into Doubt's hypnotizing eyes, I seized her by her narrow waist, and thrust my pelvis in between her thighs. "Westoxicated," and holding each other closely, tightly, we danced freely through the night, separated only by the fabric on our skins, both feeling high.

"Damn you, Ali," I said to myself smiling inside, by which I really meant, "Thank you, tequila-bearing Ali."

My inhibitions had melted away.

"What's that book you're reading?" asked Doubt, next to me on the couch.

"Oh. Here, it's called *The End of Faith* by Sam Harris," I showed her. "*Religion, Terror, and the Future of Reason,*" I read the subtitle.

"Sounds interesting."

"It is. He's not like the others—Richard Dawkins or Christopher Hitchens. Sam Harris is different, he doesn't dismiss spirituality and mystical experience. Heck, he's even open to the idea of psychic phenomenon if we find more evidence for it. He does have some pretty horrendous stances though. I mean the guy defends torture on philosophical grounds, basically. So yeah, he can be kind of crazy, but he's definitely the most interesting of the bunch, and I very much appreciate many of his numerous refreshing insights," I explained.

Indeed, in his article *The Problem with Atheism*, Harris acknowledges on the basis of his own study and experience that "people have improved their emotional lives, and their self-understanding, and their ethical intuitions, and have even had important insights about the nature of subjectivity itself through a variety of traditional practices like meditation.

"Leaving aside all the metaphysics and mythology and mumbo jumbo," Harris writes, "what contemplatives and mystics over the millennia claim to have discovered is that there is an alternative to merely living at the mercy of the next neurotic thought that comes careening into consciousness."

Then he gets even more intriguing. "To judge the empirical claims of contemplatives, you have to build your own telescope. Judging their metaphysical claims is another matter: many of these can be dismissed as bad science or bad philosophy by merely thinking about them."

Upon reading that refreshing perspective for the first time, a loud voice in my head blurted out, "Wait, did he just say 'the *empirical* claims of contemplatives'?"

"So does this mean that the uplifting experiences I had during my childhood days under the echoing dome of my neighborhood mosque and later in life have an empirical basis? That they're empirical in nature?" the voice kept asking excitedly.

Harris articulated an incisive criticism regarding how "many atheists reject such experiences out of hand, as either impossible, or if possible, not worth wanting.

"Another common mistake," he went on, "is to imagine that such experiences are necessarily equivalent to states of mind with which many of us are already familiar—the feeling of scientific awe," or "artistic inspiration," and he found this attitude problematic.

As someone who has made his own modest efforts in this area, let me assure you, that when a person goes into solitude and trains himself in meditation for fifteen or eighteen hours a day, for months or years at a time, in silence, doing nothing else—not talking, not reading, not writing—just making a sustained moment-to-moment effort to merely observe the contents of consciousness and to not get lost in thought, he experiences things that most scientists and artists are not likely to have experienced, unless they have made precisely the same efforts at introspection. And these experiences have a lot to say about the plasticity of the human mind and about the possibilities of human happiness.

For some reason, something about this explicit acknowledgment resonated with me, and the fact that it came from one of reason's fiercest heroes and advocates in my mind at the time made it especially powerful, because it meant it couldn't be based on mere faith-based propositions or delusions lacking in evidence. On a deeper level, I felt that the views Harris espoused perhaps held potential for some valid meaning and purpose in one's life, meaning and purpose that I felt Dawkins and Hitchens did not and could not offer in their wholesale attack on religion and religious belief.

"*The End of Faith*, you say? Let me read it for a bit," requested Doubt. "He does sound interesting." And with that, I temporarily passed her my new bombshell of a book.

We sat huddled together onboard the long bus ride to the Highlands, and suddenly, something in the conversation Doubt and I were having touched a raw nerve, and provoked me into a long incoherent rant.

"I mean, seriously, how are my views that different from Ibn Rushd, whom you guys call Averroes? He was a Muslim, and even *he* held those 'heretical' opinions, but they were only heretical in the eyes of those damn traditionalists. Screw those buggers. Plus, it's not like I'm dismissing revelation all together. Reason is supreme to me, but revelation can have its place, you know."

"Amir."

"It's like what An-Na'im said. You've read the guy. 'Every orthodoxy once started out as a heresy,' right?"

"*Amir.*"

"And when it comes to human rights, it's not like we have to go around imposing them just like that. We *do* need to look at the different cross-cultural situations in their implementation for them to take root and really work. And again, it's not like people don't naturally want to have their rights. I mean, who the hell wants to live in indignity anyway?"

"Amir!"

"What?" I was startled into silence, eyes wide open, and stopped ranting.

"Are you trying to convince me, or are you trying to convince *yourself*? My dear, it's okay, you don't have to be afraid.

Come on, it sounds like you have wonderful parents. I don't think they're going to disown you. You're worrying too much. It doesn't matter whether you call yourself a Muslim or not, just be honest with yourself."

I wanted to believe her, but I couldn't.

9

Discovering the Dark Side

In order for one to experience painful heartbreak, one must first be deep in love. And deep in love I certainly was with my childhood beauty, my faith. It's the kind of love and relationship that can only survive, thrive, and be sustained by trustworthiness, compassion, and an ongoing renewal of commitment whenever the ride gets bumpy.

For well over a decade, I cultivated that kind of love and relationship—through thick and thin—imagining I'd live and die a loyal Muslim.

Yet, despite the struggles and sincerest of devotions, I gradually woke up from my beautiful dream world, only to face a nightmare I was still trying to deny, and I found myself at an unexpected crossroads on the dark side where critical life-changing decisions had to be made.

Decisions that could make you, or break you.

"Will I survive the path I was about to embark on?" I silently wondered. As before, I wished I had the answers to the lingering uncertainties, but I didn't. And hence, I had no choice but to continue down toward the forked road that lay ahead.

• • •

"I'm moving out," I told my dad.

"Why, for what reason?" he said, putting aside the book he was reading.

"It takes me two hours every day to go to the office and come back, valuable time I could use more productively instead of wasting it onboard the LRT train," I explained. I had recently taken the job with the tech start-up and incubator, ditching in the process the two prospective corporate job offers.

"Then read a book when you're on the train," my dad replied ingenuously.

"That's what I'm already doing," I answered annoyed, "but still, sometimes I need to be in the office really early in the morning because of conference calls and the time difference between us and clients and authors in the United States," I explained. "The place I'll be moving into is just a ten-minute walk from the office. It'll make my life so much easier, and again, more productive."

"Fine, we'll see," responded *aboi* dismissively with a slight frown.

"*Ya aboi*, come on. This isn't possible anymore. *Khalas*, I finished university, and I'm working now and earning my own money. All these years, I was a student already living on my own in the hostel, so what's the difference today? Must one wait until he gets married first? I'm back in KL, and I'll be living only forty-five minutes away from you guys. I can always come on weekends. It's even easier now."

Pausing for a moment, my father sighed in retreat, and finally said, "*Khalas*. Fine, but just make sure you come and spend time with us on weekends, and during the weekdays, too, when you're not busy."

"Of course I'll come visit. Where else will I find delicious home-cooked food?" I said jokingly in relief before walking away, with other ideas in mind.

Living on my own for more than four years on the university campus hours away from the city made the expected custom of returning to live under my parents' roof a discomforting and alienating experience. I needed my space, and by then, even more desperately so, thanks to my quietly growing anger and hatred toward religion, and anything with a hint of suffocating traditionalism.

I had grown extremely intolerant of anyone or anything messing with my mental, emotional, and physical space. It was rightfully mine, and nobody would claim it from me. At least not without putting up a good fight. From then on, I'd live how I'd want, the way I'd want, and I wouldn't look back.

By late August 2008, Doubt had returned to Paris. Saying good-bye at the airport wasn't easy, but it wasn't crushing or too sad either. We knew we'd stay in touch and remain friends. One thing that wasn't destined to remain the same however, was the status of my relationship with Islam. It was set to deteriorate further.

Standing outside the shisha lounge after a cold jug of beer, Ali and I chatted for a while before heading home our separate ways.

"Anyways man, it was good seeing you. I guess this is the last time we'll be drinking for a while. Ramadhan is coming.

It's just around the corner, dude. Crazy how time flies," Ali observed.

I sighed. "Man, I think I need to tell you something. I haven't told this to anyone, and I need to get it off my chest," I admitted reluctantly. "If there's anyone around who'd understand, then I'm hoping it's you," I said slowly with a heavy heart.

Concerned by my tone, Ali, whom I had known for nearly a decade, asked "What's up, dude? Is everything okay?"

"Yeah, it's just . . . Man, I don't know. I just—" I hesitated for a bit. "I don't think I'm going to fast this coming Ramadhan," I finally said.

"Oh-kay. You mean like the whole month, or just a few days?" he checked, clearly hoping I meant the latter.

"No, as in the whole month. Maybe I'll fast a few days if I want to, but honestly, I don't have the intention, and I just don't care anymore," I admitted.

"Wait, what?" he said, eyebrows raised, in a bit of shock. "But, dude, it's Ramadhan. Okay, so, yes, sure, I drink and all, and someday I'll maybe quit, but it's still Ramadhan. It's the holy month."

"Bro, I don't even think I believe in this stuff anymore," I said.

"Okay, hold on, hold on." Ali raised his open palms. "I understand you've got your issues with all those idiotic bearded monkeys who belong in a zoo. Even I hate them and think they're giving Islam a bad name, but what about the Book, dude?" he asked. "*The Book!* You know fasting is mentioned in there, and it's one of the five basic pillars of Islam. What about that? At least you still believe in the Book, right?"

I looked at him in grief, and shook my head in dismissal.

"Honestly, I'm not even sure if I believe in the Book anymore, either," I said.

Astonished by what he had heard, Ali sat down on a ledge, trying to internalize the seemingly apocalyptic revelation that I had lost much of my faith in Revelation.

"I know, I'm sorry, but it's the truth," I said.

"Dude, this is a big deal. I didn't know it was that bad. I mean, I know you have your reasons and all, but maybe this is just a phase. It could be, right?"

"I don't know. Maybe. All I know is that right now, I'm tired, man. I'm just really tired."

"If that's the case, bro, then I hope things work out well for you, and you manage to figure things out, you know? Just keep reading. Either way, I'm still your friend," he said with a heartfelt laugh, a good sign and gesture I appreciated very much.

And I most definitely did keep reading. Only Ali didn't know that the material I was reading wasn't exactly the kind that makes one appreciate faith more, but rather less. A lot less.

The holy month of Ramadhan came and passed uneventfully in September 2008, that is, pretty much without fasting or worship on my part. Largely removed from my family and Muslim surroundings, I soaked up the solace of my free solitude among an international group of friends and North American housemates—Mike and Alexandra—who were neither religious nor conservative. Not even close.

Unfortunately, the solace was never the sustained paradise cocoon I wished it could be. For I had a promise to keep to my family whom I regularly visited, and in doing so, found myself constantly reminded of the double life I was adopting.

"Welcome home, we missed you. How has your day been?" my mother would ask lovingly. "I left you three missed calls. Hopefully the fasting didn't exhaust you too much?"

Slowly growing sick of myself, I'd conveniently and inconveniently lie. Again. "The day has been normal. I'm fine *ya ummi*. I've been mostly relaxed indoors anyway, so it's not like I did anything exhausting."

"Okay, then go say *salam* to your father upstairs, and tell them all to come down now so we can eat soon. It's almost time. The *azaan* will sound off in a bit."

Sitting around the dining table, we'd eagerly wait for the *azaan* to blare from the nearest mosque's minaret speakers so we could break our fast with dates and water.

"Look eager and starving, Amir. You don't want to appear full of food and water," a concerned inner voice reminded me.

The hypocrisy. The pretending. The acting.

It made me sick of myself.

And all for the sake of not wanting to hurt the feelings of those who raised me and cared for me—not wanting to disappoint them. All for the sake of maintaining some semblance of balance.

Funny enough, I didn't care about the potential anger I could incur if the truth emerged. Anger, unlike hurt disappointment, was another matter I knew I'd be able to withstand witnessing and receiving, because if I were to face fireballs of wrath, I'd simply swing back a ginormous galactic star of raging infernos.

I really was determined to ensure that nobody would ever again mess with my mental and emotional space. I'd defend

it with anything I could, and I was sure as Hell ready to un-
leash Hell at anyone and ready to consume myself in the
process if I had to.

Especially if it was against the treacherous, politicized,
prostituted guardians of the order—the maintainers and en-
ablers of "Islamdom's Industrial Complex." The enforcers of
its horrendous, brutal authoritarianism.

Against them, again and again, I pledged to myself, "No
submission!"

Never.

As 2008 progressed, and even as I rejoiced among my friends
and work colleagues, deep inside, I walked around lost in the
shadows of my disowned selves, aflame with intensifying
hatred and anger.

Feeling increasingly stuck in limbo, I knew I could not
maintain my inner and outer double acts for much longer.
Something had to give. And fast.

Khalas. I was fed up.

I needed to settle for a final position.

"Are you still in, or are you done and out, Amir?" asked
the voices in my head repeatedly.

While I was happily mentally liberated from all the suffocating religious dogma I had been indoctrinated with growing up, it felt as if Islam still had a faint hold on my heart.

If it hadn't, I wouldn't have had to question myself if I
was still in.

And so, I decided to give my "marriage" a final chance. I
ventured into cyberspace in search of the conclusive answers
for my final position, and in doing so, stumbled upon a very
dark side of the Internet: jihadist forums.

They were the real deal. The places were al-Qaeda and its self-organized global network of followers and supporters congregated online and persistently spread their propaganda videos and proclamations. Plus of course, step-by-step instructions on how to build homemade bombs using easily obtained materials, readily available in large supermarkets and gardening stores.

It was in forums and cyber territories such as those that discontented individuals like Umar Farouk Abdulmutallab— the twenty-four-year old Nigerian "underwear bomber" whose explosives luckily failed to detonate—got lured in, indoctrinated and recruited into al-Qaeda. And Colleen Renee LaRose, aka "Jihad Jane," the blond, blue-eyed American female Muslim convert who allegedly intended to use her appearance to more easily blend into Western society, and who hatched her plots online with other coconspirators.

I knew the forums existed. But I had never expected that one could so easily visit many of them simply by Googling patiently, and typing in their domain names into a browser.

I did just that, and what I found shocked me, as if I hadn't experienced enough shocks already. It terrified me into fully confronting the toxicity and dangers of a militant religiosity hell-bent on terrorizing and causing harm to "the Other," even if it included women and children, all in the name and service of a fiercely sectarian God whose compassion extended only to a loyal few, and denied itself to the rest.

I clicked around discussion thread after discussion thread and witnessed the theological debates that raged there, and how sophisticated they were.

It was abundantly clear that the members of those forums weren't simply a bunch of crazed lunatics. They could not be dismissed as such. No, these were smart, ruthless individuals who referenced a great deal of religious texts in support of their views and agendas. They didn't sugarcoat, and they didn't bother with conveniently interpreting away the dark side of religious texts that many others find troublesome. No, if anything, they actively sought out this dark side and incorporated it into their discourse.

They took in everything terrifyingly literally and did it with such fervor and bloodlust, they put the overwhelming majority of other Muslims to shame, and made them look like utter sissies.

"What if religion really *is* all about this?" I began asking.

Mainstream and liberal Muslims often seemed to require performing some admirable mental gymnastics to arrive at their tolerant and nuanced readings, I felt as my skepticism increased. It's the same with Christians and teachings of the Bible.

But why all that complexity and need for rigorous historical and linguistic contextualization?

"If God had really intended for His message to be internalized and practiced well by humanity, why is it so complicated to understand the Qur'an 'properly' then? Why is there so much endless disagreement, and often around trivial matters? Why couldn't religious teachings be more straightforward?" I wondered with growing frustration.

Maybe the texts *are* meant to be understood literally, for better or for worse. Taking them literally certainly made them easier to understand more objectively, it seemed to me at the time, but it also made many of their claims more ridiculous and far-fetched.

"Perhaps the literalists really are being more objective and intellectually honest, while the rest are engaging in well-meaning, but ultimately false, deluded, wishful thinking, because they can't accept the difficult truth. That it's all just a man-made lie," told me the whispers inside.

Who knew?

The deeper I angrily delved into virtual Jihadistan, the more I felt I couldn't just stand and do nothing. If the majority of scholars and Muslims were busy condemning the heinous atrocities and senseless violence of al-Qaeda and its ilk, then I'd go further, I dramatically visualized and decided. I'd fight the organization and its affiliates stealthily. Online. Where they congregated.

Utilizing Tor, a special tool that safeguarded one's identity and made surfing activity on the Web anonymous, I "heroically" went in during my free time. Undercover. Determined to infiltrate some of the jihadist forums to earn the trust of system administrators, and gain special access to password-protected areas where actual terrorist plots were apparently being discussed.

I was high on the aspirational fantasy that my one-man mission could stop some potential carnage and might save some lives. And so I decided that upon learning of any important information or uncovering any plot, I'd make a report to the relevant authorities who could then take the necessary steps and precautions.

It didn't take too long for those anger-fueled, and rather self-deluded, fanciful ambitions to completely fade away over the weeks and months that followed.

The closest I came to uncovering anything of significance was landing on a well-hidden forum thread that contained calls for planning attacks on targets in Germany for its role in supporting the war in Afghanistan.

"Ah, what about this, Amir? This looks useful. Maybe the German Embassy should get alerted to this. It could put some of these lunatics behind bars, and save some innocent lives," I naively thought, abandoning the idea afterward.

As I'd come to learn from various media and think-tank reports, numerous Western and international intelligence agencies were and always have been keeping a close watch on the forums in virtual Jihadistan. It was an industry populated with experts, and analysts whose work I consumed and found fascinating. That is, before I decided to move on and refocus my attention elsewhere: the Internet's neutrality as a technology for information sharing.

By October 2008, it was obvious to me that my marriage with Islam was in the gutter, streaming downward agonizingly into the abyss. My infatuation with atheism seemed to have also reached its peak and was starting to flatten out on the graph. As for reason, my love for her kept growing stronger and more passionate. And as it did, I thankfully developed a great relationship with my job as well.

The company I joined didn't disappoint when it came to growth and learning. Every day, I jumped out of bed with excitement, and got to witness the power of the Internet in marketing ideas, and generating money seemingly "out of thin air," as they say.

The consistent experience almost never failed to inspire me to keep learning about psychology, technology, and on-line advocacy. What I saw in the jihadist forums only added fuel to that desire. As far as I was concerned, it was war, and to win this war of ideas for a *free* marketplace of ideas, I affirmed to myself that one not only has to know how to craft honest, persuasive messages, but one also has to master the digital communication tools of the age.

How else could we maximize the potential of the Internet for good?

"We cannot, and must not let those who are spreading bigotry prevail. One day, soon, I'll put this knowledge to good use. Just wait, and see, Amir. Wait and see," I quietly plotted.

I failed to realize that I was becoming similar to those I claimed to be fighting: intoxicated on hatred and anger.

While the contents of my hatred and anger and theirs were markedly different, and we stood for very different values, the feelings we carried inside were nonetheless the same: toxic hatred and anger. I wasn't aware of it. I was too caught up in the dramas of my heart, and too busy partying with friends in escapism to notice.

Even as I was surrounded by many wonderful and beautiful work colleagues, I often felt miserably lonely and increasingly in despair.

As my not-so-snarky Drima once blogged on an October evening under a post entitled "Reading Your Way to a Lonely Place," "I feel lonely when I'm around members of my traditionalist Sudanese community. I feel lonely when I find myself the only one cringing at some of the ridiculous remarks being uttered among friends. I feel lonely when I'm at a mosque on the day of Eid feeling disgusted as I listen to a heinous, heavily politicized sermon that has little to do with Eid itself. I feel lonely because I can't express my newfound voice sincerely or on an articulate level others in my surroundings will be able to grasp and relate to. And so, I drift away, further toward those who do or merely toward more books, and as that happens, the situation only worsens as I come into contact again with those with whom I parted ways into a different and highly 'radical' perspective.

"In times of weakness," I wrote, "I wish I could just go back to the orthodox comforts of yesterday, but I can't, and I won't.

"This status quo is dead, and I am free. This liberation is worth the anguish and loneliness that comes with it sometimes. Nonetheless, what matters most to me now is how I put it to good use. Back to reading and writing."

And indeed, it was back to reading and writing. Writing the foundational ideas of what would eventually become the book you're reading right now.

Part of the reason I picked my job at the tech company wasn't just because it provided a great learning opportunity to master digital marketing, but also because I knew I'd be able to learn more about personal development thanks to the company's online publishing activities, and its relationships with major figures in the Human Potential Movement like Jack Canfield of the *Chicken Soup for the Soul* fame, and later, Tony Robbins.

Having read nearly every single one of Robert Kiyosaki's books on entrepreneurship and financial literacy, I was hungry for more self-empowerment insights, but the more exposed I became to personal development literature and the self-help industry, the more unsettled I felt.

While most of my colleagues were more into traditional

practical personal development, some were hard-core fans of New Age spirituality—a loose category and very broad body of literature that draws its ideas from the Human Potential Movement, Eastern esoteric wisdom, and sometimes even shamanism and the occult. The book, *The Secret*, and the similarly titled film fell right smack into the middle of it all.

The more I heard some friends talking about the film, the more I knew I had to investigate its claims, and so I decided to watch it from beginning to end.

By the time I was done, I knew where I stood: not a fan.

I could see why Oprah had put her influential weight behind it. She fell in love with its core message of self-empowerment, overcoming victimhood and taking responsibility for your own life. I very much appreciated that aspect of the film, too.

What I was disturbed by, however, was the film's metaphysical claims, pseudo-science, and encouragement of simplistic wishful thinking.

The Secret basically says that your thoughts *literally* send out vibrations to the Universe, and that you *literally* attract whatever you desire, no matter how big or small. If you aren't, and shitty things are happening to you, well, it's essentially because of your shitty thoughts—*literally*. In other words, the Universe is at your service, it is an ATM, and you are the center of your existence. According to the film and many of its gurus, it's as simple as that.

I found those claims troubling. "Where's the evidence for all these woo-woo ideas?" I wondered. "Oh and what about all of those people who died in tragedies like Darfur and the Holocaust, or due to natural disasters? Did they attract those fates to themselves, too?"

Even personal development literature seemed to have its own dark side. Just like religious texts, and just like the virtual wonderlands of the Internet.

Other nontraditional offerings like the Silva Method were a lot more nuanced than *The Secret*, despite wrapping up some teachings in metaphysical claims.

"I liked Laura's explanation of the different brainwave frequencies," I admitted to an accompanying friend after a certification seminar that was facilitated by Laura Silva, daughter of Jose Silva, the pioneer of the Silva Method. "What were the frequencies again? Beta is the waking state, Alpha is light sleep and meditation, and Theta is deeper sleep and meditation, right?

"What's weird is that before I began the guided audio meditation," I continued, "I followed the instructions and set the intention to solve a specific problem that was bothering me, and then as I went into Alpha, this strange forgotten childhood memory suddenly got unlocked and came back to me like a film reel. I just sat there, and felt it, and then I had this emotional 'knowingness.' I don't know how to explain it. But the imagery that came to me helped me resolve my dilemma and enabled me to understand something about myself that I had been really struggling with for a while now. It was . . . relieving."

Despite that experience, my stronger preference remained toward the more practical Stephen R. Covey– and Tim Ferris–types of personal development.

Simply put, I held my relationship with reason in the highest esteem, and valued rigorous evidence. I knew too well the price one could pay for wishful thinking and faith-based belief, no matter how enticing the ideas may be.

• • •

By the end of 2008, I finally arrived at the forked road that
had lain ahead all the while.

"You've done your reading, and you've had your time to
think, Amir. So, are you still in, or are you done with Islam
and out?" demanded my inner judge and jury.

Khalas, I needed to end my limbo. I needed to settle for a
final position.

The theological debates in the jihadist forums. The religious literature that made up the Islamic tradition. The core
sacred Islamic texts of the Hadith and the Qur'an.

I went through what I could, closely and passingly, patiently and impatiently, and felt I had to make a decision that
would have been difficult had it not been for my anger and
disillusionment.

"If every single part of the Hadith Sahih volumes and the
Qur'an is indeed valid for all times and all places, as Muslims
are expected to believe according to the Islamic tradition,
then I want nothing to do with Islam," I reasoned.

Moreover, I faced what I felt were irreconcilable issues
with certain verses in the Qur'an, like the controversial
wife-beating verse.

These were verses that I vehemently refused to accept
literally, which is how I felt they were intended to be understood. I wished to interpret them away, conveniently through
acceptable metaphors, but I still strongly felt that interpreting verses metaphorically and freely without some proper
objective methodology would constitute wishful thinking
and personalized cherry-picking—an approach I felt wasn't
intellectually honest or valid.

Needless to say, I also ceased to have faith in miracles and stories like Noah's Ark, the virgin birth of Jesus, and the feats of Moses. At best, I found them to be full of useful parables, and at worst, nothing but comical archaic mythology.

At the end of the day, the tradition won. It defeated me. It imposed itself, defined the "proper" parameters of "Muslimness" as it desired, and left me no choice but to conclude, for better or worse, that "I'm done. If this is what one has to do and believe to be a Muslim, then I can no longer honestly continue calling myself a Muslim."

And hence, my relationship with Islam had to end.

But how would it?

PART IV

The Messy Divorce

10

No More Mercy

It's 10:35 A.M. on a cloudy January 2009 morning, the start of a new year. I'm still in bed lying awake under my blanket, burdened by more than just thick woolen fabrics. Burdened by intensifying contempt for all religions and the vast majority of religious leaders.

Feeling sickened by the filthy liars who are blinded by their dogmatism and driven by the polarizing divisiveness inherent in their beliefs. Feeling disgusted by their pretentious claims to respect other people of different faiths when they in fact believe those same people are going to Hell because of their deviant ideas. And above all, feeling seething rage at their desire to keep me, and others like me—Muslim, Catholic, Mormon, Orthodox Jew, Hindu—married to religious traditions that we neither chose nor want anything to do with anymore.

Bogged down by the emotional terrain, one early morning while lying distressed in bed, I recalled something I had forgotten about for many years.

"You're divorced. Divorced. Divorced!"

I remembered the dramatic scene from the Egyptian television series I saw my mother watching in my childhood, and in my mind, heard the angry husband's divorce proclamation and his wife's weeping from the shock and stinging slap. "What did she ever do to deserve getting divorced so fiercely?" returned the question.

Frustrated by the lack of an answer, I concluded that it doesn't matter. Regardless of what happened, nobody should have to put up with such abuse.

Now imagine if after all of that, the divorced wife argued to a friend, "But I still love him."

"Gosh, he smacked you, and beat the hell out of you, and you still want to be with him?"

"Yes, I can't help it. I still love him," argue too many women in similar situations every day.

Men, too, albeit in different ways and under different circumstances.

What's to be said to such people who remain too nice, too naive, and unassertive?

Often, we're told about the virtues of love, patience, and compassion, and encouraged to embody them into what essentially becomes a form of pacifism. Yet, I'd argue that doing so is immoral under certain situations, (as long as we don't lose sight of the humanity of our opponents).

Just picture if Gandhi, the "poster-boy" for change, had to deal with the Nazis instead of the British, while still maintaining his philosophy of nonviolence. What would have happened then? Here's what: Gandhi and his followers would have most likely gotten mercilessly exterminated in the gas chambers of concentration camps.

Maintaining nonviolence and pacifism would have been defeatist, suicidal, and utterly unacceptable.

As unacceptable as remaining in a loveless, dysfunctional, abusive relationship with religion became to me.

The reprehensible indoctrination. The emotional blackmail. The treacherous infidelities. The denial of my full rights. The lies about the reasons for Islamdom's decline. The dirt on the dark side. The list just kept getting longer, and longer.

Sometimes, you just need to take off the gloves, and revolt with three words in mind.

"No. More. Mercy."

I awaited my copy of Ibn Warraq's book *Why I'm Not a Muslim* with bated breath. It represented a bigger heretical bombshell than books by Harris and Dawkins, because it was written by an ex-Muslim.

When the copy arrived at last, safely delivered to me by a Western diplomat friend of mine, I sat alone in my apartment's living room, and held it with caution.

Palms sweating, heart rate increasing with a bit of hesitation, I flipped the cover, knowing I was about to read the blasphemous words of an apostate who had the clear intention of convincing his readers to leave Islam behind as he had. Thus to comfort myself, I reminded myself that I was sincerely searching for the truth, and since one of Allah's ninety-nine names or characteristics is called al-Haqq, or the truth, then my quest did at the very least honor that aspect of God—that is, if He existed. I then took a slow breath to calm down, and felt the images of Hell's flames disappearing from my mind's eye.

In the introduction of the book, Ibn Warraq, which isn't his real name, began by distinguishing what he calls the "three Islams." Islam 1: the teachings of the Qur'an and Prophet Muhammad. Islam 2: the religion as expounded, interpreted, and developed by the scholars and jurists into a corpus of dogmatic theology. And lastly, Islam 3: what Muslims actually did do and achieve, meaning the Islamic civilization.

As I continued reading, Ibn Warraq made it clear that he despised Islam 1 and 2. As for Islam 3, he elaborated on what he wrote in the introduction, which is that "Islam 3, Islamic civilization, often reached magnificent heights despite Islam 1 and Islam 2, and not because of them."

While I appreciated his brutal attacks, I wasn't very impressed with the book by the time I finished it. To minimize and often outright deny some of the positive roles of Islam 1 and 2 seemed disingenuous to me. Nonetheless, I didn't dwell on it.

Ibn Warraq's writings were precisely the sort of medicine I needed at that time. And it worked, because something odd happened in the immediate aftermath of reading *Why I'm Not a Muslim*.

I lost all my subtle remaining fear of the possibility of Hell.

If my mind hungered for blasphemous anti-Islamic material with an intellectual basis, "What other book could possibly be more scathingly anti-Islamic?" I thought.

It felt like I had reached the very edge.

"You do realize there's a high possibility I won't end up with a Sudanese girl," I told my mom puckishly one afternoon.

Now that I had graduated university and I was working and earning my own money, the topic of marriage had become a recurring one.

"But why?" she'd asked, quite annoyed as usual at the prospect of a non-Sudanese daughter-in-law.

"Come on, let's get real and practical, *ya ummi*. As it is, even guys in Sudan who already graduated and are now working have trouble finding the right one. And this is *in* Sudan, where there are hundreds of thousands of interesting girls who may qualify. What makes you think it's going to be easier for me here in Southeast Asia where there are only a handful of Sudanese girls, the majority of them being the complete opposite of what appeals to me?"

Most of the time the conversations and debates were light-hearted and friendly, but on that specific afternoon, I went ballistic.

"What do you mean she doesn't have to be Muslim? Are you really serious?" my mother blasted me.

"Why? Why does she have to be Muslim? Why is it a must? Who cares? She can profess to be a Muslim, but also be a totally messed-up person at the same time, so why does it matter? Shouldn't her conduct as a person matter first and foremost? Shouldn't that be the most important factor?" I ranted angrily.

My mother's question, asked so unflinchingly, did it for me.

"Dude, help me understand, what's the main issue?" Ali asked me as we sat chatting over mint tea and shisha after a delicious meal of hummus and shawarma.

"Man, I'll tell you what my problem with religion is. Let's conduct a little thought experiment, shall we? You've got a person named Omar, and another named Mousa. Omar happens to be a strong believer in all the Islamic doctrines. He believes in God and the Prophet, believes in the Qur'an and the stories in it, fasts and prays routinely, but happens to be one lying, stealing, back-stabbing, demeaning, cruel son of a bitch. On the other hand, Mousa happens to be kind, generous, and very compassionate toward others. In fact, he's a wonderful member of his community and contributes actively to its well-being. But there's a catch. Mousa doesn't necessarily believe in all the Islamic doctrines. Poor Mousa, he has some doubts. I'm not even saying he rejects the doctrines. No, I'm just saying he has some doubts and has trouble believing the Qur'an is the word of God. Now here's the fun part, and let's be honest with ourselves. When it comes to Omar, what's the usual reaction to someone like that in typical Muslim circles?"

"People will be upset by Omar's sinful behavior and his character, obviously," replied Ali.

"Exactly. People will say 'Oh, look at Omar. How sinful, may Allah guide him,' and so on, right? But what will happen if Mousa goes into the same Muslim circle and openly confesses his strong doubts in Islamic doctrine, say his doubts in the Qur'an. What will happen then?"

Ali started chuckling.

"People will go batshit crazy, dude. That's what will happen!" I said.

"True," Ali admitted calmly, exhaling the shisha smoke.

"And *that's* my main issue! We're so freaking obsessed with beliefs and doctrines, we elevate them to such a high status that our conduct toward others becomes much less of a priority. Isn't there something horrendously wrong with that picture? Oh, and better yet, we fight and bicker over trivial details that we cannot even prove! Jesus was born from a virgin, Jesus was not born from a virgin. Jesus wore a purple T-shirt. Jesus did not wear a purple T-shirt. Moses parted the sea, Moses didn't part the sea. Who gives a shit?" I asked rhetorically.

"Why does believing or not believing in such trivial matters have such enormous weight that it negates who I am as a person in the eyes of so many? Why does doubting or disbelieving in these stories and the doctrines automatically make me condemned to Hell? What, all of a sudden I'm now an immoral, horrible person? And for what? Doubting a bunch of stories? Really? I mean, how idiotic is that? Sure, let's all get penalized for not believing in unicorns. 'But it's a miracle!' they say. Well, good for you. You can go ahead and believe in all that mythology if you want to. As for me, thanks but no thanks. I'm done. I will doubt and disbelieve whatever the hell I want, and it shouldn't matter. Only my conduct and integrity should."

Leaning back in his chair, Ali sighed and said, "Yeah, I guess you're right, but that's just people, and people can be real idiots."

"No, it's organized religion, dude. That's what it is," I said. "*Religion*. And by the way, it's not only in Islam, it's in Catholicism, too. Try being a good human being who happens to be Catholic, and then go to the Pope and tell him you no longer believe in Jesus as the son of God, or that you reject the doctrine of the virgin birth. You'll be out. Bye-bye, no more salvation through Jesus. Hell will await you, you bad,

bad person. Same thing in Mormonism. Reject some of the key doctrines, and announce it to your community. Good luck keeping them happy."

"Okay, so never mind the people and the system. Have you considered just accepting the stories as moral parables perhaps?" asked Ali with genuine curiosity.

"Yeah, like the story of Abraham, and his dream about God telling him to slaughter his son, and his son willfully complying after getting informed the sacrifice is God's wish? Gosh, yes, what a wonderful parable: blind obedience. How lovely!" I declared, to which Ali chuckled again, before turning serious.

"What if you're wrong?" he asked. "What if your doubts are wrong? Aren't you worried that you could be wrong? Doesn't that possibility scare you a little?"

"You know, Christopher Hitchens puts it nicely. The simple truth is, we're all atheists. Every single one of us. You, me, everyone. We're all atheists when it comes to Zeus, Osiris, the Mayan gods, and just about every other god. But do you go to bed each night worrying if you're wrong about one of them, and if you'll be punished in an afterlife? No. And speaking of an afterlife, do we truly know what happens after death? Sure, Islam offers ideas about what will happen when you die, but even then, do we really, really know what happens? No. At the end of the day, what matters is just being good, and doing good, for its own sake. For the sake of an honorable purpose larger than yourself. I cannot for the life of me understand why creed and doctrines have to matter so much. If you were born in India, chances are you'd be Hindu and you'd end up believing Hindu supernatural notions, ones you can't empirically prove or disprove, so again, why bother? Hence, my philosophy. Do good, be good."

By mid-January 2009, Google was performing a ruthlessly effective job as my "private investigator"—my weapon of choice for uncovering all the remaining dirt I could find about my unchosen spouse, and former love. I watched every You-Tube video I could find of Harris, Hitchens, Dennet and Dawkins. I read article after article by them. And once in a while, I got my dose of Ayaan Hirsi Ali, too.

With every piece of anti-religious content I consumed, my anger at the injustice of organized religion grew, and my position cemented. Moreover, the ongoing Israeli-Palestinian conflict cemented that position further. The way Hamas brainwashed children into hatred. The way Israeli Zionists and settlers demolished Palestinian homes, and occupied the land claiming God gave it to them. The way all dogmatic religious sides—Muslim, Christian, and Jewish—uncompromisingly insisted on their claims to the Holy Land as Christiane Amanpour had so brilliantly documented in CNN's three-part special, *God's Warriors*.

It was enraging.

In retrospect, I realize it was a decidedly immature and simplistic way of assessing the Middle East's most infamous conflict, but that's how I saw it. That's how I saw virtually everything at the time: through the lens of religion.

It was a gloomy January weekend in 2009. I woke up in my room in my family home with a heavy chest, feeling miserably depressed at how I had lived so much of my life not according to my own terms or in alignment with my inner

voice, but in accordance with someone else's suffocating expectations. That of the guardians of the order.

"You're divorced. Divorced. Divorced!"

The dramatic scene from the Egyptian television series
came to me once more, this time percolating through me.
Slowly. Silently. *Fully.*

That's when it hit me.

All my life, I had been in an arranged marriage, forced to
be with a spouse I neither chose nor truly desired on my
own. Forced to suppress my true yearnings, and to live in
bondage.

No more. And so I gathered the strength to assert my will
forcefully, and that's when it somehow happened, internally
in the heat of my anguish.

"You're divorced.

"Divorced!"

I paused for a second.

"Divorced," I muttered.

The third time was difficult. I verbalized it but deep inside my heart, I couldn't mean it. I wanted to, but I couldn't.
For some mysterious reason, it didn't register.

The first two divorce proclamations were full of rage, full
of hurt, and contempt, but the third, oh no, the third was
different. It was full of empathy, full of longing, and strangely,
still full of this odd, resilient love. But it was a love in tension
with an irritable raging fire, which then took over and overwhelmed everything.

"Good-bye, my Islam."

Unlike the other preceding days, this time I got up from
bed, and hopped into the shower with a certain sense of glee
and satisfaction.

I would now be free.

Or would I?

"Hey, Veronica. Listen, next week a friend of mine is arriving in KL and will be staying with us for a few days. She'll be crashing on the guest couch, just so you know," I told my Venezuelan apartment-mate and work colleague as we cleaned up our home together.

"Ah, okay, sure, but did you tell Alex?"

"Alexandra? Yeah, she knows, I told her already."

"Where's your friend from anyway?" asked Veronica.

"She's an Egyptian journalist living in New York. We've never actually met in person before, but I've been reading her stuff online for a while now, and she's read my blog, too. She's awesome. I saw her update her Facebook status saying she's coming to Malaysia for a conference, so I told her to come a week earlier so we could hang out and I can show her around. She liked the idea, and she knows I live with you and Alex. You'll like her. She's cool."

"Nice, does she write about religion, too?"

"Religion, liberalism, social media, the Arab world, and especially women's rights. She's a hard-core feminist. Oh, and she doesn't like Chavez, either," I added with a smile.

"She better not, dude," cautioned Veronica with a semi-serious face. Her writer mom had apparently been a victim of threats and intimidation in President Hugo Chavez's Venezuela.

I laughed at Veronica's predictable reaction.

One normal Saturday afternoon, Veronica and I spent our time strolling around the Suria KLCC shopping mall. Her being the ever-touchy Latina she was, she had her arm momentarily locked in mine as we walked together looking for the shop she needed to find.

Slowing down outside the Swatch store, the mini-skirt-wearing Veronica elbowed me and asked, "Dude, why is that woman staring at us? She looks pissed. Do you know her?"

Standing opposite us a short distance away was a Sudanese lady I recognized as one of my mother's acquaintances. She was standing with her daughter, and both of them looked unmistakably, unpleasantly shocked.

In the past, especially during my confused and confusing high school years, I would have panicked and felt caught red-handed in the midst of such a moment. But not now. Not this time while I relished my newly formed sense of clarity and conviction, because there's nothing wrong about strolling arm-in-arm with a close female friend from a different culture, and because I respectfully sympathized with my mom's acquaintance, understanding fully well how disturbing the scene must have looked from her very Sudanese perspective.

"One sec, Vero. Let me go say hi."

I strode calmly and assertively toward the lady and greeted her as if nothing significant was going on. "*Salam ya khalto, kafik?* Hi, Auntie, how are you? It's been a long time since we last met."

It took her a few seconds to collect herself. "I'm fine *ya ibni.* How's your mother?" she asked, trying to act normal and maintain eye contact with me, instead of eyeballing Veronica from afar.

"My mom is doing good. I'm out here today doing some shopping. That's my friend and colleague from work over there," I said, pointing at Veronica. "She arrived in Malaysia recently, and I'm showing her around because she's got some stuff she needs to buy. Anyway, I just stopped by to say hello. It was nice seeing you. *Yalla, salam.*"

"Yes, nice seeing you too, send my regards to your mom," she replied half-heartedly, not having fully recovered from the shock of seeing a Sudanese youngster in the deviant company of a Western-looking girl who, God forbid, could be sleeping with him, and together could be doing all sorts of nasty sinful things, since it's impossible for a male and female to just be friends if they're in physical contact.

"What was that about?" asked Veronica after I walked back to her and continued strolling around the shopping mall.

"She's my mom's acquaintance."

"Why was she staring at us?" Veronica wanted to know.

"She was shocked. Because she probably thought we're a couple and we're banging. The way I was walking with you as an unmarried Sudanese guy is very inappropriate. Especially with you dressed like this. She's traditional and very conservative, so I don't blame her for seeing things in this sexual way."

"That's fucked up!" exclaimed Veronica.

"Nah, it's just a different perspective. Out of respect, I wouldn't stroll around like that in a Sudanese setting, and neither would you. But in a public place like this, it's nobody's business how I live or act."

I doubt Veronica got it. But then again, I didn't expect her to. She's never had to constantly straddle East and West, or deal with the constant pulls of different cultural norms— the downside of growing up a third-culture kid. And for that, a part of me envied her, and people like her.

People whose lives and identities seemed simpler and easier to comprehend.

On a late night in the first week of February, I heard the expected knock on my apartment door and the noise of luggage being dragged outside. Our apartment was just about to receive another guest.

I opened the door, and there she was: the hard-hitting, provocative, Egyptian-born columnist Mona Eltahawy, standing before me.

"*Mona! Izzayyik ya hanem?* How are you? *Akheeran.* At last. Welcome, you made it safely," I greeted her enthusiastically.

"*Amir, izzayyak?* God, thank you for talking to the driver, we couldn't find the place at first."

"Glad you made it. How was your trip?" I asked after hugging her and helping her with her luggage.

"It was okay, it was okay. I fly all over the place, so I'm used to it," she replied hurriedly.

Something struck me. "You know, I did not expect you to speak with a British-sounding accent at all. I thought you speak English with an American accent since you live in New York," I noted.

"It's because I lived in the UK first—Egypt, Saudi Arabia, *and* the UK."

"Oh my, Saudi Arabia and the UK? No wonder you've got that whole feminist thing going on. I bet you absolutely loved Saudi Arabia when you lived there, no?" I poked in amusement.

"Saudi Arabia? Oh please don't get me started. How can you not love it! Especially when you're a woman!"

For some time, Mona had been rising in visibility thanks to her fiery, courageous activism, and unapologetically polarizing liberal articles on all kinds of issues in the Arab world.

At a time when much of the liberal Arab blogosphere wrote anonymously, Mona stood out as an anomaly. Not only did she tackle taboo subjects, she did so openly, boldly, and as a progressive Arab woman, albeit a controversial one under the glare of a growing spotlight. I had always been inspired by her ability to do that, even when I disagreed with some of her stances. Hence I looked forward to the opportunity to spend much one-on-one time with her in person.

Tired from attending the previous night's crowded Thaipusam Hindu celebrations in Batu Caves with other expats and tourists, Mona and I sat chilling in the apartment living room, surfing the Net on our laptops and replying to e-mails.

"How did you get to do this?" I asked.

"Do what?"

"Travel the world speaking about issues and causes you're passionate about."

Mona explained to me how she started out as a journalist at a young age, reporting actively from numerous countries throughout her career in the Middle East until she got fed up dealing with her employers and editors.

"My ex-husband basically told me, 'If you're so sick of your job, then go create your own.' I don't think he meant it, but you know, Amir, I said to myself, 'Huh, maybe I should do that.' And so that's what I did. I quit my job and became a freelance writer and columnist," she said matter-of-factly.

"Nice. It must be great doing your own thing," I confessed.

"It's been wonderful! I can't tell you how much better it is, especially when you're a journalist who has so much to say. You don't have to deal with your editors, or stick to all this BS 'objectivity' crap they teach you. I'm now free to say what I want," rejoiced Mona, who spoke fast, with passion, and in true Arab style, with her arms and hands gesturing all over the place.

"It sounds like blogging, and the freedom we bloggers now have to say what we want," I concurred.

"It is, it is!" Mona said excitedly.

To which I clarified, "—as long as you're anonymous though. Because some issues are just too sensitive," I remarked drily.

"No, but why? Why do you say that?" she protested. "You don't have to be anonymous. We need to speak up, and to say what needs to be said. We have to, and you need to do it with your real name and show your face, because it has more power. We have to expose the hypocrisy, *ya Amir*. We have to. Otherwise, how are we going to move forward?"

Feeling slightly defensive, I said, "Um, have you seen what I've been blogging about lately? I've been a lot more open about my heretical ideas on religion, and some of the responses I've been getting are not pretty."

"Who cares? People write crap about me all the time."

"Still, you're in New York. I'm here, so some of us need to be anonymous," I reminded her.

"Of course, of course, I'm not saying you in particular need to stop being anonymous, because, yes, some of us do need anonymity. But if we can, it's better if we speak our minds openly!" she insisted.

"Obviously," I concurred again. "Thing is I have been

thinking about it. Revealing my identity. And eventually writing openly with my real name, and you, among a few others like Mahmood in Bahrain and Ahmed al-Omran, aka Saudi Jeans, have been inspirations of mine. But what I write is more controversial, and I don't want to have to be all vague and diplomatic if I begin writing openly. I like that I can be blunt right now."

I revealed to Mona the extent of my disillusionment with religion, but for all her liberalism and progressive views, I still couldn't completely share how I truly felt. I worried it might be too much. Too heretical. Maybe offensive.

Despite that, Mona still understood where I was coming from, and we spent the next twenty minutes or so talking about religion again. We were both big fans of the Sudanese-born American scholar of Islam, Abdullahi An-Na'im, whom she knew personally. On top of that, she too had read about my heroes, the Mu'tazila. They were her heroes as well, and at one point in the conversation, she lamented their defeat by the Ash'ariyya just as I had, saying, "If only the Mu'tazila had won! Can you imagine how different Islam would be today?"

It felt comforting to know she knew like I knew. I really was not alone in my feelings and frustrations.

"Amir, we exist!" exclaimed Mona. "Don't be fooled by the lies. People like us exist! And because of the Internet and social media we're all finding one another and coming together just like the two of us connected, and that's the exciting thing. This is huge, Amir! It's huge!"

"You're damn right it's huge. We're waking up, my friend," I concurred once more with a mixture of pride and doubt. Doubt in whether our growing online awakening and spirit of virtual self-empowerment could actually bring tangible change on the ground, in our tyranny-ridden lands. It just didn't seem feasible. In fact, it seemed impossible.

"Until when are we going to remain silent?" instigated Mona rhetorically. "*Khalas*. We're fed up. Enough of these tyrants. *Enough*. Change is coming. Change *has* to come."

She was relentlessly defiant, and unforgiving. I smiled at her impassioned declarations, and in my mind repeated my three-word mantra, "No. More. Mercy," hoping to completely rid myself of the remaining faint sympathies and sensitivity I still mysteriously had within me for my former love, my faith, my Islam.

II

Loneliness

It was around 2:00 A.M. on a dark, lonely March night, and I had been sobbing in my bed as silently as I could for over half an hour. Sobbing and learning an important lesson the hard way.

In my eager quest for the truth, mental liberation from the shackles of dogma turned out to be just the beginning. Inner happiness and peace didn't automatically follow.

Heartbroken. Crushed. Disillusioned. The love of my life had betrayed me, her mesmerizing beauty lifting like a veil worn by an old Bedouin woman, to reveal a harsh face beneath its folds. My romanticized childhood love, she who I had trusted, had been exposed. Her voice, her haunting minaret calls to blissful prayer, the way she made me feel as if I knew my place in this world—all these felt like a cruel trick played on my unsuspecting heart.

I didn't know who I was anymore. In deconstructing and tearing down the bulk of my now crumbled Islam, I unknowingly tore apart my own identity as an Arab, as a Sudanese, as a Muslim. And now my love was gone. Divorced, discarded, and buried away. Leaving me with a painful and unexpected inner void I needed to fill.

Never before in my twenty-two-year existence had I felt so deeply betrayed. "It's okay, Amir. Forget it. It's all bullshit anyway. Seriously, just man up and face it. Religion really is a lie!" tried a consoling voice in my head. "How could this be? I can't believe it. After all those years of love and devotion? This can't be true. I know what I felt. Every time I immersed myself in prayer, I felt it. It was real," agonized another voice in response.

The pain I was feeling had been building up inside of me for a while. On that night, it was no longer bearable. The betrayal filled my chest to the brim, and mercilessly tore it open. It grabbed my heart, ripped it out, sliced it into a thousand pieces, chewed on them, and spat them out all over the dusty deserts of the earth.

As I stared at the ceiling, I kept sobbing, not knowing what to do, not knowing how to reconcile the torn pieces of my being.

Lying in bed, consumed by the poisons of hatred and anguish, I plotted my revenge against the faith of my forefathers and all of religion. But then I stopped and imagined the kind of pain my actions could cause my loved ones. In my betrayal and outrage, I wanted to go from ardent devotee to sworn enemy, but by turning against the religion my family held dear, I felt that I was betraying them, just as religion had betrayed me. After all they had done for me, I felt that I was going to wrong them. And so, slowly but surely, the scorpions of guilt crept under my skin and stung me into temporary silence.

It was during moments like these that I longed for the

days of yesteryear, when everything was simpler, and life made more sense. But those days were gone, and were now replaced by voices in my head waging against each other a war of ideas with an intensity that was gradually driving me crazy.

My mom was right. "Stop thinking so much, Amir," I remembered her always telling me. "It's not good for you." But I couldn't help it, not then, not now. "Maybe I should have listened to her," I told myself in that weak moment. "Maybe I should have listened."

By the middle of March 2009, it had become very clear to me that reason—she whom I had loved (and still unequivocally continue to passionately love)—failed to be my salvation. She miraculously nourished my mind, but failed to nourish my heart into peace.

Continuing to read parts of Immanuel Kant's *The Critique of Pure Reason*, along with reviews of its ideas by some scholars, including conservative American writer Dinesh D'Souza, made me recognize that my expectations of rationality and logic might have perhaps been too high.

I strongly hesitate to say that I properly understood the majority of what I read in *The Critique of Pure Reason*. It's a very dense read, but whatever I grasped in my self-taught quest was enough to make me aware that reason has her limitations. She is incapable of revealing the full truth about reality to us.

The way we understand the world is through our bodily sensory perceptions. Therefore, our understanding is limited by what we can empirically perceive through those very senses. Our understanding is also mediated, and hence influenced by them.

Just because a blind person is unable to see, it does not mean that objects he cannot see don't exist. And even if he could see, the way a frog would see a given object is different from how the man would see it.

At the same time, that very blind person also shouldn't go around claiming matter-of-factly that certain objects exist when he has never touched them, and can't even see them.

Because the simple truth is, the blind person does not know if they exist. *That* is the intellectually honest position. Similarly, when it comes to matters of an afterlife, or the resurrection of Jesus, empirically speaking, we don't know, but given the mutually exclusive faith claims of various religions, we can reason through them and safely conclude that the improbability of those claims is pretty high.

Hence, while I did feel more satisfied intellectually, my heart could not deal with the uncertainties and the lack of "valid" answers to the deeper philosophical questions (despite not being sure what the parameters of valid in this case entailed).

Where did we come from? What is the purpose of life? How can we arrive at an objective morality? Do we have free will?

What is the truth?

And so the internal void grew, but despite that, I knew there was absolutely no way I'd go back to organized religion and its dogmatism, for in my eyes, it provided a false sense of assurance and stability that individuals like D'Souza refused to admit. He was certainly right about the limitations of reason, but that's no excuse to make room for a god of the gaps, or to flounce faith-based notions with arrogant certainty and moral superiority in our faces. No excuse at all.

"Salvation through Jesus only—or else!"

Thanks, but no thanks.

I understand the desire to defend faith. After all, we do need faith. We should encourage faith. All of us, even atheists, live everyday with faith. But it's a kind of faith that's different from "bad religious faith," and the divisive separation theology that comes with it. And herein, I define "good faith" broadly as the conviction in certain positive notions and outcomes for which there can be no compelling evidence to back or refute them. Hence, in the presence of evidence, one would not require faith.

So what's this good faith I speak of? And what inspired me to increasingly contemplate the idea by March 2009? I can't remember how exactly I got there, but here's an excerpt from a blog post series I wrote entitled "The 7 Categories of Faith, Explained—The Uplifting Sacred, the Downright Ugly and Everything In-Between." I never finished the series, but in my clumsy attempt to define good faith, I wrote the following fictional anecdote to help me develop the idea and to stir up debate with some of my atheist readers.

Aicha's son is addicted to cocaine. She's worried about him. She's distressed with pain. She's disappointed and at times uncertain about what the future holds for him.

Yet, Aicha believes he'll get better. Yet, she showers him with unconditional love and maintains her faith in him.

And as Aicha believes all of this, she can't provide any sufficient rational evidence to support this unfounded belief of hers. The truth of the matter is that she does not know what will happen to her son.

Nobody does.

Rationally speaking, her belief's validity is neither provable nor disprovable. We're all agnostic to it. We don't know if it's true or false. It's just faith, an intangible, uplifting and empowering faith.

Indeed, Aicha's son could very well end up fully recovering . . . or also dying from an overdose. But it doesn't matter. Aicha remains faithfully optimistic.

That's good faith. It is the kind worthy of respect and reverence. It is necessary for basic survival, let alone making our world a better place. Even atheists have it whether knowingly or not.

We need more of it.

Yes, we do need more of this good faith. Faith in ourselves. Faith that certain things will turn out better, even if dark circumstances might say otherwise.

Faith in humanity.

Jamal, who read the blog post, disagreed in the comments section and wrote, "I'm not sure I'd quite call what you're referring to here as 'faith.' I think perhaps a better label for it is 'hope.'

"But then again," he reconsidered, "(obviously I'm thinking as I type here), perhaps that hints at a different level of what you're referring to that could be categorized as faith."

I considered the disagreements that came in from various readers, and how many of them were essentially a matter of vocabulary and semantics, but in my mind, "faith" was the ideal world.

Good faith, that is.

But that kind of faith is not a belief system. It's not a world-view. It doesn't answer where we came from, or how the universe came to be. It's an attitude, one that I was trying to nurture in myself. It helped temper my anguish. Nonetheless, I remained in tatters—confused, torn, and scattered.

"This can't just be it," I thought repeatedly. "There's got to be something else, something that can help me make meaning of the world, and feel at peace, but in a way that's evidential, and empirically valid. Not some wishful thinking, religiously divisive, faith-based mumbo jumbo."

But what is it and where would I find it?

"Have you read *A New Earth* by Eckhart Tolle? You should," said a colleague at work who was quite familiar with my journey until that point.

I had already heard of Eckhart Tolle by then and knew about the giant orgasm he gave many people in the New Age movement, with which he has come to be associated. His ideas in his preceding book, *The Power of Now*, which I had flipped through months before were interesting, but somewhat too idealistic, it seemed to me. And now there I was hearing about his newer book, which sounded even more naive and "Kumbaya-ish."

Nevertheless, my curiosity got the better of me, and so I walked to the office bookshelves, grabbed a copy of *A New Earth*, and flipped through it for about twenty minutes.

For a while, the book was quite intriguing.

Tolle patiently detailed how our ego-based thinking causes much suffering in the world, and how we can learn to overcome this suffering both within ourselves and on earth by awakening to our true essence and the beauty that lies inherently within us. He explained this by drawing from different mystical traditions, especially Eastern ones like Zen Buddhism.

"When you yield internally, when you surrender, a new dimension of consciousness opens up," wrote Tolle in *A New Earth: Awakening to Your Life's Purpose.*

Still, the book wasn't good enough for me. Not only did it not sustain my attention, it felt irrelevant to the predicaments of a very cynical Amir at the time.

"Yes, yes, let's all awaken to our true beautiful nature, love each other, and sing Kumbaya in front of a backdrop of rainbows and butterflies. I'm sure we'll save the earth."

Tolle didn't give me something to sink my teeth into.

The pages felt too fluffy and simplistic.

"Yup, not for me," I concluded, and put the book away.

I was desperately yearning for something bigger and more comprehensive, yet I still had not found it, which obviously sucked. Big time. But Tolle did do something critically useful for me though. He pointed my attention into a direction I had not seriously pondered in my quest before: Sufism, Islam's mystical tradition.

And so I delved quite a bit into Sufism, but a lot of what I read, I couldn't understand. All this nice-sounding stuff about the Unity of Existence, annihilation of the ego, and union with the Beloved, was too poetic and too vague for me to grasp. It was nowhere near intellectually satisfying as I had hoped it would be. And emotionally, it did nothing to ease the pain I still felt.

I also had severe problems with the traditional Sufi practice of pledging an oath of loyalty to the master and head of a Sufi order. In some cases, there was so much reverence from followers for their Sufi masters, it felt excessive. "Blind guru-worship. Not for me," I thought again.

Was there any hope?

Would I ever find my answers?

Maybe I was destined to end up a little like Ayaan Hirsi Ali—an outcast I empathized with, out and alone in the wilderness thanks to the espousal of controversial atheistic views.

Maybe.

But even if I were to face such circumstances, I still vowed to myself that there would be no submission.

As the days passed by, my outspoken demeanor against religious dogmatism emerged into greater view on my blog, to some of my readers' dismay and disappointment.

But I didn't care. Even though I had felt held hostage by my Sudanese and Western audiences at certain points before, and I did try to adjust my tone accordingly, this time, I had other concerns—and chiefly among them was my blog pseudonym and persona, Drima. Myself. Or was it my fictitious self?

"Which one is it, Amir?"

I didn't know. And that precisely, was the torturous problem. After almost three years of consistent blogging, I arrived at an unavoidable crossroads.

Was I Amir Ahmad Nasr, the transformed young man still quite afraid to share his true thoughts with those around him in the real world? Or was I Drima, the snarky, irreverent, anonymous blogger behind The Sudanese Thinker, who had a few thousand fans and readers around the world, and was unafraid to speak his mind?

The pressure kept building, and the questions became more pressing.

I loved Drima. It was because of him that I found the courage and tools to confront and destroy the troubling question marks I tried ignoring since childhood. And yet I also hated Drima. Hated him for leading me astray, away from my community and family. I wanted to disown him, forget him. Pretend he didn't exist.

"But Drima *is* you, Amir. And *you* are *him*," told me a gentle voice from deep within.

Sinking deeper into the quicksand of my loneliness as my transformation continued, I felt that I would no longer be able to maintain the same kind of relationships with those around me who were religious or Muslim, even my family. I was convinced they wouldn't understand, and when Drima burst from cyberspace into the real world, they proved me right. "They" being a few close individuals who reacted explosively.

Let's just say the reception to my formerly held-back ideas wasn't exactly the kind that included red carpets and ribbons waiting to be ceremonially cut.

"That's it! From now on, our relationship is never going to be the same!"

"I don't want to know you anymore. In fact, *I don't know you*!"

"You better rethink your thoughts, Amir. Otherwise, you're a traitor, and you deserve to be treated as such."

My parents were disappointed, to say the least, but displayed sensitivity and restraint, and more than anything, great surprise. "Why this? And why now? What changed? You've always been the most religious and practicing of all your siblings!"

"I don't know how to explain it to you," I told them remorsefully and begrudgingly. "But I have my reasons. And I don't expect you to understand them. Just leave me alone, please. If you want me to be fine, if you want things between us to be fine, don't ask me any questions about religion or bring up the topic again—ever. Please. If you'd just do that. Ask me anything, talk about anything—just not religion. Please. Not religion."

By early May 2009, it had been many, many months since I had gone to a mosque or prayed. The poison of hatred and anguish at all the betrayal I felt reached its zenith, consuming me from within, and depleting me emotionally. And yet, I vowed to keep "fighting," or in actuality, vowed to keep drinking poison and waging my hatred-driven battles. I hadn't gotten that far only to then collapse in defeat and lose. But I was getting tired and fed up with everything. My only consolation was my work colleagues and circle of friends, my growing pile of books, the Internet, and the solitude of my apartment.

"Maybe you need a break, Amir."

One day, as I walked back to my apartment with bags of groceries, I passed by the mosque near the grocery store and heard the call to sunset prayer. For the first time in a long, long time, it wasn't easy.

The *azaan* from the minaret sounded beautiful, melodic, and haunting, but also treacherous and dangerously seductive.

I had to resist the powerful intoxicating nostalgia it induced in my soul. I had to fight it off, and overcome the sense of longing it aroused in me.

Responding instantaneously, a fierce, almost uncompromising voice in my head insisted, "No Amir, no. Don't fall for it. This is how they lure you in. They make it all nice and melodic, and once you're in, you're in forever. They'll cage your mind, and you'll have to abide by all that dogmatic bullshit again. It's all just treacherous nonsense, unworthy of your empathy or sensitivity. Fuck it. Don't fall for it, Amir. Don't fall for it!"

Then I saw a poster hanging on one of the mosque's fences featuring large bloody images of decapitated Palestinian babies, and calling for a boycott of Israeli products. In a fraction of a second, there was nothing to resist.

PART V

The Reconciliation

My Three-Eyed Beauty

An hour past noon in mid-May, I'm standing in the majestic interior of a four-hundred-year-old mosque under the colossal dome. I am accompanied by a Jewish WikiLeaks hacker, a Tunisian digital activist, a Syrian citizen journalist, and my camera. The mood is tranquil, and the energy serene, restful, and temptingly sacred.

Resigned to being a tourist for the day, I had tagged along with my new friends when the opportunity presented itself. We arrived at the mosque just as the congregation of worshippers and the Imam were about to begin the afternoon prayer in the spacious building.

Rather than explore the evocative calligraphy and artistic works that surrounded me, I sat alone quietly at a large side window, and like some other tourists, watched the worshippers from afar.

"*Allahu Akbar*, God is Greater," the Imam called out, and began the silent recitation of the Qur'an. Again, "*Allahu Akbar*, God is Greater," he called out, bowing forward toward Mecca. "God Hears who thanks Him," he reminded the worshippers. "Oh Lord, to you, thanks is due," the congregation responded in unison and what felt like sincere gratitude, their modest voices reverberating hauntingly under the almost celestial dome of the mosque.

For four hundred years—from the peak of the Ottoman Empire to its fall and transformation into modern-day secular Turkey—millions had walked through the gates and doors of the Sultan Ahmed Mosque. Fathers mourning their sons, sons mourning their fathers, the doubters, the devoutly faithful, and those whose hearts were filled with greed and envy, love and compassion.

The mosque must have witnessed it all, and the variety in those supplications.

"What a pity," I mused. "As if there's a God who really does answer our prayers."

"*Allahu Akbar*, God is Greater," recited the Imam. It felt like he was taking forever, so I took out my camera and snapped a picture. And then my thoughts drifted back to the preceding days.

On May 12, 2009, I had found myself onboard an Emirates flight on my way to Istanbul, Turkey, for a three-day workshop on online anti-censorship tools. In my hands, I held a little book that gripped my attention by the neck and held it throughout the long journey. Every word, every sentence, every chapter had enthralled my mind, heart, and soul. Now the words came back to me as I sat in the echoing mosque.

"Unless science can be shown to be compatible with certain deep features common to all of the world's major wisdom traditions, the long-sought-after reconciliation will remain as elusive as ever," wrote the American philosopher of consciousness Ken Wilber in his thin but elegant book, *The Marriage of Sense and Soul: Integrating Science and Religion.*

A digital marketing colleague, Sam Rosen, whom I had gotten to know over Twitter, recommended it to me after a Skype conversation in which I had shared with him my peculiar views. I had hesitated, having encountered Wilber's writings before and found them dense and full of obscure lingo, but Sam assured me that *The Marriage of Sense and Soul* was one of his more accessible and introductory works.

Wilber, I found out, was the most prominent voice in a newly emerging philosophical movement known as integral theory. Thousands of miles away from Malaysia, in places like Boulder, Colorado, and the Bay Area in the United States, a new way of looking at the world was starting to take shape and gathering a small but growing tribe of advocates.

Initially, the body of literature seemed "New Agey" to me and, I suspected, lacking in intellectual rigor, but upon closer inspection, I discovered it was anything but, and that integral theory, as well as its cousin, evolutionary spirituality, actually have a lot to offer. For a start, the integral perspective makes a simple but incisive distinction in matters of religion that I believe is supremely important, and desperately ought to be part of any meaningful discourse on the subject.

Broadly speaking, when we look at religion through an integral lens, we realize there are two different dimensions of religious experience. Firstly, we have religion in its exoteric or "outer" dimension, which mainly consists of the rituals, beliefs, and codified dogmas and doctrines of a particular

religion. And secondly, we've got the esoteric or "inner" aspect of religious experience—by definition one "hidden"
from sight, and hence not adequately discussed. Both the
exoteric and esoteric aspects are intertwined together with
varying combinations in different religious communities and
wisdom traditions.

The exoteric form is the standard form of religion for
the majority of the faithful. It's a kind of religion that's pre-
dominantly centered on certain beliefs and doctrines, and
dedication to an exclusivist sectarian God. On the other
hand, the esoteric form of religion, the less standard form,
is mainly centered on systematic practices such as meditation, fasting, and prayer that can be deeply transformative
and enriching, holding great potential to heal us and change
us for the better. Best of all, we can directly experience the
gifts of this second type of religion for ourselves, instead of
accepting it merely based on faith or because we've been
slyly forced to.

Every religious tradition offers within it variations of the
two aforementioned exoteric and esoteric approaches to religious experience. In Judaism, you can choose to live by the
confining rules of Orthodoxy, or opt for the mystical path
Kabbalah. In Hinduism, your lack of fortune could mean being born into a low caste, thanks to the lovely caste system,
or living a traditional yoga-inspired lifestyle with all the benefits that entails for one's self and the environment. Similarly,
in Christianity, you may treat yourself to some Rick Warren
and Pat Robertson, or explore the teachings of Christian
mystic Father Thomas Keating. And of course in Islam, you
could resign yourself to a very doctrinal existence like the

one my bearded teachers had prescribed, or nourish your heart and soul by embarking on the Sufi path. Even if one were to examine shamanism and tribal rites, one would find exoteric components as well as esoteric aspects.

According to Wilber, in order for there to be a reconciliation between religion and science, one needs to come up with a working definition of the two, and initiate the integration on terms acceptable to both parties. This sounded great to me—as a passionate lover of Reason, I sure wasn't going to accept the integration thesis if it weren't first and foremost presented on terms acceptable to science. And so I read on.

First, religion needed a definition that located something common in all of the various traditions, despite their competing truth claims. Wilber points out that beyond the apparent differences in their exoteric rituals and dogmas, all the traditions contain a similar "map" of the inner esoteric landscape of mystical and spiritual experience. This commonality is often called the "Great Chain of Being," or as Wilber renames it, "the Great Nest of Being."

What Wilber wrote struck me as very revelatory. At their esoteric mystical core, the world's major religious traditions aren't that different after all. It is the exoteric components that too often create and promote the troubling exclusivist sectarian truth claims. But when we look at the esoteric insights reported by the men and women who've tasted them through the mystical tools of their different religious traditions, they tell us a very different story. Their insights are remarkably similar and they poetically describe the same experiential observations.

Feelings of peace and "oneness" with everything. Out-of-body experiences. Losing one's socially-constructed sense of identity and tapping into a deeper knowingness. It's pretty profound, but what is perhaps even more intriguing is that the wisdom traditions have mapped out levels of consciousness and "spiritual development," which according to Wilber, correspond with one another, and in many cases correspond to Western developmental psychology's maps, too, along with anthropological and sociological maps as well.

I wondered for a moment if Islam describes any of the spiritual levels. Then my father's words rushed back into my memory from early childhood, filling my awareness with a sense of ease. "When it comes to prayer, there is something else I didn't mention. It's called *al-nafs al-mutma'innah*, the tranquil self. . . ."

In Sufism, the levels are elaborately described, highlighting in some cases seven levels in the following order.

1. *Al-nafs al-ammaarah bissu':* the manifestation of our "lower self" or animal nature. Anger, aggression, hatred, jealousy, and the sexual impulse are raw expressions of this self.

2. *Al-nafs al-lawwama:* the admonishing self, or the voice of our conscience that encourages us to resist the negative aspects and temptations of the "lower self."

3. *Al-nafs al-mulhimah:* the self that communicates inspiration from God, or the Supreme Self, to improve our nature.

4. *Al-nafs al-mutma'innah:* the tranquil self that emerges when a person becomes free of self-sabotaging behavior and is in a state of willful, peaceful surrender to the Supreme Self.

5. *Al-nafs al-radiyah:* the accepting self that accepts life as it is, regardless of the good or bad that's happening, and is in a state of humble gratitude.

6. *Al-nafs al-mardiyyah:* the self of one who is not only experiencing a state of gratitude, but better yet, embodies it and other spiritual qualities in daily life.

7. *Al-nafs al-safiyyah:* the purified self of one who's in a state of harmony.

Apparently, each level and state of self is associated with a "station" on the Sufi path to mystical union with God—a journey that other traditions like Zen and Vedantic mysticism also describe with similar levels of development and inner enlightening realizations.

This brings us to another crucial point. These mystical experiences are virtually universal and have been described in great detail by the world's wisdom traditions. Therefore, experiencing such heightened states of consciousness within a certain tradition does not lend credence to that particular tradition's doctrinal sectarian truth claims. It doesn't prove that Jesus is the son of God, or that accepting Islamic doctrine is the only valid path to avoid hell, which is unfortunately how most individuals who go through such experiences interpret them, falsely concluding that their religion must be the right one, and exclusively so. And this of course brings us back to the exoteric dimension of religious experience and worldviews.

Another idea that intrigued me in Wilber's writings was the notion that there are different stages of evolutionary development in worldviews, through which cultures around the world have passed or are currently passing. A very simplified model of these various worldviews goes from *tribal* to *traditional* to *modern* to *postmodern* and now, slowly, to *integral*.

Hinduism and the three Abrahamic faiths—Islam, Christianity, and Judaism—for instance, emerged in traditional and tribal societies, long before the rise of modernity, which first emerged in Europe starting in the form of the Enlightenment, thanks partially to seeds passed on from the Islamic civilization. To a great extent, the Enlightenment project emerged as a response to the domination of the Church. And then of course, more recently, postmodernism emerged in certain parts of the developed world, largely as a response and rejection of modernity's strong emphasis on objectivity in discerning truth. Emphasizing the important roles of interpretation and contextualization, for better or worse, postmodernism injected into various cultures the notions and consequences of relativism. In its more extreme forms, it claims that truth is merely relative and all perspectives have equal validity and value.

I shared Wilber's apparent dislike of postmodernism's relativism, and appreciated his passionate desire to assert the validity of objective truth. But more importantly, what really struck a chord with me was his articulation of the stages of cultural development—how no stage is inherently better than others, how each can have a healthy or problematic expression, and also how each has its pros and cons. I appreciated how integral theory is an attempt to integrate the best of each of these worldviews, including modernity's almighty science, and the premodern world's "Great Nest of Being."

Some people may object to the idea of stages of cultural development, on the grounds that it is a reductionist way to think about the rich tapestry of human civilization. But once I started peering through this lens for the first time, I found it to be anything but reductionist. It made sense of so many of the confusing and contradictory situations I had encountered in my own life and in the world around me. Moreover, it was clear that the stages are merely maps, and as Wilber likes to often remind his readers, "the map is not the territory."

To an extent, the worldviews explained why an illiterate man in a rural village in Pakistan would embody Islam in a traditional unsophisticated way, compared to say, an affluent Western-educated Pakistani man living in modern New York, or Dubai. In terms of moral development, it explained why the aforementioned hypothetical village Pakistani could very possibly be more moral than the affluent educated Pakistani.

It also explained to me parts of my struggles growing up in Malaysia as a third-culture kid torn between my conservative upbringing and my Western education, and desperately trying to craft an alternative path that combined the best of both. I started to understand that it wasn't just the external circumstances in which I moved that seemed so contradictory—my own consciousness was shifting from a more traditional mindset to a modern and postmodern one, and even beyond.

Based on my trials and tribulations, and those of others I knew, it also made sense of the softening and dissolution of my formerly hardline exoteric religious beliefs about the

Other going to Hell for not believing in our doctrines. During my life, in matters of religious belief, I realized I had spiraled upward from a tribal "warrior consciousness" and a traditional worldview, to a very modernist, rational perspective, to a somewhat postmodern view, and by then was reaching for a more integrated place that I intuited but struggled to see clearly or to articulate. In other words, a more *integral* view.

The ideas that Wilber discussed also made me wonder about different regions on the planet, and the stage of cultural development they're in or moving into. According to the developmental system called Spiral Dynamics, on which much of Wilber's work in this regard is based, the United States' "center of gravity" is modernity, with traditionalism dominating in the Bible Belt, and postmodernity flourishing in pockets and on the coasts. In western Europe, postmodernity is more firmly established. The Arab world, on the other hand, has its center of gravity in traditionalism, with the exception of significant parts of its urban populations in more developed places, such as Tunisia, Dubai, and Cairo that have transitioned into modernity, and to a lesser extent, even postmodernity.

There's no way I can do Wilber's ideas or the theory of spiral dynamics justice in these brief pages. You'll have to further explore them yourself. And you really should. What I have shared here are just brief, simplified glimpses of the eye-opening and stimulating thoughts that captivated my attention on my flight to Istanbul. But there was more to come.

And then, from between the covers of that slim book, she appeared: my Three-Eyed Beauty. Or as I like to sometimes call her, Neo's Trinity.

Having discussed the inner esoteric core common to all the religious traditions, Wilber came to one of the essential features of the scientific method: empiricism. To be an empiricist in a broad sense, Wilber noted, "simply means to demand evidence for assertions, and not merely to rely on dogma, faith, or nonverifiable conjectures."

That was essentially what I did in my neighborhood mosque in Qatar as a child. I questioned ustaz Ashraf's assertions to better understand them, but I was bullied into belief through his invocation of hellfire. And it was what I essentially failed to do in my Islamic international school in Malaysia when ustaz Raheem talked to us in class about the torture of the grave. I didn't ask for evidence for his assertion, but accepted it on faith and dogma, and I surely learned my lesson afterward. As Carl Sagan famously put it, "extraordinary claims require extraordinary evidence."

Now according to Wilber, evidence can be gathered in three domains, through three modes, or "eyes of knowing" available to humanity, whereby "there is evidence seen by the *eye of flesh* (e.g., intrinsic features of the sensorimotor world), evidence seen by *eye of mind* (e.g., mathematics and logic and symbolic interpretations), and evidence seen by the *eye of contemplation*," for example, Buddhist satori and nirvana, and the spiritual Sufi experience of *fana'a*.

A narrow empiricism only deals with the experience of the five senses in the material physical world, whereas a broad empiricism accepts all three: sensory, mathematical, and spiritual evidence.

But how can one accept intangible "spiritual evidence?" What's that even supposed to mean? How do you test and verify that? These would all be fair questions to ask.

And this is where things get interesting.

Science, as it is, already accepts mathematical truth. In fact, it cannot operate and carry out its mission without mathematics, and the last time I checked, I couldn't taste, smell, or touch numbers, let alone a complicated physics equation. As such, dealing with nonmaterial evidence is already part and parcel of the scientific process.

Now how do we discern the validity of such knowledge and evidence? Through science's process of firstly following an instrumental injunction (eye of the flesh: examine the cells under a microscope; eye of the mind: solve this mathematical equation), followed by gaining a direct apprehension of "data" via the performed injunction, and then thirdly checking the "data" with a community of trained fellow experts for communal confirmation (or rejection).

And so just as biologists and mathematicians perform certain injunctions that they've been trained in, reach certain findings, and then publish them in peer-reviewed journals, attaining mystical knowledge through the eye of contemplation essentially works in the same way.

Perhaps that is why I longed for something spiritual, because I knew how it felt from experience. I knew the assuring transcendent bliss of meditation and prayer, and I wanted to taste it again from a place of gratitude, but I also wanted to honor reason. And so I didn't want to engage in any practice of wishful supernatural thinking even if it felt good. I was certainly open to something valid though. Can spirituality become a science then? Is it? According to Wilber, yes.

Become the student of a Sufi teacher or Zen monk, follow specific injunctions (meditation, zikr, or whirling), experience an apprehension of "data" and insights, check with a community of fellow students and experts whether they had the same results you did, and presto! You've got a science of spirituality—a process that's repeatable, falsifiable, and verifiable. And so as long as we don't commit "category errors"— for instance, using the eye of contemplation's findings to discern truths in the domain of the eye of flesh—we'll be fine. Otherwise, we'll begin mixing spirituality and quantum physics, which will end up producing what many have rightly termed "quantum quackery."

I was elated by what I had read. Integral theory's elegant and more sophisticated epistemology, my Three-Eyed Beauty, opened up a whole new world of possibilities for me.

At last, I knew I had found something special: an evidential and coherent big-picture approach that made room for the spiritual nourishment my heart craved. And more importantly, an approach that honored my deepest love, my reason.

If Islam were to harmonize itself with life in the globalized twenty-first century, I concluded, it really ought to upgrade its exoteric dimensions appropriately, and express its esoteric mystical heart more powerfully, openly, and widely in order to become all it can. Otherwise, it was clear to me that the rotten state of affairs would continue, thanks to the ignorance of too many among the guardians of the order.

By the time my long flight landed in Istanbul, I had gotten so much out of my little book, I felt as if a burden had been lifted off my battered chest.

It had been a day since I arrived in Istanbul. Once done with our coffee break, our caffeinated group of fewer than twelve participants—consisting of facilitators, journalists and digital activists—returned to the small conference room in the hotel to start the next session of the workshop.

Over the previous intensive hours, we had discussed and shared with each other knowledge on everything from on-line censorship circumvention tactics to setting up our very own individual and customized encrypted communication systems for security purposes using open-source tools.

"So let's say you've got some important information you wish to communicate with other activists, but you want to do it securely, the scary truth is, everything you're using right now—Skype, Gmail, Facebook—all of that can be tracked by governments, especially the U.S. government," explained Johnny, who closely resembled a computer-wiz character out of a cyberpunk movie. "They can find their ways if they really want to."

"Even Skype?" I exclaimed in surprise.

"Yes, some hackers discovered a backdoor that can be used to spy on you. I know this for a fact, and it's confirmed information," he replied confidently with a tone bordering on paranoia.

It had the desired effect.

"Once you've generated the key," continued Johnny, "pass it to the person meant to receive your secure communications, not over the Internet, but offline, so he or she can decrypt your encrypted messages from that point onward. The higher the encryption level, the better, for obvious reasons."

The sessions went on, and later, one of the participants, a Tunisian digital activist, shared some of the successful strategies he'd been using together with his compatriots for years to expose the corruption and tyranny of the Ben Ali regime. I watched with admiration, and took down notes.

I was impressed by the tech-savvy brilliance and dedication with which those guys advocated their cause relentlessly, both from outside and within Tunisia.

When my turn to present came, I talked about numerous tactics, including the usefulness of encouraging your blog readers to sign up as subscribers to your e-mail list or RSS feed.

I explained, "If they block your site, you can always e-mail your loyal core readership and announce your new domain name or mirror site. As for those subscribed to your RSS, they'll still be able to read your blog updates on their Google Reader anyway. Unless your government blocks it, which will of course be a dumb move."

I had much to digest after the workshop was over. It was focused and serious, but it made part of me question whether there would ever come an occasion on which we'd put to use some of the more elaborate and sophisticated tactics we learned.

Clearly, I didn't own a crystal ball.

The insights I had encountered in Wilber's writings quickly began to change the very eyes through which I was seeing the world around me. One late evening after workshop sessions, we went out together for dinner at a popular tourist location and restaurant near Taksim Square in Istanbul. The wind was cool and gentle, and the smells of Turkish cuisine and kebab, deliciously enticing, found their way quickly to my eager nostrils. I examined the nearby tables after the waiter had seated us outdoors, and observed two large Turkish families dining.

Sitting just a few feet apart, the two families seemed like embodiments of two dramatically different worldviews, and yet were part of the same interwoven Turkish societal fabric. At the first table, the women wore no headscarves, but at the other, they did. At the first, the adults drank wine and beer with their meals, but at the other, they didn't.

It was a beautiful contrast and a peaceful coexistence, supplemented by the Middle Eastern tunes and melodies gracing our ears from nearby speakers as well as a small traditional live band away in the distance, down the stone alley, performing just outside another restaurant.

"*Allahu Akbar*, God is Greater," came the reverberating call from across Istanbul's mosques and minarets, drowning out the sounds of music in our vicinity. Almost immediately, our waiter went inside the restaurant and turned off the music player, out of respect for the *azaan*. Nearby restaurants did the same, but some kept on basking in their tunes, including the traditional band down the alley.

No religious police arrived at the scene to arrest or fine anyone. And no dirty looks for perceived transgressions were exchanged by any parties. It was as if there was a silent agreement—perhaps a little tense, but cordial nonetheless—an agreement that said, "To you, your way, and to me, mine."

I sat gazing and taking it all in, idealizing the freedom to healthily indulge and yet in deep awe of the un-coerced sublime piety of this historic city, the former Constantinople—at one point in time, the capital of the Eastern Roman Empire, then, centuries later, the capital of the Ottoman Empire under the command of the twenty-year old Sultan Mehmed II.

Istanbul's story was one full of strife, but somehow in that serene moment—with the blended sounds of music and the *azaan* romantically flooding my ears—she seemed perfectly reconciled to me. A wonderful, elegant blend of East and West. A melting pot of tradition, modernity, and the sacred mystery of our existence. A soulful, approachable friend.

We understood each other, and exchanged a quick wink when no one was looking. She comforted me, and I hoped to comfort her, to meet her at sunrise over the Bosphorus as a loyal servant of her rhythms, and then return to her again at sunset reborn a better self.

"Amir, your food is here!" My workshop colleague broke my reverie. "Here you go. *Yalla, bismillah.* This looks good!"

In the gracious, spacious four-hundred-year-old Sultan Ahmed Mosque, only a few moments had passed, but at last, after what felt like forever, the afternoon prayer ended.

The energy inside was still serene, restful, and temptingly sacred. I put away my camera, and listened to the Imam begin rhythmically invoking Allah's names in moving gratitude, and every graceful thing but platitudes. It was the practice of *zikr*—perfected by the Sufis, and practiced ordinarily by the laymen—the practice of "remembrance."

"*Allahu Akbar,* God is Greater," recited the Imam. "*Subhan'allah,* exalted be Allah," he repeated, his voice emanating heartfelt sincerity. The colossal dome above him did the rest, reverberating the words hauntingly, dwarfing my childhood neighborhood mosque's humble form.

I resisted the intoxicating nostalgia, the sense of longing, but with each reverberating rhythmic chant from the Turkish Imam, my anger-fueled resolve to not be seduced, to not be enchanted by the spell, to not surrender, weakened.

And weakened. Quickly. Badly. Until I lost track of time, and the intention of the formless moment under the celestial dome transformed me into a psychonaut, launched into inner space, inward toward the territories less traveled.

Drunk on a long-lost love, I became a drop in the ocean, one with the ocean, and the ocean itself—all at once. Simultaneously, and without any trace of anger or agony.

In fact, there was no "I" to feel any anger, but rather, a new calm grounded "I," an "I" that felt disassociated from the angry Amir, the Amir who struggled with his social identity, his past, and his divorce. I was no longer him, and he was no longer me. He was *not* me. I observed him, and in doing that, I affirmed that indeed he was *not* me. He *is* not me. So then, who was this new "I"? This "I" of seemingly nothing yet everything? I was stillness, peace, and tranquility—gone for a millennia, and back to the present in my physical body, eyes moist with tears.

The Sufis, Islam's mystics, were right. They were right! At last, I had heartily tasted what their profound poems attempted to explain over generations, but failed to fully capture: the Beloved. My Beloved. Our Beloved.

At last, the psychological detective work, the quest, the pilgrim's journey could end, or at least cease its relentless painful march. At last, I realized a perennial treasure, a deeper truth I had yearned for. All along, it wasn't out there in the wilderness—ink on paper, binary digits through fiber optics, words on a screen. Oh no, it's not out there. It's *here*.

Right *now*. In *this* moment. If only we are willing to surrender to it. To willfully and peacefully submit to it, and awaken to its divinity and ecstasy.

From then onward, I understood that my Beloved cannot and should not be reduced to text. God, Allah, Spirit, Supreme Reality, or whatever you wish to call the Source of Being is meant to be experienced, not through the sometimes torturous eye of mind, but through the eye of contemplation. The eye of spirit, and all its available tools and systematic injunctions—*zikr*, *vipassana*, *koans*—from the various wisdom traditions. Yes, God (or again, "God" if you wish) is meant to be experienced, because in the words of Morpheous, "No one can be told what the Matrix is. You have to see it for yourself."

Sitting down on the bright maroon carpet of the grand mosque, eyes open and heart healed, fully acknowledging that I still did not understand all the answers to remaining perennial questions and the nature of ontological reality, I recited the poetic words, "I bear witness that there's no Reality, except the One and Only Supreme Reality, the Supreme Self, and that Mohammed, the mystic of Hira'a, was His servant and Prophet."

"Amir, how are you doing over there? Are you okay?" My Tunisian companion suddenly appeared out of nowhere at my side by the window where I sat alone.

"*Tamaam*, I'm fine," I replied, pausing for a moment. "Can I ask you a question?" He nodded. "I noticed you didn't pray, either, but just walked around instead. Why did you do that? Do you think you'll ever find the answers you're seeking?"

Somehow he knew what I meant, sighed, and scratched

his beard momentarily in contemplation. "Ah, it's complicated, Amir. It's complicated," he replied with a heavy voice.

"Guys," called out our Jewish friend, standing nearby, "shall we? We've got more stuff to see and explore. I want to take more pictures. And plus, we've all got planes to catch."

He was right. We had to get going.

13

Tradition, Modernity, and My Beloved

Much like the imperfect reconciliation of Istanbul's traditional past with today's modernity, I departed the city a different person—an imperfectly reconciled person—wishing the world around me would find a way to reconcile itself, imperfectly as well, for how can there be a perfect reconciliation?

It was a desire in part motivated by self-interest, a desire to find a reconciled place to which I could belong. A physical place to call home.

All around the Muslim world and beyond, the challenge of reconciliation loomed and still looms large, tearing proud communities apart, fragmenting our souls, leaving too many behind in the tracts as modernity rushes forward. As it unleashes the miraculous power of science and technology, driven by short-sighted economic measures of GDP growth, causing environmental devastation and deforming our priorities. As modernity both crashes and dashes world traditions—with some managing, the static deservedly languishing and a few adapting and thriving, hence bringing forth the best of themselves in service of a world gone slightly mad.

I knew I could count Turkey among the adapting and thriving. But even in Turkey's case, her reconciliation, at least at first, wasn't organic. It wasn't natural. It was forced by the authoritarian, not secular, but *secularist* iron-fist of Ataturk, which dragged traditional Turkey kicking and screaming into modernity. And to this day, Turkey bears the scars of that dramatic transition, with some forces in it quite determined to reverse the course, and re-establish a prominent role for religion, a sentiment that's understandable, but terribly dangerous if pursued with a vigor that could overturn a flawed, but largely democratic Turkey.

In Iran, that's what happened. Except Iran wasn't a flawed, democratic nation. Ruled from 1941 to 1979 by the United States–supported and socially permissive secular dictator, Mohammad Reza Shah Pahlavi, who brutally repressed political dissent, the nation finally said "enough is enough," and in February 1979 deservedly overthrew him in what came to be called the Islamic Revolution.

Unfortunately, the revolution brought in a vengeful religious tide that swung the pendulum from secular to religious dictatorship, sweeping away the old order, and establishing as a result a horrendous totalitarian theocracy where religion is used to control, suppress, and viciously eliminate opponents in the name of a sectarian God.

Decades of the despicable new style of affairs left millions of Iranians desperately hungry for genuine democratic change, and in June 2009, a month after I returned from Turkey to Malaysia, Iran exploded in upheaval. The opposition, which came to be known as the Green Movement, took to the streets of Tehran to mobilize against the theocratic dictatorship of the mullahs and their puppet, Iranian President Mahmoud Ahmadinejad, to protest alleged election voting fraud.

In a first major instance, Iranians inside their country used Twitter to keep the world alerted of events in their homeland, and helped spread a video of the last tragic bleeding moments of twenty-six-year old student Neda Agha-Soltan after she was shot by Iranian security forces.

Sadly—very sadly—the protests were successfully squashed by the reprehensible forces of the Iranian theocracy, as the world largely began looking the other way, thanks to a waning media spotlight on Iran once news of Michael Jackson's death took center stage.

It was a sad reminder, as many noted, of the state of mainstream media and culture in general, when celebrity gossip and news of pop stars overtake much more significant topics in countries like the United States, where the primary cultural malaise is perhaps addiction to a rabid consumerism that is depriving us of meaning.

We could all make use of some positive reconciliation—one that transcends but includes the best of tradition, modernity, postmodernity, and the better angels of our nature.

Alas, it's easier said than done, especially at a societal level.

Sometime in October 2009, I sat alone in my room in my apartment in Kuala Lumpur fast approaching the last pages of *Children of Dust*, the memoir by the American Pakistani blogger Ali Eteraz, whose writings I had read religiously in the Islamosphere earlier.

A healing, and deeply immersive book, I saw myself in Ali's story and evolution, and related to much of what he had gone through. By the end of the book, he returns home to his mother's embrace, after what seemed like a difficult period of weakened bonds.

Moved by Eteraz's evocative words, I closed the book and made my decision. I'd give up my apartment and move back home with my family. Enforcing healthy boundaries and maintaining my independence would no longer require a far-removed, different physical space. For some reason, I knew it'd be almost effortless.

One or two weeks later, I moved out.

"At last, you decided to stop being stubborn!" declared my mother in joy. "From now on, there will be no such nonsense as 'I'm moving out' until you're married and on your own," she insisted, as if drafting a new formal law. I smiled in amusement.

Strangely, that one decision led to a domino effect of other decisions, two of which were difficult, to say the least. I ended a relationship I was in, and I quit my job, taking the scary plunge into the more flexible self-employed world of freelancing, followed gradually by consulting gigs that paid well.

The inner detoxification and reconciliation needed fresh space to keep the pace, which I'd come to find in a most unexpected place: Beirut, Lebanon.

I landed in Beirut on December 7, 2009, on my way to attend the Second Arab Bloggers Summit. Seeing the hilly city's buildings from above as the flight descended reminded me of the scenes I saw on television during the 2006 Lebanon–Israel war, except there was no smoke rising up from bombed structures.

It had been nearly thirteen years since I left the conservative Arab nation of Qatar, and my family started a new life in Southeast Asia. I had been away from the region for a long time, and a lot had changed over the decade—world politics, media, and myself.

And with that kind of transformation comes the desire to grasp on a deep level what really happened, what really changed, and if there is anything you lost along the way, disowned, and needed to reconcile with. Or maybe whether what you lost has always been there within you but you've been too distracted to notice it, leading you to assume it's become nothing more but a mere relic of your past.

I'd realize shortly after arriving in Beirut that a part deep inside of me had been growing very homesick all along. I had always unknowingly longed for that Arabness that I somehow partially lost along the way throughout my corrosive years as a young Afro-Arab Sudanese Muslim in a conflicted Diaspora. And now, the nation of the cedar tree was set to facilitate the much-needed reconciliation.

When I walked into Beirut's airport, I expected to see migrant workers from the Indian subcontinent doing things like picking up luggage, but almost everyone employed at the airport seemed to be Lebanese.

Clearly, this wasn't Dubai, but was it going to be the city I heard notorious stories about when it came to the treatment of dark-skinned Arabs, especially North Sudanese?

I wasn't worried. If anything, I was actually excited and curious. "Another entertaining question mark I can tackle. Should be fun," I thought. With the exception of the grumpy immigration officer who asked me to redo my arrival card in

Arabic instead of English, everyone else at the airport was friendly and welcoming.

Within about an hour, I was outside the airport with George, the driver who was holding up a sign with my name inside the airport's arrival area. The air was wonderful to breathe and colder than hot tropical Southeast Asia. I loved it.

"Interesting, looks like the war really affected this area pretty badly," I observed as we drove to my hotel where the Arab Bloggers Summit meetings were going to be held. "It's Hezbollah territory. The Israelis really pounded it badly, but it'll get fully rebuilt in no time. That's how it is here. Every once in a while, the Israelis find an excuse to destroy the Lebanese economy and damage the country, so that many potential tourists will end up in Israel instead."

"Do you support Hezbollah?" I asked George.

"Of course, they're a resistance," he said. "They've fought the Israelis and stood up to them when others in Lebanon couldn't. Hassan Nasrallah is a brave man."

George continued sharing his thoughts. I cringed and found it intriguing that a Lebanese Christian supported Hezbollah so passionately. As much as I despised Israeli policies and atrocities, I couldn't lend my support to the Iran-backed Hezbollah or its ideology.

"We Lebanese, we come in many different sects, and in general, we've always lived in peace," replied George after I asked him what it meant to be Lebanese, and if there was real unity among the people. "It's our enemies who are determined to divide us," he observed. "And once a few members of each sect begin attacking the houses of worship of other sects, things get out of control. It's unfortunate. What can you do? Those political leaders in this country, they just make things worse. They only care about themselves, and so the rich get richer, and the poor get poorer," George ranted with frustration and resignation.

We continued deeper into Beirut, and with Hezbollah territory behind us, it was now hard to notice the damage of the recent war. It was as if nothing had happened in those inner areas of Beirut we were now driving through. Not a single visible scratch.

At the hotel, I was greeted with a big hug by Sami Ben Gharbia, director of the advocacy arm of Global Voices Online, and cofounder of the formidable Tunisian pro-democracy portal, Nawaat. It was good seeing him again after a previous workshop we had attended together. I appreciated his mentorship, and looked up to him like a big brother paving the way forward for younger bloggers and activists.

I looked around the hotel lobby and recognized many other fellow members of the GVO tribe and community. GVO was the key co-organizer of the summit, and the portal we all blogged on and had in common.

I quickly checked into my room and descended back to the lobby. Fifteen minutes later, a big bus arrived to take us, the trainers involved with the summit workshop sessions, to the Beirut office of Heinrich Böll Stiftung, a German organization that was co-organizing the event with GVO.

Aboard the bus, I had the honor of sitting next to the famed Iraqi blogger Salam Pax. Naturally, our conversation focused on the United States–led invasion of Iraq and the Iraqi blogosphere. Sitting nearby was Amira al-Husseini, the constantly giggling Bahraini Global Voicer, and an editor with the Web site. We chatted and joked around with Wael

Abbas, the Egyptian responsible for helping expose and raise awareness of police torture in his home country, and the first blogger ever to win the Knight International Journalism Award for his outstanding work.

"You know guys," shouted Amira, catching the attention of many on the bus, "I just realized something. If any Arab dictator wants to get rid of the top bloggers in the Arab world, all he has to do is just bomb this bus!" she announced, and burst out laughing.

It was a funny moment, but also a serious one that demanded introspection. Looking around me, I realized that Amira was right. Many of the people on the bus comprised the crème de la crème of the Arab blogosphere. I was humbled and honored to be in their presence, but a little unhappy about being the only Sudanese there. There should have been more, especially the more qualified activists based in Khartoum, even if they weren't well-known bloggers.

At the HBS office, we were warmly welcomed by the generous and hospitable coordinators, Doreen Khoury and Hiba Haidar.

"Drima!" Doreen greeted me by my blog pseudonym. "Wonderful to see you, thank goodness you arrived safely. I'm so glad you didn't have problems at the airport. You were the one I was worried most about," she confessed. "Sometimes, they don't treat Sudanese well."

Eventually, everyone sat around a big table, and we proceeded with our brainstorming session on planning the days ahead. A lot of opinions and ideas were exchanged, but one in particular stood out.

"Of course it's important for us to cover online censorship and how to fight it, but I think we need to have an additional

workshop on how to deal with the biggest form of censorship for us in this region. Self-censorship!" suggested Tunisian blogger Slim Amamou.

It was a significant "aha" moment for me, and it got me
thinking about the many times in the past when I hit back-
space on my keyboard before publishing certain blog posts.
Many in the room could relate.

Jamal Eid, an Egyptian human rights lawyer who founded
the Arabic Network of Human Rights Information, agreed
and proposed a workshop to educate activists on what to say
and what not to say from a legal civil rights perspective during a police interrogation.

"I also think it will be very useful if we have a workshop
on how activists can deal with fear and calculated risks," suggested Slim again. "For example, if I get arrested, I'm fine
with getting punched and kicked, but of course I'll be scared
of getting electrocuted or tortured with other methods."
The discussions continued and we outlined a number of necessary areas of focus for the summit.

Following the brainstorm session, we swarmed the streets
of Beirut late in the evening, and headed toward a restaurant
nearby Gemmayze. It was getting cozy already and a genuine
sense of camaraderie was beginning to emerge.

The Arab Bloggers Summit started with numerous simulta-
neous workshops in the Barcamp format and with nearly one
hundred diverse bloggers, journalists, and activists in atten-
dance from all over the Arab world. While there were some
preplanned sessions, anyone and everyone could propose to
present on additional topics and wait for a show of hands from
those interested.

The workshops were primarily aimed at helping participants understand how to practice free speech online better,
more effectively, and safely in the advocacy of human rights.

"Before blogging, discussions about Islam on the Internet
were dominated by Islamists who ran major centralized Web
sites like Islamonline," explained Wael Abbas and Jamal Eid
during the workshop discussion I joined. Apparently, later
on, because of blogging's individualist nature as an activity
and a blog's autonomous independent character as a medium, blogging attracted a more liberal-minded crowd open
to conversation.

That wasn't surprising to me. Social media after all is
about being social, and having two-way communication, but
at the time, the bulk of the online Islamist movement preferred old-school online forums with administrators who
could moderate discussions and delete remarks they didn't
like. Forums as a medium granted the administrator more
control.

"Surprise of the century. The Islamists want to control our
thoughts and speech. They want to preach while we shut up
and listen. How lovely," I thought.

As the day went on, I met bloggers and fellow Global
Voicers I had been reading for years, including Internet-
freedom activist Jillian C. York, and Ahmed al-Omran, the
blogger behind Saudi Jeans.

Such encounters are always profound, and enable you to
put the person's written word in the context of their demean-
ors, quirky personalities, and physical expressions, hence revealing richer layers of texture and meaning in what they
espouse.

They were a like-minded bunch. Not in their political

stances, but rather in their impassioned impulse to speak up and tell their stories freely. To express who they are, to courageously say what they believe in the face of harsh but changeable realities, and to stand behind the most basic of democratic freedoms: the freedom of speech.

Alaa Abdel Fatah, the Egyptian blogger who was jailed in 2006 and whose "Free Alaa" campaign I humbly participated in online, was also present, and demonstrated his natural leadership talents. He made his defiance known incisively and clearly, as did Syrian blogger Razaan Ghazawi and Bahraini online speech pioneer Ali Abdulemam.

The mood was informal, but very attentive, and full of networking. More importantly, it was colored by the ambiance of newly forming heartfelt friendships and alliances, and the strengthening of pre-existing ones.

The liberal Arab blogosphere—that online self-organized and self-organizing passionate freedom-fighting creature—was alive and well in Beirut on that day. No longer virtual, but physical, out on the ground, and determined to manifest its ethos of freedom and individualism in the real rotten world of Arabia's orthodox, authoritarian, and paternalistic circles.

"My 'beebull,'" I began on the day of my presentation, making fun of how some of the Arab participants had thick-accented English whenever they called out "people."

"My 'beebull,' today I'm going to exblain to you za imbortance of understanding search engine obtimization in advocacy and for growing your blog audience," I announced in my fake accent before switching to Arabic, giving the audience a good laugh. Such was the atmosphere at the summit by then. Fun, very friendly, and casual. As I spoke, some began livetweeting the main points of my presentation, and I had to remind them not to mention my real name or post my picture online. While my fears had significantly decreased, I still preferred protecting my hidden blog identity out of precaution.

The presentation was well-received, and at night, a big group of participants went out for dinner at Teh-Marboteh in al-Hamrah, a touristy part of Beirut. There, I sat chatting with the Egyptian hijab-wearing blogger Noha Atef.

After hearing Noha deliver her presentation, I admired her for her audacity. Covering torture in Egypt is no fun business. On top of that, initiating citizen journalism–based campaigns that lead to freeing unjustly imprisoned people is an outstanding achievement.

"What do you think of the Muslim Brotherhood?" I asked Noha, suspecting she might be a fan. "Do you support them?"

"No," she replied. "I believe that the nation state needs to be secular. Now, I don't know what your understanding of secularism is, but my understanding of it is that the state needs to be religiously neutral. In other worlds, Islam can't be the religion of the state," she clarified, and I nodded my head in agreement.

"In Egypt, Christians need signed permission even if they simply want to renovate an aging church. This is pathetic. Christians should be able to practice their faith freely, and so should I as a Muslim without anyone bothering me with what I can or can't do. Also, I think that religion and politics shouldn't mix in a state, primarily because I think politics damages the purity of religion and dirties it," she stressed.

Her words were comforting. "Oh, daughter of the Nile, good to hear you say these things. I didn't expect you to be a supporter of a secular civil state, because of your hijab. I assumed you could be an Islamist," I told her, and thanked her for enriching my mind with a more nuanced and intelligent perspective.

On the following day, Jacob Appelbaum, a brilliant IT security wiz, gave a technical workshop on using the online circumvention tool, Tor. Prior to that, he was telling a small group of us over a casual conversation about some of his work with WikiLeaks. It was the first time I had heard about the site.

"We basically help whistle-blowers expose wrongdoing so the world can know about it, and those responsible can hopefully be held accountable," explained Jake.

We also had a few discussions about how some Western companies repulsively participate in the repression of Arab citizens and human rights advocates by selling and providing censorship and surveillance equipment to Arab dictatorships to be used against us. Tunisia stood out as the prime example for its world-notorious pervasive practices, and all for the purpose of preserving the Ben Ali regime's totalitarian grip on power as it enriched itself at the cost of Tunisia's people.

It was an all too common story—twisted, sickening, and inexcusable, and often with the complicity of Western governments preaching human rights while turning a blind eye to companies providing dictatorships with weapons and tools to oppress their citizens.

When day six, the final day of the 2009 Arab Bloggers Summit in Beirut, had arrived, we all knew that something inside of us had transformed.

With all the interactive workshops, dinners, and consecutive late-night parties to live Arabic music and folk songs in some of the city's most enjoyable restaurants and joints, many of us had gotten pretty close over the days. We all had experienced the magic of dancing between your current and former self to the uplifting beats and rhythms of Beirut.

I'd remember my conversations with Nasser Weddady, the Mauritanian-born director of outreach at the American Islamic Congress, someone who'd later become a dear friend and mentor; Nizar Qabbani's poetry; cruising after 3:00 A.M. with like-minded comrades in search of chicken shawarma; intimate stories about pasts that shaped us; outpourings of reasons for why we do what we do; internal struggles; Islam; democracy; the Internet; what it means to be an Arab; similar deeply held values; and a staunch refusal to accept or leave things as they are.

All of those factors brought us together in a very real way, and at certain points, it felt overwhelmingly intense.

Leaving all of that was the hardest part.

Beirut's coziness and the company of my fellow activists and Global Voicers reminded me of what it means to be an optimistic Arab, among warm hospitable Arabs, in an Arab city drowned in the sounds of Arabic music. It showed me the way to feel a liberating Arabness stripped of its suffocating politicized aspects, and based on language, a rich heritage, and delicious cuisine. An Arabness that existed comfortably and naturally with the proud Nubian in me.

Yes, leaving was the hardest part. But at the airport, I bought my first book in Arabic in years, one written by the Sudanese novelist Al-Tayeb Saleh, and I left Beirut more healed, reconciled, and optimistic than I had ever been.

. . .

In late April 2010, I traveled to the Bay Area of the United States for a digital marketing and e-commerce consulting gig with a company that did some work with a few figures and teachers in the integral movement.

There, in Marine County, I met one figure whom I found intriguing and had read a little bit about. A veteran meditator and co-author of a book with Ken Wilber, Terry Patten was a big-hearted, generous teacher of integral spirituality, and a former college student activist during the 1960s before becoming a student of a provocative unconventional guru with whom he spent some years.

"Well, isn't that what it's about in Islam?" he asked me, referring to the five prayers, over a healthy breakfast meal in a small organic café. "It's about submitting our hearts in humility to the Mystery of life, the Mystery of our existence, and making that an integral part of our spiritual practice, five times a day. Every tradition has its approach, but the important thing is to have a daily spiritual practice to ground us in our day-to-day lives," he said.

"I love how you refer to 'It' as Mystery with a capital 'M'," I told him after a moment of silence to take in what he had just said.

"Well, that's because it *is* a Mystery, right? At least rationally speaking, because our minds can't really comprehend Spirit. But our hearts can, and it is through our hearts that we connect with the evolutionary impulse that has been driving the process of creativity and unfolding in the universe ever since the Big Bang. . . . We need to learn how to shift our modes of being from grappling with the questions to living the questions, Amir."

"I'm not sure I get what you mean by 'evolutionary impulse'?" I admitted.

"Keep reading, and soon you will," replied Terry with a laugh, close to completing his meal. Once done, we went outside to the parking lot and he handed me a book from the trunk of his Toyota Prius.

It's September 2010, and I'm in Khartoum, Sudan, in the blistering heat of summer and fasting in the month of Rama- dhan. In town to settle some important visa paperwork be- fore returning again to Malaysia, I took the opportunity to catch up with some old friends.

One evening, I met Waseem, a childhood Sudanese friend I grew up with in Qatar, and someone I stayed in touch with via Facebook.

"Man, your years abroad have really changed you," he noted after I shared with him some stories and told him a bit about my blog. "But I can understand some of your reasons. I went through a similar period, but not as extreme as yours. Anyway listen, while you're here, there's someone you ought to meet. He's a wise and respected young Sufi man whose relative is the head of a Sufi order in Omdurman."

"I'm not sure if that's a good idea. He'll probably get pissed once I share with him my 'heretical' ideas," I cautioned with a chuckle, but Waseem was adamant, and so off we drove after breaking fast together to meet the Sufi at his home.

"A lover of the Beloved? Why not? What's the worst that could happen? At the very least, we'll most likely have an interesting conversation," I thought.

A tall and large man in his mid-thirties with a deep and calm look in his eyes opened the door and graciously wel-

comed us in and showed us to his guest room where we sat
ánd chatted for a while.

"I'm sorry for the short notice," Waseem told him. "But I
felt that it would be crucially important for Amir to meet
you and for you to meet him. He has some interesting ideas,
and some difficulties with religion."

I began telling the young Sufi sheikh some of what I
thought after some nudges and glances from Waseem. Slowly.
Reluctantly. Until I began warming up to the conversation,
and started ranting on and on to make my point.

"We fight and bicker over confining archaic doctrines.
Why? What's the big deal about them? I can't and refuse to
believe in them. My mind can't and won't tolerate such ideas
and notions. We should be much more concerned with the
substance of our behavior and conduct toward one another.
Not dogmas, beliefs, and divisive creeds."

Sheikh Talal was more tolerant and open-minded than I
expected. More important, he was present. Not only did he
hear my words, he felt them and empathized with me without judgment, even when I spewed some harsh statements.

Talal smiled, and said, "Now, I think I've begun to understand you."

"*Ya Talal*, let's continue this some other time. It's getting
late and I have to go, but we'll return in a day or two," said
Waseem.

"There's a real crisis taking place nowadays," began sheikh
Talal when we sat with him again, "and we urgently need to
address it. The thing about you, Amir, is that you're a rationalist. You're very rationalistic, and that's why a traditional
understanding and teaching of religion won't appeal to you.

That's why religion no longer appeals to many young people nowadays. We go through the motions, but we can't internalize the ideas spiritually. In the past, the traditional education worked. Learning was built on respect for and obedience of religious authority, but unfortunately in this day and age, many have abused this authority."

"No shit, Sherlock," I thought quietly. "Relying on authority is bad evidence, and hence I reject it, or at the very least, I'm very cautious of it," I said.

"Yes, Amir, but not everyone has the same ability to demand and discern evidence. When you're dealing with the masses, reliance on authority will always be part of the way they discern truth, and this is why we need good authority. The doctrines have their place, and not only do they serve a function, but in our case, in Islam, they're based on God's Word, the Holy Qur'an. Still," Talal continued, "I've been arguing with many other sheikhs and calling for a change in how we impart religious education. We need to make it more rationalistic to better reach the urban youth of today."

"I think you nailed it," I told Talal. "You nailed it, religious education, the way it's done today, it's a real problem."

"It's a huge problem!" he said.

"So what's to be done?" I asked.

Religion is understood and followed differently by different people. Therefore, it would be false to say that religion is inherently problematic. That much is certain, but what is more so is this.

While organized religion isn't inherently problematic, what is heinously and undoubtedly so are things like dogmatism, hatred, violent sectarianism, fear-mongering, indoctrination, authoritarianism, repression, bigotry, homophobia, emotional blackmail, arrogance, intolerance, suffocating conformity, blind faith, misogyny, and the stench emanating from them all: devastating ignorance. Organized religion, unfortunately and tragically for all of us, too often happens to contain insufferable amounts of those reprehensible characteristics. Just as fervent nationalism, fascism, and communism can, did, and do, lest we forget. As such, until organized religion is cleansed of such travesties and tamed into a benign creature expressing the spirit of humanity, religion as taught and practiced today—I repeat as *taught* and *practiced* today—by too many people on the face of this earth is a disastrous problem.

The greatly wasted cognitive potential. The barriers to progress, critical thinking and scientific innovation. The relegation of women to a lower status. The rape and molestation of children. The violence and needless wars. The list of organized religion's disasters is long, and I can go on, but you get the point.

It hasn't always been this way. Religions had typically started with an onset of a mystical experience that signals the "prophet's prophethood," and launches the messenger to share the needed message of the day. Later, the teachings get codified, politics seep in, and we end up in a mess.

Mystical experience, inclusive spirituality, and the encouragement of embodying compassion toward ourselves and others should be religion's hallmarks. We should return to them. Let us value our humanity over divisive creeds, essence over form, and substance over empty ritual.

Indeed, many of the faithful lead such inspiring lives, the kind the not-so-faithful faithful could aspire to. The kind I wanted to embody day-to-day.

"So how does it work?" I asked sheikh Talal.

"What do you mean?"

"Becoming a Sufi. How does it work? Do I have to take that oath with the head of the Sufi order, is it compulsory?" I inquired.

"Only if you're ready for it," replied Talal with an understanding smile. He had noticed my discomfort around the idea. "But even if you don't, you're always more than welcome to join us during our *zikr* practice and rituals, just like Waseem and his friends often do."

On the way back to Khartoum, Waseem said, "I don't like the idea of pledging an oath to the Sufi head, either, so I didn't do it. Yet they're still so welcoming, kind, and generous, and the rituals in their mosque, man, Allah, Allah, Allah, they're beautiful. Ecstatic, rapturous, and just beautiful!"

Crossing the bridge over the Nile, I made up my mind. I'd study and incorporate Sufi practices in my life, but wouldn't sacrifice my intellectual independence and standards for evidence.

By December 2010, I was getting prepared to start life as a postgraduate student. After a period of hesitation, I figured it would be worthwhile to pursue a master's in philosophy at the International Institute of Islamic Thought and Civilization in Kuala Lumpur, Malaysia. Not only would the opportunity provide me with access to a diverse group of Muslim academics and Islamic scholars, as well as non-Muslim visiting American professors, but I'd be able to improve my knowledge and explore intriguing topics ranging from the philosophy of Islamic art and the history of Western science to international relations and the relationship between science and religion.

More relevant, I'd also be able to conduct some proper scholarly research on how the Internet is democratizing Islamic authority, and the changing relationship dynamics between Muslims and their religious establishments in numerous communities throughout the world, which to me marked the start of an exciting development with huge potential ramifications for Islam and Muslims in the long term.

My inquiry seemed straightforward: can we steer the future of Islam in the age of digital media in a favorable democratic direction, and if yes, what would it look like?

I had unrealistic ambitions with that wide-scope academic question, but I was stubborn, and felt it would be crucial to at least understand the inquiry better in hopes of playing a role— any tiny role to help facilitate some kind of positive change. Change that I suspected had to come sooner or later, and it came. Only sooner. Much sooner than anyone could have predicted, from a place few would have expected, and bigger and more euphoric than anyone could have ever imagined.

14

(R)evolution

On December 17, 2010, a twenty-six-year-old struggling Tunisian man named Mohamed Bouazizi did the unthinkable. He lit himself on fire in front of the Sidi Bouzid municipal building to protest the confiscation of his fruit-cart by an abusive female police officer whom he was too poor to bribe. Too weak to fight. Too unprivileged to overcome.

It wasn't the first time he'd been harassed by the authorities, but it would be his last, and in his single act of desperation and gruesome self-sacrifice, Bouazizi, we've been told by popular media narratives, helped spark the revolutions that came to be known as the Arab Spring.

But like most stories of this nature, what actually happened is a lot more complicated.

Here's the slightly more complicated version. After Bouazizi wrote his suicide note and following his deadly self-immolation, his family led a protest at the town's municipal town hall where a relative captured footage of the demonstration on camera phone. Next, the footage was uploaded

onto Facebook where it was noticed by a group of Tunisian
dissidents and digital activists.

One of them was the Europe-exiled Sami Ben Gharbia—
yes, that same Sami from the 2009 Arab Bloggers Summit—
who packaged the tragic piece of news into a compelling story
and used his popular pro-democracy portal Nawaat to dis-
seminate it actively. And thus, this time, unlike similar incidents witnessed before in Tunisia, the injustice of Sidi Bouzid
didn't just stay in Sidi Bouzid, but instead it traveled in near
real-time beyond its painfully limiting confines until the
story was picked up by Al Jazeera Arabic.

Al Jazeera—the Qatar-based satellite TV channel, which
revolutionized the Arab media space by making it much
more open—ran the news item aggressively, broadcasting it
onto the television screens of the Arab world and every Tunisian home and café that tuned in.

It didn't take long for other small Tunisian towns with
similar grievances to begin protesting, too, and as they did,
overnight, semi-dormant regional networks and international alliances of digital activists and journalists came to life
to engage in the media war initiated by Tunisia's Ben Ali
dictatorship.

The regime responded to the growing protests with violence, killings, and a brutal crackdown, which digital activists
relentlessly exposed. Then in a sign of the regime's growing
frustration with the failure of their attempted media black-
out, they went after bloggers and journalists.

On January 6, Slim Amamou, the well-known Tunisian
critic of censorship and AB09 participant in Beirut, was detained, causing widespread concern online about his

well-being among friends and Global Voices colleagues as
we kept track of the situation on Twitter. The next day, on
January 7, more arrests targeting bloggers, journalists, and
activists were made.

But such measures didn't and couldn't stop the shifting
tide. There was no going back as the demonstrations grew
in size and defiance, and continued to be met by unjustified
brute government force.

Tear gas continued to be fired into crowds. Snipers took
to rooftops of buildings and fired live ammunition at largely
peaceful and nonviolent protesters. Ben Ali sang songs of reform, but it was too little, too late. By January 13, the entire
country was in upheaval with crowds pouring into the streets
of the capital, chanting in unison "The people! Want! The
fall of the regime!"

At last, on January 14, Ben Ali cowardly fled Tunisia with
his family and accepted self-exile in Saudi Arabia. His twenty-
three-year ruthless dictatorial rule had finally come to an end.
It was only then that the news became a prominent story in
Western media.

I sat in my chair watching celebratory videos online in
disbelief. Tunisia's people had achieved the impossible in my
lifetime, and showed us what's possible.

But would it be possible elsewhere, too?

In mid-January 2011, a young Dubai-based Egyptian Google
marketing executive named Wael Ghonim posted an invite
on a popular Facebook page he administrated in his spare
time. The name of the page, We are All Khaled Saeed, was
in reference to the twenty-eight-year-old middle-class Egyptian from Alexandria who was beaten to death by tyrannical

police officers. After his murder, a picture of Khaled's disfig-
ured bloodied face was circulated widely over the Internet,
sending appalled shockwaves across Egyptian society

Wael Ghonim was one of those repulsed by the image. It
was the last straw, and soon after, he put his digital marketing experience to use and launched the Facebook page dedicated to exposing police abuse, poverty, and corruption in
Egypt, all issues that mattered to everyone in the nation regardless of political affiliation.

In just three months, the page's members grew to more
than 250,000. Then came the Tunisian revolution and the
toppling of a modern-day Arab dictator, and all of a sudden,
the impossible became vividly possible in a concentrated
part of Egypt's ambitious imagination—primarily that of its
liberal, defiant, tech-savvy youth.

"Now is the time," Ghonim felt. Aiming to be as inclusive
as possible, he posted his Facebook event invite and call to
action with the bold title, "January 25: Revolution Against
Torture, Poverty, Corruption and Unemployment."

Why January 25? Because it's known as Police Day in
Egypt, a symbolic date, a date that shouldn't celebrate the
police but should instead admonish them and their heinous
abuse. Quickly, the call spread and other digital activists
began doing exactly the same: spreading the call.

Of them all, perhaps the most powerful call-to-revolt came
from none other than Asma Mahfouz, the young Egyptian
woman and activist cofounder of the April 6th Youth Movement, whose online recorded video message went viral all
over Egypt.

Looking defiantly at the camera, she unleashed her righteous words and moral outrage. "I will not set myself on

fire," she said in reference to Tunisia's Mohamed Bouazizi's self-immolation. "If the security forces want to set me on fire, let them come and do it! And to every man in this country who's really a man, come down with me," on January 25 to Tahrir Square, Asma insisted.

"And to everyone who says that women who go to protests will get beaten, or that it's inappropriate for them to do so, should have some honor and manhood, and come with me on January 25. And whoever says the number of protesters will be small, and nothing will happen, I want to tell him you're the reason for this. Yes, you're the damn reason! And you're guilty. Just as guilty as the president, the corrupt, the abusive police . . . Your presence will make a difference. And no, it won't make a small difference, it will make a huge difference. Talking to your neighbors, your friends, your colleagues, your families, encouraging them to come down . . . will make a difference. Sitting at home, watching the news, or surfing Facebook, *that*, that will screw us. It will screw *me*. So if you have dignity, and you're a human being, and you're a real man in this country, then you have to come. Come to protect me and protect all the other girls. And if you stay at home, then you deserve everything that's happening to you . . . God says that He 'does not change a people's lot unless they change what is in their hearts . . .' Come and demand your rights, my rights, your family's rights. Our rights! I'm going down on January 25th, and I'm going to say 'No to Corruption,' and 'No to this Regime.'"

Asma's courageous and vulnerable words minced nothing and went straight for the jugular, challenging as well as simultaneously testing the chivalry of the men of her patriarchal society. But would her words work? Would her call, and the similar calls for revolt spreading via mobile phones, word-of-mouth, Twitter, Facebook, and the blogosphere bear fruit?

As January 25 drew closer, debates ensued on Twitter, where I was most active by then. Naysayers and skeptics doubted if what happened in Tunisia could take place in Egypt.

"Tunisia is much smaller compared to Egypt. Egypt is too big."

"After Tunisia, Mubarak is going to be very prepared. He's a military man."

"Tunisia's literacy and Internet-penetration rates are a lot higher compared to Egypt."

"They got lucky in Tunisia. The protests spread fast. Won't happen in Egypt."

I was one of those skeptics, containing my reluctant enthusiasm.

"Will Egypt rise against those who corrupted her and dragged her into regression?" I wondered. I wanted her to. But could she?

Many nervously contemplated the question knowing full well that an Egyptian revolution would be more significant than any other in the Arab world.

Like millions of Arab children and recent generations before us, we grew up on a steady influential diet of Egyptian cultural exports—movies, books, television shows, music, and comedy—that shaped and molded us as we transitioned into adulthood. So much so that if American pop culture's fingerprint could be found everywhere in the world, then Egypt's was seared onto the consciousness of every Arab, even those claiming to dislike Egypt and Egyptians. In short, Egypt is the main psychological center of the Arab world, and so unlike Vegas, what happens in Egypt does not stay in Egypt.

"Could she revolt? Could she, like Tunisia, erupt?" I kept wondering anxiously.

Then came January 25, and suddenly, like a volcano that had been dormant and rather inactive for too many years, Egypt erupted in fury, turning the nonideological flames started by Tunisia into a raging inferno, and triggering an earthquake that shook the entire Arab world, and instantly glued us to our television screens and computers.

Battling with violent security forces firing rubber bullets, water cannons, and obscene numbers of tear gas canisters labeled "Made in U.S.A.," the real heroes—the demonstrators, students, laborers, men, women, rich, poor, Muslim, Christian, secular, religious, young, and old—braved through the streets and poured downtown in the thousands until they gathered defiantly in Egypt's new sacred ground: Tahrir Square.

From there came the electrifying, nerve-wrecking, liberating, historic scenes and chants broadcast all over the globe. "The people! Want! The fall of the regime!" chanted the huge crowds in Tahrir Square. "The people! Want! The fall of the regime!" And with every chant, Tahrir reclaimed our dignity, our power, our voice, our self-worth in our own homelands, and our entire being. It was an exercise in spiritual-cleansing of epic proportions. A dramatic exercise in revolution, in awakening and the unshackling of the self.

I watched the euphoric footage on television and read the fast-moving fiery stream of tweets by comrades and journalists on the ground feeling overwhelmed by intense emotions. Feeling ecstatic and also upset at myself for not being in the

Square, because in that charged moment, and over the following days, I knew with unshakable certainty that if I were to die anywhere in the world, for any cause, it would unquestionably be in Tahrir Square.

In Liberation Square.

Nowhere else.

In Wael Ghonim's words, "the revolution of the youth of the Internet" quickly became "the revolution of the youth of Egypt, which in turn became the revolution of all of Egypt."

Then in a drastic move unprecedented in its scale and in the lead up to the "Friday of Rage" protests, the Mubarak regime shut down the Internet, leaving operational only the obscure Noor Data Networks that provided a connection to multinationals and the Egyptian Stock Exchange.

"Shit," I blurted at my Twitter time line. The volume of tweets by Egyptians like @Sandmonkey, @Gsquare86, and @3arabawy had disappeared.

Panic.

Hactivists, such as Tor's Jacob Appelbaum and others from the AB09 meeting in Beirut, jumped at the center of efforts to maintain communication, utilizing their tech-wizardry to teach and advocate the how-tos of using the old dial-up methods to connect online. The war to establish the authoritative and valid media narrative advocating the revolution had to continue, and since I couldn't be in Tahrir, I did the only thing I could and knew best. I loaded up my Internet browser, and readied my humble digital tools.

"Dude!" I excitedly called Sandmonkey via Skype. "It's me, Amir. Drima, The Sudanese Thinker."

"Ho ho! Drima! Long time dude."

"Listen," I shot back quickly, "I'm going to hit the record button on my special Skype plug-in software, and we're going to start an interview. Let's keep the stories flowing. Cool?"

"Hell yes. Do it!" he said.

"Sandmonkey, tell us what the hell is going on there," I began the interview.

"We are currently entering . . . the end of the first week of protests. It all started with a national call . . . inspired by the Tunisian revolution. More than inspired, actually. They made us feel as if we're not men. So we figured we might as well have our own. They're not better than us. So we went ahead with it, and nobody expected it to be this big, honestly." Asked about the situation on the ground, he replied, "It's fantastic . . . even with the economic situation going badly, we're actually participating in building up the nation."

I was curious if Sandmonkey was aware of the comments made by United States Vice President Joe Biden about Egypt's Mubarak and the protests. "Dude! I have no Internet. *I have no Internet!*" Sandmonkey reminded me, so I read to him what Biden had said.

"Mubarak has been an ally of ours in a number of things," the vice president had explained. "And he's been very responsible on, relative to geopolitical interest in the region, the Middle East peace efforts; the actions Egypt has taken relative to normalizing relationship with . . . with Israel . . . I would not refer to him as a dictator."

As if everything should always revolve around Israel and the one-sided, biased, AIPAC-influenced, so-called Middle East peace efforts.

To make matters worse, as if not satisfied with refusing to

refer to Mubarak as a dictator, Biden went on to question the legitimacy of the protesters' demands.

"Expected," replied Sandmonkey in one word. "We know that none of those governments are with us in what we are trying to do. But we know that the people . . . The people are with us! So we're okay with that. We'll take that. Screw the governments. I'm happy with the people . . . Let people govern themselves."

Finally, Sandmonkey articulated the crucial consequential point and what was at stake. "If Egypt just manages to get Mubarak to leave . . . I'm *guaranteeing* you, changes will happen everywhere else in the region. Where Egypt goes, the Middle East follows . . . I hope it all ends well."

The subversive awesomeness was just beginning.

By February 2, the Internet was reinstated by the Egyptian authorities due to growing pressure.

"The Internet is back in Egypt! FINALLY!" tweeted Egyptian human rights activist Dalia Ziada. "I have more than 500 e-mails in my inbox! Oh my God!"

The regime's move backfired and thousands more poured onto the streets. And best of all, the digital media war for the revolution was back in full force.

At the heart of the regional action in the cyber sphere was the AB09 network, and our allied affiliates of trusted friends, journalists, and organizations. Like a large flock of furious birds flying together—some big, others tiny—everyone's efforts and contribution to the collective intelligence played a role in the continuing and raging media battles on two primary fronts—fighting the Egyptian regime's propaganda, and keeping the world abreast of the truth with the assistance of big media.

Abdu, a Somali journalist and producer with Al Jazeera who was present in Beirut's bloggers meeting, frantically tweeted with other AB09 folks asking for the contact information and phone numbers of relevant people on the ground in Cairo or Tahrir. Thirty minutes later, a relevant person would appear on Al Jazeera English speaking to millions across the globe, advocating the demands of the revolution.

Hours upon hours, as the digital war raged, thousands of online soldiers armed with the digital media equivalents of pistols kept up the onslaught. Others, like behind-the-scenes master strategist Nasser Weddady, used the media equivalents of deadly machine guns and well-aimed artillery shells to incisively destroy counter-revolutionary memes. And a few online soldiers, like the Emirati Sultan al-Qassemi, Egyptian-born journalist Mona Eltahawy, and NPR's Andy Carvin, who each had tens of thousands of followers in their lists that included influential figures, amplified revolutionary voices, and conducted the digital media equivalent of devastating missile strikes.

The online juggernaut fought on—reporting, tweeting, organizing, translating, curating—*influencing* the international media until our narrative became the established authoritative narrative: that this really was a legitimate revolution of the people for freedom, dignity, and justice. Not some crazed plot by the Muslim Brotherhood to create another Iran. (Fox News would of course continue to spin the story, and spew the latter.)

Meanwhile, on the ground, despite heinous violence by

armed government thugs, live ammunition, and getting run over by speeding security forces vehicles, the hundreds of thousands of demonstrators—once more, the real heroes and ones truly deserving of praise—persisted with admirable restraint and mostly, with nonviolence.

Finally, on February 11—after eighteen days of revolt, thousands of injured protesters, and more than eight hundred dead later—the resignation of Egypt's tyrant, Mohamed Hosni Mubarak, the Arab world's "Berlin Wall," was announced on live television to massive jubilant crowds all over Egypt's squares and ecstatic viewers across the globe.

Almost immediately, where Egypt went, the region did expectedly follow, with protests of varying sizes and intensity happening next in Libya, Bahrain, Oman, Yemen, Jordan, Saudi Arabia, Sudan, Morocco, and Syria.

But what wasn't expected was what followed in Europe and in the United States.

Months before the tenth anniversary of September 11, the youth of the Arab world—those "evil" Muslims, those "backward ignorant fools" and "terrorists"—inspired the world with their ingenuity, nonviolent mobilization, and passion for liberty, freedom and democracy. And shortly afterward, similar protest movements against corruption and advocating accountability, would emerge in Europe, and in the United States in the form of the Occupy movement.

It was the start of something special. Clearly, the ethos of the youth of the Internet had now begun spilling over into the real world in Arabia, America, and beyond. The train had left the station. The toothpaste was out of the tube. There was no going back, and the world would never be the same again.

• • •

"This is the problem with the Internet, and modernity today. Everything is about speed. Information, information, but what about knowledge? And what about taking the time to digest this knowledge so you can form wisdom?"

By March 2011, I was well underway with my first semester at the International Institute of Islamic Thought and Civilization in Kuala Lumpur, Malaysia, and my Iranian professor Amir H. Zekrgoo was discussing the importance of tradition, the philosophy of Islamic art, and the downside of the Internet. He didn't seem like much of a fan of the medium. I tried paying full attention in class, but I was too distracted on my BlackBerry tweeting, retweeting, and reading revolutionary updates from protesting friends on the ground around the Arab world.

Then the professor said something that gripped my attention. "Of course technology is good, but our conception of the world cannot get caught up in the speed of things. In order for us to be well-grounded individuals, we need a deep and rigorous cosmology. What many are suffering from today is the effects of living in a world with a fast-food cosmology."

"He has a point," I thought to myself. But then I wondered, "What would a deep and rigorous meaningful cosmology that's not necessarily traditional but primarily evidence-based look like?"

Not long after that, I got a satisfactory answer from Michael Dowd, a fundamentalist Christian turned "evolutionary evangelist." Dowd advocates "Big History"—our fourteen-billion-year cosmological unfolding toward ever greater complexity and cooperation—as the mother of all cosmologies. Dowd and his science-writer wife, Connie Barlow, have been criss-crossing North America since 2002, sharing "an inspiring evidential view of our inner and outer nature"—what they call "The Great Story." The couple presents this science-grounded grand narrative as "humanity's common creation story." It is, they assert, a *sacred* narrative, and it offers a fresh understanding of our evolved instincts. The story charts a magnificent journey of transformation from stardust to cells to humans to cities to satellites.

When I met Dowd in person sometime later in Chicago, he left me with some profound heart-expanding evolutionary insights.

"It's all about coming into right relationship with reality, Amir. That's really the only thing that matters. Religions, of course, speak of this as getting right with God, but it's the same thing. When you realize that 'God' is reality's mythic name and 'reality' is God's secular name, it becomes obvious that scientific, historic, and cross-cultural evidence should be considered modern-day scripture. Surely, facts are God's native tongue."

"I'd encourage you to be more generous toward tribal and traditional mentality," he advised. "It served its evolutionary purpose. Yes, today it needs to evolve beyond itself, to include the best of itself, and transcend its limitations. But before you bash traditionalists with harsh language, I suggest that you deeply appreciate how tribal, mythic mentality helped our species survive and cooperate at scales that we would not otherwise have been able to do. When you come from a place of gratitude, of honoring what was necessary to get us to this place, you'll develop a more generous tone, and you'll become a much more effective change-maker."

Michael was right. I still had a lot more to learn, and more forgiving to do to reclaim more of my disowned selves from the shadows of my psyche.

It's May 2011, and I'm in cold breezy Oslo, Norway, standing in front of the 130-year-old Grand Hotel tingling with mischievous anticipation and getting ready for the day to deliver my opening speech at the Oslo Freedom Forum's panel "Dawn of a New Arab World."

With my real identity revealed on my blog at last, the moment had finally come when I'd speak on stage, cameras rolling and all, with my real name and my face exposed, unafraid to say what I think, and mean what I say.

One by one, the BBC's Philipa Thomas introduced the speakers to deliver their opening remarks, starting with the Egyptian Wael Ghonim, who delivered his speech virtually from Cairo. Next, each of us, the panel speakers present in Oslo—the Libyan Ghazi Gheblawi, the Tunisian Lina Ben Mhenni, the Bahraini Maryam al-Khawaja, and I—gave our openings then sat together for the group panel. Notably absent was Ali Abdulemam, the online free speech pioneer I met a year earlier in Beirut at the AB09 Summit.

Jailed for months, Ali was released at the height of the Bahraini revolution, but disappeared into hiding after Bahrain's absolute monarchy imposed a wide-ranging crackdown, and began its appalling witch-hunt for activists who mobilized peaceful protests.

So much had changed and dramatically rocked the region since the fall of Mubarak in Egypt.

In Libya, NATO-assisted revolutionaries were in a state of civil war against the brutal forces of Libya's dictator, Muhammad al-Ghaddafi, who had ruled for forty-two years and who'd have turned the rebel stronghold city of Benghazi into a bloodbath had the U.S.-supported NATO not intervened with the notable diplomatic support of Qatar.

In the more complicated Iran-neighboring Syria, numerous towns were up in revolt, their rebels dealing with a horrific military onslaught waged by their China- and Russia-backed dictator, Bashar al-Assad, whose forces would not even hesitate to slaughter and slit the throats of women and children, gruesome crimes the world would probably not have found out about if it weren't for the immensely courageous Syrian digital activists armed with camera phones, YouTube, and an Internet connection.

Yet despite the nightmares of the Arab uprisings, there was still much to rejoice and be pragmatically hopeful about. As I had concluded in my opening remarks at the Oslo Freedom Forum, "Yes, there are challenges, but I think the fear barrier has been broken and that's why we should be optimistic."

Back in the institute where I pursued my masters in philosophy, I was making progress with my question on how the future of Islam could or will look like in the digital age. To gain some fresh insights, I hosted an online audio seminar entitled *The Future of Islam in the Age of New Media* that featured sixty speakers in sixty seconds each for a total of sixty minutes.

In light of the Arab uprisings, the media had put an increasingly bright spotlight on the impact of social media on politics. But I felt that wasn't the real big phenomenon taking place. If anything, the bigger deal was new media's impact on contemporary Islamic thought, and its facilitation of the ever-increasing democratization of Islamic authority.

Why? Simply because in the Muslim world, Islam permeates virtually all aspects of Muslim life, including education, culture, and politics. Therefore, any evolution and new trends that emerge within Islam and contemporary Islamic thought, even in cyberspace, have the potential to influence important matters beyond Islam itself.

Already, the religious establishments have lost and continue to lose their monopoly on the interpretation and dissemination of religious texts.

About damn time.

On top of that, more and more Muslim women are participating in the reinterpretation of Islamic texts from a feminist perspective that is ridding the traditionalist Islamic corpus of its patriarchal toxins. In fact, one of the most interesting things that emerged out of the online audio seminar was what the women participants had to say and on what they agreed. Fatemeh Fakhraie, founder of Muslimah Media Watch, captured the echoing sentiment well when she said, "With greater Internet access will inevitably come greater female participation. Muslim women are already actively engaging online through blogs, Facebook pages, and Twitter accounts. The future of Islam is bright because Muslim women can use new media to access knowledge, participate in conversations, and shape Islam equally with men."

Another speaker, American Pakistani playwright Wajahat Ali, captured the overall spirit nicely when he said, "Islam doesn't speak, Muslims do. And the Muslim youth is speaking, living, and identifying with Islam using a new language: the new language of new media. . . . Muslims have a microphone for the first time. They're no longer sealed off behind a wall at the mosque. They no longer have to go to a pulpit and beg for the microphone."

On the other hand, Haroon Moghul, the former director of public relations at the Islamic Center at New York University, shared a rather contrarian view, expressing caution about the potential of the Internet in transforming Islamic thought. "I think that the Internet is going to be a very destabilizing force among Muslim communities worldwide," he began. "I say that because in the Muslim world right now, the biggest problem that we have . . . is the absence of voices that are authoritative. There are a lot of voices that are authoritarian, and believe themselves to be authoritative, but we have a huge gap between people who see themselves as primarily engaged in what they call the modern world, and we have people who primarily identify through a religious lens. And in the absence of institutions that can produce people who can navigate both those streams . . . the danger I feel with the Internet is the possibility of magnifying some of these negative tendencies and encouraging people to stay within their own points of view."

"A valid concern, certainly," I thought.

Nevertheless, the Internet is but a neutral technology, and it is up to us to make the best use of it, and utilize it for the greater good. And use it and utilize it for good we must.

Otherwise, there could be much at stake as July 22, 2011, painfully demonstrated. Inspired by rabidly anti-Muslim Web sites, such as Robert Spencer's Jihad Watch, which I used to track in my earlier years in the blogosphere, the Norwegian Anders Behring Breivik went on a killing spree targeting Norway's Labour Party.

His motive as documented in his manifesto? Annihilating multiculturalism, and the deportation of all Muslims from Europe, among other objectives. The terror attack left seventy-seven dead and 151 injured, and shook the small, peaceful nation of Norway.

Yes, use the Internet and utilize it for good we really must.

It's October 2011. I had just arrived in free Tunisia to attend the Third Arab Bloggers Summit, the follow-up meeting to Beirut's December 2009 meeting, the previous meeting where in the words of Apple's Steve "Abdulfattah" Jobs, we were "the crazy ones. The misfits. The rebels. The trouble-makers. The round pegs in the square holes. The ones who see things differently."

We were crazy enough to think we could change the world. Crazy enough to think we could change things in our societies, some things, anything. But as crazy as we were, none of us imagined in 2009 that we'd be meeting again in the capital of what used to be one of the most sophisticated Internet-restricting dictatorships on the planet. Fast-forward nearly two years later and that's precisely what happened. I arrived and met my old friends and comrades in Tunisia, and by then, a lot had indeed changed. So much that it took us all by surprise, giving us one of the best damn feelings anyone can experience. Giving us an incredibly powerful validation, because we knew beyond a shadow of a doubt that our collective efforts were not in vain.

"Ghazi, good to see you again brother!" I embraced my Libyan copanelist from Oslo, at the Golden Tulip Carthage Tunis.

"Good to see you, Amir!"

"Look at you, man," I said to Ghazi pointing at his belly. *"Masha'allah,* you've been eating well since Ghaddafi finally got overthrown and killed, huh? No longer stressed like you were in Oslo? *Alf mabrouk,* a thousand congratulations to you and the people of Libya for finally getting rid of that monster."

"I can't tell you how happy I am," confessed Ghazi. "It's still hard to believe. We did it. It happened. It finally happened. It's crazy!"

Indeed, at some level it all felt crazy: the roller-coaster ride of 2011, as well as our bloggers' gathering in Tunisia, which just a year earlier would've gotten us thrown in Ben Ali's jails.

But there we were, gathered to discuss how our collaborations can strengthen and improve in the face of new censorship efforts by Arab regimes, as well as so-called democratic governments around the world that had awoken to the Internet's potential in enabling people to exercise their inherent power.

This time, the summit witnessed many new faces since the organizers focused on inviting a new generation of Arab bloggers to prepare them with the necessary skills and networking opportunities. Notably, some of us old-timers also began waking up to the importance of thinking and operating like entrepreneurs for leverage, scalability, and larger impact. The momentum had to continue, bigger and more efficiently, despite the challenges.

We all also very well knew that in some Arab countries, things might have to get "worse" before they get better. Nonetheless, most of us felt that the regional psychological shift triggered by the uprisings from victimhood and apathy, to self-entitlement and self-empowerment was set to grow. "It has ended over forty years of political stagnation, and it's here to stay," I blogged.

Especially in the era of the digital age, more freely flowing information and a time of rapidly changing demographics and evolving belief systems.

Especially at a time when the majority of the Arab world's population consists of frustrated youth under the age of thirty with dreams of a better future. The psychological shift in the Arab world is only bound to grow and continue, and it is the duty of all optimistic netizens and citizens to continue feeding it with pragmatically optimistic fuel to keep burning and raging.

Secretly though, in the middle of the company of wonderful friends in the hospitality of Tunisia, a part of me still harbored resentments and pessimism around an issue that I felt was so battered, so damaged, so regressed, no positive change could be expected from it anytime soon: Sudan, my home country. For the second time in a row, I was the only Sudanese present at the Arab Bloggers Summit, and I didn't like the feeling. One invited Sudanese blogger I recommended couldn't make it. On one level, it felt a little lonely in some moments. Thankfully, the organizers promised me to invite more Sudanese bloggers and activists for the following summit. I was grateful for the voiced commitment.

Sitting during one of the workshops, I continued to wonder, "Would Sudan's turn ever come? Would Khartoum ever rise against Omar al-Bashir?" Previous attempts at revolutionary protest mobilization had failed miserably.

It was my last night out with the gang in Tunisia for our farewell group dinner. Feeling the gentle breeze that carried with it the scents of the nearby free sea, I walked momentarily in quiet introspective solitude to soak up the profundity of the moment.

"Hey, can we wait a bit here to buy some stuff? Let's do that," shouted one of the participants on our way uphill through the alleys where many had stopped at a traditional shopping spot to purchase some items.

Standing alone a distance away to keep a watchful eye on the crew was one of our hosts, Sami Ben Gharbia, home in a free Tunisia at last, and a hero in his country after thirteen years of exile in Europe.

I strode slowly in his direction and stood next to him. He didn't notice me. As usual, he seemed lost in thoughts, gazing away into the air, with a content smile on his lightly bearded face.

"So how does it feel?" I asked him, capturing his attention.

"What do you mean?" he asked in a low, deep voice.

"How does it feel to be back? To finally be a free man in your country after all these years? To be standing here, the troublemaker you are, in the company of all these troublemakers you've helped invite for the event?" I clarified with a laugh.

Maintaining his reserved, nonanimated composure, after a deep sigh came out his deeply heartfelt reply, carried by the breeze of the sea, "It's a beautiful feeling, Amir. It's a beautiful feeling."

"What did you buy?" he asked me seconds later.

"This," I showed him my left pinkie finger. "It's a Tunisian-made silver ring. I just got it from that shop, right there. I wanted something that will forever remind me of the past few days. Of Tunisia. Of the importance of speaking your truth. So basically the next time I'm writing and typing something, if I hesitate to speak my mind, I'll hopefully notice the ring on my finger and remember to still speak up. To say what needs to be said. To write what needs to be written," I explained, feeling the tranquility of the wind on my skin, and that of my heart. "Thank you for this," I told him. "Thanks for everything."

"My pleasure, *ya sadeeqi*." He nodded. "*Yalla*, let's get everyone moving for dinner."

By June 2012, the critics and naysayers were back with loud proclamations of doom and gloom that the Arab revolutions had failed to bring democracy. But they forgot that Eastern Europe didn't transform overnight after the fall of the Berlin Wall. They forgot that the French Revolution didn't last for two years. It lasted for one, long messy *decade*.

Most of the time those reminders worked. On other occasions they didn't.

Some will always choose to dwell on pessimism, even the outright unwarranted kind.

And just as I had predicted, the role of Islam in post-uprising nations like Egypt and Tunisia would come to occupy most discussions. "Look, the Islamists have won in Egypt's elections. They got the majority of votes," critics would say to dismiss any notions of real progress.

"True. But their victory isn't an indication of popular support for Islamism in the Arab world necessarily," I'd begin to explain. "Rather, the Islamists mainly won because for decades they've been the only well-organized, disciplined political opposition force in the region with a message and platform that resonated with the masses. As for us, the young liberals, we're just getting started, and we'll definitely need to move our asses to get self-organized to play politics. Plus, so what if the Islamists won in Egypt? I say good. Because now, they'll have to deal with the scrutiny of the ridiculous levels of free speech we're witnessing after the fall of dictators. And for the first time in Egypt, the Islamists will be held accountable and will need to deliver on their promises. If they don't, they can be voted out. Finally, keep in mind that in the first round of elections, the majority of the votes decidedly went to non-Islamist and secular candidates clearly and unequivocally supporting a civil, not religious state, so what does that tell you? There's still a great deal to be optimistic about. If I'm worried about anything, it's the horrible economic situation. Islamist or secular, we'll really need to fix the situation and combat corruption. So let's do our part to bring things to fruition rather than bitch and complain."

It's July 2, 2012. Revolution fever had finally arrived in Khartoum, Sudan, beyond a shadow of a doubt. Our turn had come. Hopefully. Days earlier, on Friday, June 29, a day before the twenty-third anniversary of Omar al-Bashir's military coup, Sudan witnessed nationwide demonstrations against the government.

"The big bright spark happened!" I celebrated, knowing the mood wouldn't remain the same. Not when you've got thousands in towns all over the country chanting "The people! Want! The fall of the regime!'"

But it was still too early to truly rejoice. There was still more work that needed to be done and no guarantees the protests would succeed. I went on Skype to talk to a fellow Sudanese media activist from Girifna, the nonviolent youth resistance movement that had helped mobilize the dozens of thousands of protesters in Khartoum and throughout the country.

Circumstances had changed over the previous six years. At last, we had a sizable Sudanese online community of activists to be reckoned with. At last, I was no longer a lone social media voice of dissent like in April 2006.

"The recent Friday's #SudanRevolts protest was a success," I noted to my colleague. "More people, even women and older men, have joined in large numbers at last, and the media coverage went well. The Twitter hashtag received the attention we were hoping for. We're getting there, but how do we keep up the pressure? I'm doing all I can to advocate for more crucial international coverage. So far we've had all the big media outlets cover things. CNN. *The New York Times.* France24. BBC. *The Los Angeles Times.* Also, I know my *Foreign Policy* piece is being used by other journalists doing research for their own pieces. Al Jazeera Arabic is still behind though, surprise, surprise. Nothing significant from them. The Qataris are worried about their friend Omar al-Bashir falling in Sudan."

"Yes, all of that is true," replied the activist I was talking to. "But I'm worried more about the real possibility of a low turnout for next Friday's protests. The NISS are arresting our Girifna members left and right, even from their homes! There are more than fifteen hundred demonstrators and key activists in detention now. It's going to be hard to mobilize. We need ideas," she said.

I felt her frustration. "Those NISS bastards are finding out about who's involved because they're going through mobile phones belonging to those they've arrested. I'm also guessing they've managed to torture and force some of our guys to give their e-mail and Facebook log-in passwords. I know it happened to one detainee who got released. I suspect that's how they're finding out who the members are and then arresting them. It's almost as if they've got a list now, or something."

"So what do we do? I can't reach the others right now."

"Here's our potential next move and strategy then," I told her. "We need to reach out to the Manaseer. Months ago they were demonstrating fiercely demanding their compensations, as I'm sure you can remember. They're motivated, and they've proven their assertiveness. Oh, and what about the detainees' families? Why not unite them?"

"They're already grouping together."

"Excellent! Then that's the main media story we could push. Let's frame things to emphasize the role of brave women and mothers in these planned protests. Hopefully that will give journalists something more compelling and newsworthy to report about."

"Okay, I just forwarded the message to those who can work on that," she said. She was efficient. "By the way," she added, "I don't know if I should send e-mails to our guys anymore. What if the NISS have access and read the messages?"

"Screw the NISS. They probably already know who you are, and I'm pretty damn sure they already know about me," I replied.

"I'm not worried about myself," she said. "I'm worried that my e-mails could piss them off and make them torture or harass our guys more."

"Shit. Yeah. Good point," I realized, and paused to think. "Fingers crossed, then. Let's reach out to those who aren't detained, and let's see how this coming Friday turns out. Hopefully we'll be able to maintain our momentum. Let me know how else I can help with any other media stuff. Gotta run now."

"Cheers."

Sitting in my swivel chair in Kuala Lumpur, my thoughts drifted back to Sudan, to the garden where my grandfather and I used to play chess when I was a child, where he used to tell me grown-up things I struggled to understand, where I wished to stand in again without nagging concerns about the all-too-real possibility of getting detained upon arrival at the airport in Khartoum.

"My son, life is like a chess game," my grandfather's words came back to me. "In life, just like in chess, you always need to understand what goes on around you. . . . You need to see where you're standing, because if you don't know where you're standing, the circumstances you're in, and how you got there, if you don't understand all the factors involved, well, you won't know how to progress. The pattern is in the relationships. It's in how the dots connect. Do you understand me?"

My grandfather's words held a deeper meaning by now. Looking back at my coming-of-age journey, I connected the dots and saw the pattern in the relationships. I saw how my life would have probably taken a very different course had I not landed on the blogosphere. I saw how I most likely wouldn't have been sucked into virtual wonderland had I not gone through the indoctrination of my childhood. I saw how one's early fate contains a code to be unlocked so one can consciously choose to determine one's destiny. To unlock that code or not, the choice is yours.

Feeling a little tired, I got off my swivel chair, closed my MacBook, and went for a walk. "Fingers crossed," I repeated to myself smiling nervously, thinking about the protests. "Fingers crossed."

Epilogue

One of the most central acts of our humanity is the act of storytelling. Throughout this book, I've employed storytelling and metaphors in a way that I hope you have found relatable and insightful, and has made you question and think critically for yourself. I'd like to think I succeeded somewhat in doing that without being preachy. Despite learning a lot on the path, I am still learning and growing, and my mind remains hungry, which is why I weaved the appropriate tales together for you from which to draw your own conclusions. Conclusions which I suspect will evolve and change if you return to the stories I shared when you're at a different point in your life journey.

Nevertheless, storytelling has its disadvantages. While it leaves numerous parts of the book open to various possible and valid interpretations along the philosophical spectrum, it also opens up numerous opportunities for misinterpretations by different readers. And herein, I'd like to speak to you more directly to articulate a few important points with some precision and clear up any possible misunderstandings that might have arisen during your reading.

For a start, it's important to note that the religious and political indoctrination experience I underwent as a child is not representative of what all Muslim children go through, at least certainly not in its intensity, effectiveness and content. After all, the Qur'an recitation class I voluntarily attended at my neighborhood mosque in Qatar was run by an Imam who subscribed to the problematic Salafi ideology and interpretation of Islam, which is known for its rigidity and extreme stances on many issues. Salafism, of course, is but one of varying currents within Islam.

Moreover, to be fair, despite its many remaining and persistent flaws, Qatar has thankfully made some commendable strides forward since my childhood days. It has revised its education system, and put in place many good improvements. Unfortunately, the same cannot really be said about neighboring Saudi Arabia, which urgently needs to improve a lot more. In a *Foreign Policy* piece entitled *Teaching Intolerance* published in May/June 2012, fellow blogger and Saudi colleague Eman al-Nafjan details how the ultraconservative religious establishment of the oil-rich Kingdom continues to inject its toxic bigotry into the education system to further its propaganda against the Other. It is the same cancerous bigotry that has spread its tentacles all over the world and poisoned previously tolerant Muslim communities and societies. Therefore, the fight against such indoctrination practices and lies about the Other—which let's not forget, also includes millions of supposedly "lesser" Muslims—must continue everywhere it's found, because the dangers are real and hideous.

Speaking of the Other, it would be useful to revisit the issue of Muslim relations with Jews and the topical mine-field that is the Palestinian-Israeli conflict. There's no way I can do justice to such a broad, emotionally charged subject in these short pages. Nonetheless, it deserves a few conclusive and clarifying words for the purpose of this book.

Historically, I believe Israel is at fault, and continues to be to a large extent. The colonialist creation of what too many Jews insist must remain the Jewish State has been unjust and very problematic for the region. I also believe that our reaction to Israel's creation has been just as, if not more problematic. The rise of Muslim anti-Semitism has been one of those problematic and unhelpful reactions. To be sure, anti-Semitism has always existed in the region long before the creation of Israel. But it was nowhere near where it is today as evidenced by the numerous Jewish communities, some of them very privileged, that lived in relative peace and harmony from Tehran all the way to Egypt and Morocco just as recently as the early 1900s. But the start of the Arab-Israeli conflict and the region's reaction to it sadly changed that.

Where do we go from here? Well, less polarization and demonization of the Other in our discourse on all sides would be a nice start. Whether it can happen will depend on the realities on the ground, which influence the political climate. Can those realities change anytime soon? I don't know, but we, as individuals, can certainly do what we can to heal the rifts caused by the perils of identity in our communities, and combat the messages of those who seek to exploit them for their own heinous gains—anti-Semites, white supremacists, Hindu nationalists, Muslim radicals, the Islamophobes and anti-Muslim zealots exposed in Fear Inc., the investiga-

tive report produced by the Center for American Progress—
and the list goes on.

Having read my journey, and hopefully seen a part of yourself in it, you also may be wondering where I stand now in
regards to my own identity, Islam, and activism.

It is difficult to provide any answer in response to this inquiry simply because I'm obviously still evolving, and always
will be. Fortunately, there are some aspects I can perhaps
answer with 99 percent evergreen certainty.

I am neither just Arab nor just African. Neither just Eastern nor just Western. I am Sudanese Afro-Arab by birth and
proud heritage, Qatari and Malaysian by migration, Western
and American by post-elementary knowledge, affinity, and
education, science-affirming mystic by integral philosophical contemplation, lover of my Beloved by Sufi orientation,
libertarian-leaning by political persuasion, writer, activist and
entrepreneur by life vocation, and cosmopolitan world citizen
by choice and dedication. I am the influence of all those parts
in motion, but not their sum, for they have no sum.

And no, being a Sufi lover of my Beloved does not mean I
re-embraced Islam after my messy divorce. I didn't, because
the fact of the matter is I never was a true Muslim to begin
with when I came into this world. No Muslim ever is. The
vast majority of us don't consciously choose Islam. With the
exception of converts, we are simply born and socialized
into the faith just as Christians and Mormons are into Christianity and Mormonism respectively.

So no, I didn't re-embrace Islam. I embraced it. Once.
Consciously. I heartily and proudly embraced it as a cultural
identity along with a Sufi orientation to my spiritual path and
practice, (one also informed by a secular, evidential approach

to wisdom traditions such as Vipassana, Qigong and Tantric yoga). I embraced Islam not because I think it has a monopoly over spiritual truth, but because its mystical poetry and the language of Sufism resonates more with my heart than does the language of Christianity or Buddhism. It has more familiarity.

As such, I honor my Islam as part of my heritage and my religious tradition, but I'm no longer blindly beholden to it nor dogmatically bound to it. And neither do I believe in the traditional and wide-spread understanding of a personal theistic God anymore as is quite evident by now. Rather I accept the admittedly hard-to-define God (or "God") accessed through mystical experience, which has made me delve into reading up on the mystery and hard problem of consciousness. And so far, it's clear that eager attempts to reduce consciousness to the physicality of the brain are hugely inconclusive. Consciousness is a very open question, and it's time we challenged some of science's prevalent definitions of what counts as "physical" reality, especially when physicists are talking about things like quantum vacuum fluctuation.

As for my call to challenge religious dogmatism, it's only because I hope we Muslims, especially the Millennials among us, start discussing the serious problems we face more frankly and assertively online and offline, begin reforming our appallingly broken current fear-based models of religious education, and revolt against the abusive dinosaur preachers of our times as required. I hope other religious groups do the same as well. The digital media tools are now available at our fingertips for us to make full use of in this battle against ignorance and closed-mindedness, and I predict like many rightly have that the Internet will be to Islam what the print-

ing press was to Christianity—a major driving force for
reform.

So let us strive toward ridding ourselves and the world of
dogma, especially the fervent divisive kind. The kind that
keeps us separate, and keeps us from attaining outer and inner peace. Let us embody the activist ethos and embark on
our individual and collective journeys of self-discovery, self-
growth, and self-empowerment. Let us fight for what we
care about: social justice, the environment, conscious business, a meaningful vocation, abundance and equality, genuine health and vitality, or simply, the freedom to be yourself.

And yes, of course it's easier said than done, because
there will most definitely be struggles to overcome and battles to be won. Every day, every morning in every corner of
the globe, many of us wake up to face them.

We struggle to uncover the first steps of our path, let alone
find the courage to walk it. We struggle to hear our life calling
in the midst of all the internal and external noise. We struggle
to pick and choose our battles strategically, and with how to
fight them assertively yet compassionately. We struggle to
heal our wounds, and thus become ineffective "wounded warriors." We struggle to break free from the effects of years of
formative conditioning aimed at making us comply with society's limiting conventions and disempowering norms.

And you know what? That's all perfectly fine and normal.
Countless men and women before us have been there, and yet
slowly but surely they progressed forward in small steps, and
then leaps and strides, because they chose to. And so can you.

The ethos of activism isn't just about going out and protesting on the streets. It isn't just about bearing witness and
speaking truth to power. It is and can be about more than

just that. And it can certainly be exercised beyond the political realm in business and in culture. In its broadest sense, it's about standing up for what's right, and doing work that matters.

Micro-lending site Kiva.org. Online free education provider, the Khan Academy. Microcredit institute, the Grameen Bank. TOMS, which gives a pair of shoes to a child in need every time you buy yourself a pair. These are fine examples of social entrepreneurship initiatives, or as I see it, activism, non-profits and conscious business coming together to bring about desperately needed positive social change.

Sometimes though, activism can be as simple as engaging in that vulnerable act that is so central to our humanity: storytelling.

And so I ask you, what's your story? I'd actually love to know it briefly. In fact, I'd appreciate it if you visited my blog at www.AmirAhmadNasr.com and e-mailed it to me, along with your constructive feedback on the book, if any.

There's a lot more that I would've liked to write and include in these pages. Alas, I had to keep things short. For this reason, I want to leave you with five solid book recommendations that elaborate on much of what I have not. These are books I urge you to make time to read if you're interested in going deeper into the relevant subjects.

On the complexities and controversies surrounding Islam and democratization, I highly recommend the brilliant book *Islam Without Extremes: A Muslim Case for Liberty* by the Turkish author Mustafa Akyol. On the question and challenges of identity in an increasingly globalized world, you'd be crazy not to get your hands on the slim, elegant book *In the Name of Identity: Violence and the Need to Belong* by the

French-Lebanese author Amin Maalouf. Those two afore-mentioned books are absolute must-reads. Get them.

Thirdly, on the fight for Internet freedom and online free speech, check out the incisive book *Consent of the Networked: The Worldwide Struggle for Internet Freedom* by Global Voices cofounder Rebecca MacKinnon. Fourthly, for a well-written, accessible, and introductory understanding of integral phi-losophy and evolutionary spirituality, read the wonderful book *Evolutionaries: Unlocking the Spiritual and Cultural Po-tential of Science's Greatest Idea* by Carter Phipps. And lastly, but just as important, be sure to read the provocative and important book *Defeating Dictators: Fighting Tyranny in Af-rica and Around the World* by George B. N. Ayittey.

And once more I ask, what's your story? Write it. Write it, tell it, and share it. And of course, pursue your heart's cause. Who knows who or what it may inspire? You'll never know until you do.

Acknowledgments

It would be totally uncool to end this book without thanking the key people who've been a big part of this project and helped bring it to fruition.

First, I want to heartily thank Ellen Daly, my publishing consultant for believing in me and working with me on putting together a better book proposal to pitch to agents and publishers. She's been instrumental in helping me shape the narrative during the early stages. Huge thanks also go out to my wonderful agent Linda Langton for taking me as her client, and securing my publishing deal with St. Martin's Press, which is exactly what I wished for and had in my top choices. And of course, I gratefully thank my editor at St. Martin's, Daniela Rapp, for believing in the book and for her patience and flexibility throughout the editing process. I'm deeply grateful for the opportunity. I also thank Terry Patten and Byron Belitsos for helping make the publication of this book, my first, possible.

A big thank you goes out to Wajahat Ali, G. Willow Wilson,

and Aziz Poonawalla as well for inspiring me from afar with their admirable levelheadedness and wise insights.

I'd also like to acknowledge and thank Irshad Manji for inciting me to write a book when I had no plans to. In October 2007, we were having a friendly debate on Islam after the CSIS conference in Washington, D.C., when I jokingly said, "I don't know, maybe I'll write a book about what I think." "Do it," she replied. "Write the book." She was dead serious. I was twenty-one, and she believed I could do it, which made me believe that I could do it, too.

I completed the book after five years of blogging, reading, self-doubt, mental torture, temporary stops, introspection, and synthesizing a raging hurricane of insanity and ideas into something coherent. And I am grateful for the warm support I've continuously received during those years from my many "MV" friends and colleagues. You guys have been awesome.

Moreover, I am thankful to Ethan Zuckerman, Michael Dowd, and Rebecca Hamilton, for their valuable advice at various stages of the writing process.

Furthermore, I of course want to thank my parents for being as understanding as possible despite their concerns and some of our intellectual differences. It is only natural that they raise some worries given the controversial nature of what I've stubbornly chosen to write.

Last and ultimately, my praise and thanks go to my Beloved, the Mystery of all existence and the reason for our being in this vast universe. Any shortcomings detected in the book are mine, and mine alone, and any and every piece of stirring beauty that resonated with you is all but mine. It is His. I am simply the servant.